Gambling: Hazard and Reward

Gambling: Hazard and Reward

OTTO NEWMAN

Principal Lecturer in Sociology
Polytechnic of the South Bank, London

THE ATHLONE PRESS
of the University of London · 1972

Published by
THE ATHLONE PRESS
UNIVERSITY OF LONDON
at 4 *Gower Street London* WC I

Distributed by
Tiptree Book Services Ltd
Tiptree, Essex

U.S.A.
Oxford University Press Inc
New York

ISBN O 485 11133 O

Printed in Great Britain by
WESTERN PRINTING SERVICES LTD
Bristol

Acknowledgments

This book, though focused on Britain in particular, is an attempt to describe and analyse the activity of gambling as a sociological phenomenon. It incorporates much of the substance approved for a doctorate by the University of London.

I wish to thank Professor Terence Morris and Dr David Downes of the London School of Economics for their conscientious supervision and critical advice; Professor David Glass who, though not directly involved, generously and unstintingly gave much more of his already heavily committed time than I had any right to expect and whose immense experience and penetrative insight provided invaluable illumination; my ex-colleagues at the University of Stirling, Professor Max Marwick and Dr Sheila Mitchell, for their stimulating comments and encouragement. I also gained great benefit from my discussions with Professor Robert Herman of Pomona College.

I wish to express my warmest gratitude to Messrs Gerry Levens and Paul Harrison of Research Services Ltd for their personal efforts and active assistance in affording me access to valuable private survey material; to the officers of the National Opinion Poll, the Gallup Poll, the Statistical Division of the Department of Customs and Excise, as well as to the Town Clerks and Clerks to the Justices of the various London boroughs for their valuable help with statistical material, frequently involving time consuming research on their parts.

I wish to make public acknowledgment to my wife, June, for her patient help, her percipient advice and her unfailing good humour, without which the project would have foundered at an early stage.

My principal debt is due to the large, anonymous body of

informants—in particular those kindly representatives of that much maligned profession of bookmakers, H. and J.—who made this study possible and whose generous help and friendliness acted as constant spur.

Mrs Margaret Bilsland deciphered and typed the difficult script with impressive speed and efficiency.

I naturally bear full responsibility for any errors of fact or judgment.

December 1971   O.N.

Contents

List of Tables

Introduction

It is advisable to start with a definition. Wherever I speak of gambling in the text to follow, I take it to mean either betting on a future event or series of events, whose outcome is uncertain and beyond the direct power or control of the bettor, or the placing of stakes in money, or in tokens passing as money, on a future chance event, in conditions in which a commercial organizer, manager or promoter, or any group or combination of these, seeks to derive, individually or collectively, a profit or share from this activity. This definition—following along generally adopted lines—excludes from discussion and consideration the large field of private gambling where money circulates exclusively among the participants—in other words where there is no leakage out of the system—as well as institutions such as Insurance and the Stock Market where, even when gambling speculation does take place, this activity is no more than marginal and subsidiary to the principal aims of finance, investment and commercial development.

Eminent leaders of public opinion have rarely spoken of gambling in any other than the most pejorative terms. George Washington held that 'Gambling is the child of avarice, the brother of iniquity, and the father of mischief!'[1] Benjamin Disraeli, Earl of Beaconsfield, called gambling 'a vast engine of demoralisation'.[2]

Winston Churchill, who as Chancellor of the Exchequer had for the first time introduced a Betting Tax in this country could only admit, on moving the withdrawal of the Tax in 1929: 'In practice it has failed. The volatile and elusive character of the betting population, the precarious condition in which they disport themselves, have proved incapable of bearing the weight even of the repeatedly reduced burdens we have tried to place upon them.'[3]

William Temple, then Archbishop of York, told the 1932 Royal Commission on Lotteries and Betting that 'Gambling challenges the view of life which the Christian Church exists to uphold and extend. Its glorification of mere chance is a denial of the Divine Order in nature. To risk money haphazardly is to disregard the insistence of the Church of every age of living faith that possessions are a trust, and that men must account to God for their use. The persistent appeal to covetousness is fundamentally opposed to the unselfishness which was taught by Jesus Christ and by the New Testament as a whole. The attempt (which is inseparable from gambling) to make profit out of the inevitable loss and possible suffering of others is the antithesis of that love of one's neighbour on which the Lord insisted.'[4]

The first British Labour Prime Minister, Ramsay MacDonald, spoke of gambling in the following terms: 'The spread of the gambling habit is one of the most disquieting events of the time for those particularly who believe in self-government and in an intelligent democracy using its political powers to secure moral and social ends'.[5] The most recent Labour Prime Minister, Harold Wilson, claimed, in leading his party's denunciation of the Premium Bond scheme, that 'In 1951 the Conservative Party had promised a Britain strong and free. Now Britain's strength, freedom and solvency apparently depend on the proceeds of a squalid raffle . . . There are hundreds of thousands of people in Britain who will be outraged by this proposal.'[6] Roy Jenkins, the Home Secretary in 1966 declared: 'This country has become a gamblers' paradise, more wide-open in this respect than any other comparable country.'[7]

Nor have writers who, over the years, have devoted their attentions to the subject of gambling taken a more charitable view of the activity described by them. Geoffrey Chaucer wrote in the fourteenth century:

> Gaming is the mother of all lies,
> And of deceit and cursed villainies,
> Manslaughter, blasphemy and wasteful sore
> Of cattle and time. And furthermore,
> 'Tis shameful and repugnant to honour
> to be regarded as a hazader.[8]

The poet Charles Cotton, whose 'The Compleat Gamester', written in 1674, still survives as a classic had this to say:

Gambling is an enchanting witchery, gotten between idleness and avarice: An itching disease that makes some scratch their heads . . . It hath this ill property above all other vices, that it renders a man incapable of prosecuting any serious action, and makes him always unsatisfied with his own condition; he is either lifted up to the top of mad joy with success, or plunged to the bottom of despair by misfortune, always in extremes, always in a storm; this minute the gamester's countenance is so serene and calm that one would think nothing could disturb it, and the next minute, so stormy and tempestuous that it threatens destruction to itself and others; and as he is transported with joy when he wins, so losing, is he lost upon the billows of a high and swelling passion till he hath lost sight both of sense and reason.[9]

The moral philosopher, John A. Hobson, wrote in 1905:

Gambling involves the denial of all systems in the apportionment of property; it plunges the mind in a world of anarchy, when things come upon one and pass from one miraculously. It does not so manifestly sin against the canons of justice as do other bad modes of transfer—theft, fraud, sweating—for everyone is said to have an equal chance; but it inflicts a grave damage to the intellect. Based as it is on an organised rejection of all reason as a factor, it removes its devotees into a positive atmosphere of miracle, and generates an emotional excitement than inhibits those checks which reason more or less contrives to place on emotional extravagances . . . The essence of gambling consists in an abandonment of reason, and inhibition of the factors of human control . . . A practice so corrupting to the intelligence not only of the habitué, but even of the casual spectator, stands condemned as formidable enemy of education and of intellectual order.[10]

In more recent years Virgil W. Peterson, who as operating Director of the Chicago Crime Commission has made a life-long study of gambling and its consequences, has declared that 'Mass gambling has always resulted in great social and economic ills. And almost every civilised nation in the world has from time to time found it necessary to resort to anti-gambling legislation to protect its citizens', that 'Gambling is merely a method whereby wealth is redistributed from the possession of the many into the hands of the few', and again, 'There is no place for legalised gambling in an enlightened society.'[11]

One is able to cite the sporadic, untypical apologist for the activity of gambling. Charles Lamb states that 'A number of moralists condemn lotteries and refuse to see anything noble in the passion of the ordinary gambler. They judge gambling as some atheists judge religion, by its excesses, and denounce the innocent because of the peccant minority.'[12] Bernard Baruch, the American statesman and economist declares: 'You can't stop people from gambling on horses and why should you prohibit a man from backing his own judgement? It's another form of personal initiative.'[13] But undeniably the majority view is represented by those who claim that 'Gambling now perhaps does more harm than drink', that 'Gambling implies the implicit abandonment of reason', that 'The amount of gambling in Britain is now stupendous' and that 'Britain is in the grip of a gambling fever'.[14]

II

The Mass Media, though largely confining themselves to the legal and economic implications of gambling, overwhelmingly concur with the views expressed by the leaders of public morality and opinion. With almost one voice, the introduction of the Betting and Gaming Act, transforming Britain in 1960 in respect of gambling from a prohibitionist into the leading permissive country, was greeted with assent and approval. It was widely assumed that legalization and institutionalization of practices widely indulged in by large sections of the population would operate in the direction of control and restraint. 'It is warmly welcomed,' stated *The Times*, 'for the lines laid down by the Willink Commission were sound and ought to lead to the rationalisation of the law'.[15] 'Sense at last', claimed the *News Chronicle* on the same day, 'this reform would take a heavy burden off the police, who, under the present law, waste time and energy and make themselves thoroughly unpopular with millions of ordinary citizens by chasing street bookies and their runners.' 'Betting and Gaming Laws', said the *Daily Telegraph*, 'are a nettle which at last the Government—to its credit—has grasped. When there is one law for the rich and another for the poor, when no relevant law is respected, when attempts to enforce the law cause undiluted hostility towards the police—then it is high time that something is done', while the *Evening Standard* carried this message: 'A good bet . . . The aim should be a body of law which reflects the beliefs of today instead of perpetuating the prejudices of the past'.[16] These sentiments were echoed across a large spectrum of the provincial press: 'A commonsense reform'; 'New regulations in keeping with modern ideas will be widely welcomed'; 'A long-awaited reform that will be workmanlike and so, in its own terms, worthwhile in making for better law' and many others.[17]

Even the spokesmen of the country's major religions, as a rule implacably hostile to gambling, expressed views sympathetic to the legal changes being brought about. 'While the Church of England regards betting and gaming as so bound up with sinful desires and habits as to be always under grave suspicion,' said the Archbishop of York in his diocesan letter, 'it may still support the State in trying to exercise a more effective and defensible control over the activities of organised betting',[18] while the *Catholic Herald* stated: 'it would seem that the provisions of the Betting and Gaming Bill are calculated to regularise the present habits of betting, especially by the less wealthy, and subject them to control and scrutiny. As such, the Bill, in our view deserves praise . . . Catholics usually have to stand up against the lax views of the majority affecting marriage and personal life. It is a comfort to find ourselves in this subject-matter at one with the feelings, we believe, of the great majority.'[19]

Paradoxically it was only the major group of direct beneficiaries, the bookmakers, who, it seemed, had any qualms in this matter. 'Who wants these shops' headlined the *Daily Express* in an article based on bookmakers' reactions to the legislation of betting shops, 'Big S.P.* Bookies say: Not for us'.[20]

In spite of this virtually unanimous response of welcome it did not take long for disillusionment and even alarm to set in. As early as February 1961 the *Evening News*, in featuring an article 'Betting's new Klondike', was telling its readers that 'The more you have, the less you gamble. This is one of the interesting facts which appear to be emerging from the setting up of betting

* Starting Price.

shops.'[21] Britain was referred to as 'The Betting Shop Society'; the *Sheffield Telegraph* was asking, 'Are we really as decadent a nation as this? A nation of bingo players, Premium Bond holders, tax-dodgers, speculators, and take-over bidders?'[22] A year later the Financial Editor of the *Sunday Telegraph* referred to betting shops as 'a licence to print money' and went on to say, 'This week, I am deliberately devoting a disproportionate amount of space to turning the spotlight on Britain's newest, least documented and in many ways most depressing growth industry—the Betting Shops'.[23] The *Evening Standard* asked, 'Why have the English become gambling mad?'[24] and the *Sunday School Chronicle* wrote in an article entitled 'Easy Money': '. . . Gambling is on the increase. It has become a national vice. There is no doubt that all the legalising of betting shops and of other forms of gambling has encouraged the gambling habit. Gambling is closely linked with the widespread desire for easy money. Love of money, St Paul said, is the root of all evil.'[25]

A National Opinion Poll undertaken in 1963 disclosed that fifty-five per cent of the adult population gambled in some way or another and that more than half the men and two fifths of the women in Britain regularly gambled on horses.[26] This disclosure aroused vehement comment from among a large spectrum of publications, such as 'Gambling fever', 'A Gambling Island', 'Bookies hit the jackpot in gambling spree' and '£853 million was spent on gambling in Boom Year'.[27] 'London: The Wide-Open City' lamented the *Evening Standard*, going on to ask, '£10,000 an hour. Is this what Parliament really intended?'[28] 'Gambling crazy?' asked the *Evening Times*, Glasgow, 'we have gone from partial prohibition to an emancipation so complete that it may bring more moral and social danger than gambling left to flourish underground. Have we gone too far?'[29] 'We spend more on gambling than we do on roads', stated the women's magazine *Nova* authoritatively, 'much more than we do on hospitals. The £915 million gaming turnover is bigger than the balance of payment debt at its worst. As a nation we spend £175 million on aid to underdeveloped countries. We spend nearly four times that amount backing horses. The amount we spend on bingo is equal to the entire national budget of Uganda.'[30]

III

That gambling, particularly when legally sanctioned, and criminality, racketeering, extortion, and corruption travel hand-in-hand has long been held as an article of faith by social scientists. 'Wherever gambling is legalised,' says Kirson Weinberg, 'it contributed to community disorganisation, enriched the underworld and criminal, while its openness did not change the form of gambling or diminish its scope.'[31] Lundberg, Schrage and Larson speak of 'criminal syndicates which have assumed control over such tremendously profitable activities as gambling, bootlegging, slot-machines and prostitution.'[32] Broom and Selznick assert that 'The largest criminal associations are the vice hierarchies. Part of the public demands illicit gambling, narcotics and sexual intercourse; the syndicates capitalize on the demands,'[33] while Landis states that 'Gambling is the very heartbeat of organised crime, both on a local and national scale.'[34] *The Nation* in a special issue affirms that 'Professional gambling today is the most lucrative, most destructive and withal most widely tolerated form of crime in this country ... Each year the revenues that pass into the coffers of "Gambling Inc." are used to bribe elected officials, to oil political machines and to corrupt police and other law-enforcement agencies on a scale so staggering it has not yet been truly measured.'[35] Virgil W. Peterson, one of the most prominent world experts on the legal issues of gambling, expresses the view that, (1) It is doubtful whether law enforcement agencies, unable or unwilling to control illegal gambling, will be able to administer and control legalized gambling. (2) Gambling has at all times provided the sources and resources of the underworld racketeers and has produced political and law enforcement bribery and corruption. (3) That it is its lucrativeness and not its illegality which causes it to be dominated by organized crime, which in pursuit of the 'loot' will engage in violence, retribution, widespread use of a large variety of crooked and fraudulent paraphernalia. (4) That a wide-open policy results in alliance between the underworld and officialdom, in corruption, extortion and gang warfare.[36]

It must however be borne in mind that all these quoted sources comment upon conditions in the United States where all forms of gambling with few exceptions, are strictly outlawed; where a different set of historical, cultural and social factors operate and where, for instance, underworld control of gambling might still be a legacy of prohibition. To what extent these conditions are similarly true of Britain is impossible to assess with any degree of confidence. Undoubtedly since the establishment of casino-type gaming, allegations of criminal infiltration and control, underworld warfare, protection, racketeering, and mutual reinforcement between gambling, organized vice and criminal gangs have periodically hit the headlines.[37] It is impossible to assess how firm the foundations are on which these charges are made, whether any or all of these criminal implications are a natural and necessary by-product of gaming,* just as we cannot know whether, if they do exist, these criminal chain reactions are more prevalent or merely more visible now that one of the major links has achieved legal establishment, and whether they are part and parcel of the tactical and technological breakthrough in gang organization. Public and police authorities, though in favour of legalization, are uniformly reticent in the release of opinion and information. The only observation I wish to make in the present context is that arrests for street betting which had numbered over 4,000 in 1953 in London alone had by 1967 declined to three or four.

IV

That gambling activity is deeply ingrained, universal and ubiquitous, prevalent wherever there are groups organized in societies, cannot be disputed. That, for a substantial section of inhabitants, past and present, in all types of societies and under a large variety of cultural and social systems, gambling is and has always been a prominent, even if not dominant, component of their existence has amply been documented and agreed.[38] Where sociologists have largely abandoned consideration of the subject of gambling to a host of social reformers, *a priori* predisposed to

---

* Continental European experience, where Casino gaming, apparently entirely free of criminal control and association, has had a long tradition would tend to refute the view that the linkup is inevitable.

regard gambling as analogous with corruption and vice, sociological analysis is overdue and will, within the present context,
commence with examination of the perspectives presented by the
few contributions within this framework available to us. Although
it is recognized that such distinction is necessarily heuristic, and
to some extent, even arbitrary, it has been decided to divide
sociological contributions to the subject of gambling into two
categories. One group consists of contributions concerned with
the causes and functions of gambling within the social structure
and the other seeks to explain the sociological factors which
might impel individuals as well as sub-cultural groups to indulge
in gambling activities. The first category is largely directed at
accounting for the prevalence of gambling and yet the moral and
social devaluation imposed upon it, and seeks to determine the
social function fulfilled by gambling. The second category
attempts to explain the covert rather than the overt motivation of the individual gambler, the social norms and processes
involved in gambling within informal groups, as well as the
non-material satisfactions derived by the gambler from his
activity.

We must from the latter category exclude psychopathological
accounts of gambling, such as those presented by Bergler,
Lindner and Reik, who all attribute the urge towards gambling to
subconscious neurotic desires for self-punishment aroused by
inadmissible death wishes towards the father.[39] Not merely are
such assumptions entirely speculative, but, in particular, by
virtue of their concern with the psychologically impaired compulsive, rather than with the 'normal' regular and habitual
gambler, they are beyond the scope of this present enquiry. John
Cohen's stimulating contributions regarding psychologically
determined predispositions towards the taking or rejecting of
risks must, for similar reasons, be excluded.[40]

E. C. Devereux, whose 'Gambling and the Social Structure' is
the most extensive as well as best documented sociological study
falling within the first category, considers gambling to be a
corporate 'safety valve' needed to balance and reconcile the con-
current subscription of Anglo-Saxon societies to the conflicting
heritage of Puritanism-cum-Capitalism and the ideals of Christianity.[41] Puritanism—implying normative subscription to the

supremacy of the virtues of systematic effort, economic rationality, strictest adaptation of means to ends, thrift, frugality and
self-denial—while persisting as a motive force in Western
societies until the present day, had suffered debasement by
infusion of the Capitalist real-life practices of acquisitiveness,
self-seeking and hedonism. These, furthermore, needed reconciliation with the syndrome of beliefs enshrined as Christianity,
exhorting the social totality to bear constant witness to the moral
imperatives of love of one's neighbour, mutuality, charity and
humility. Western industrial society, continuing to be based on
the complementary cornerstones of Puritanism and Christianity,
is unable to abandon either the one or the other and yet these
remain mutually exclusive and incapable of logical reconciliation.
However, as the pursuit of material commodities and gratifications
will usually exert a more powerful pull than commitment to
remote spiritual salvation, we follow the path of competitive
rivalry, self-aggrandizement, egotistical self-interest and vent our
anxiety and guilt on the functionally necessary scapegoat, the
grotesque and defenceless *alter ego*. Gambling, which, parallel-
ing in its alleged materialism, ruthless competitiveness and
opportunism, the dominant and yet intolerable characteristics of
the economic system, affords a perfect target which, were it not
already to exist, would need to be invented.

An alternative version of the same basic theory proposed by
Bloch stresses the fundamental ambivalence between morally
disapproved and publicly enjoyed practices and ascribes to the
economic system itself certain internal inconsistencies which,
unable to achieve self-reconciliation, will relieve themselves by
discharge on a substitute object.[42] According to this view
Puritanism, still the generating force impelling us in the direction
of pursuit of duty, work and effort, has long ago lost its spiritual
content of asceticism, self-denial, other worldliness, and communality. It has increasingly needed to integrate with an economic order in which self-centred pursuit of privilege, power and
wealth and more recently hedonism and supremacy of consumption have found themselves dominant. As, furthermore, the very
elements considered to be the major characteristics of gambling,
namely competitiveness, chance and uncertainty are, at the same
time, part and parcel of the market economy as it has evolved on

the foundation stone of Puritanism, the utilization of gambling as a scapegoat allows us to sustain two mutually contradictory value systems in double harness.

Ingenious and superficially plausible though such hypotheses may be, they fail to stand up to systematic analysis. Even were one prepared to overlook the principal logical objections to Functionalism,* what comparative empirical evidence exists, stands in direct refutation of the explanations advanced. Were gambling to be regarded as a scapegoat, functionally vital in order to unify the conflicting ideological tenets of Puritanism-cum-Capitalism on the one hand and of Christianity on the other, it would need to be shown that it prevails to a similar significant extent within the various societies subscribing to this value system, as well as being of only minor social import in other societies based on a different set of values. Yet, though gambling, as has already been documented,† is a universal activity prevailing wherever groups have been organized in societies, its incidence and impact continue to be differentially distributed throughout the various cultures. Countries such as West Germany and Switzerland, both posessing a Puritan-Calvinist as well as a Christian tradition no less potent than is to be found in Anglo-Saxon communities, are by all accounts involved in gambling only relatively little,[43] whereas non-puritan Catholic countries such as Italy and Spain, as well as others such as China and the Middle-East, differing not merely in religious belief systems, but also in economic structure and orientation, are considered to be no less immersed in gambling than we are. Nevertheless, gambling is equally subjected to moral denunciation. Since, however, the commercial superstructure is lacking, privately organized gambling is more prevalent than it is here.

Equally, if gambling is to be considered as a functionally vital scapegoat, necessary to reconcile the economic disequilibrium between the ideological imperatives of Puritanism and the actual practices of profit-seeking economic pursuit, what are we to say of societies such as the Soviet bloc, where similar economic internal

---

* The main defects of Functionalism are in all probability its tendency of treating effects as causes and the fact of its being empirically untestable. For a very penetrating recent discussion of Functionalism see *Modern Social Theory* by Percy S. Cohen, Heinemann Educational Books (London 1968), chapter 3.

† See note 38.

contradictions can be postulated and where gambling is contained within insignificant proportions? Nor are the alleged internal contradictions within the economic system inevitable, necessary, or even factually valid. In its original unadulterated version, Puritanism did regard gambling in a recreational context as legitimate and condemned it only when it induced misspending of time and money.[44] Neither is decision-taking by reliance on chance absent in conventionally legitimated fields of our social order. One can readily think of the traditional methods of jury selection, the means of introduction of Private Members' Bills into Parliament, as well as the emphasis on 'happy accident' in scientific research and discoveries.[45] Thus, even if the alleged correlations between gambling and inherent contradictions within the value system were to exist, to what extent can these be claimed as being structurally functional when they seem to be counterbalanced, if not hopelessly outweighed, by the structurally dysfunctional elements of disruptive and destructive social antagonism? If moral condemnation together with practical toleration of gambling is claimed to be the safety-valve of a 'sick society', then, as a logical corollary all other societies in which gambling does exist, while being morally unacceptable, must be regarded as 'sick'. References to sickness, ambivalence, internal contradictions then cease to have any meaning and the 'explanation' does not explain anything at all.

A more credible explanation, still marginally within the same school, suggests that since gambling is a form of activity almost exclusively confined to the aristocracy on the one hand and the working classes on the other, it has traditionally found itself the target for denunciation by the middle class, which, being morally the most articulate group of modern society, feels free to criticize it. Partly impelled by motives of disapproval of the squandering of time and other resources, partly disenchanted and morally indignant at others' preferment for amusement over self-improvement, the middle class castigate gambling as a vice. Being, furthermore, activated by resentment of social exclusiveness and by envy of the spontaneous fun enjoyed by those assumed to be inferior, they gain from such devaluation moral impetus towards the promotion of self-interest.[46]

Unfortunately, even this theory—affirming Ranulf's generalization that moral indignation characteristic of middle class psychology in reality represents repressed and displaced envy— seeming reasonably to fit British social conditions, still fails to account for the motivations of the morally articulate sections condemning gambling in societies in which the middle classes fulfil no more than an insignificant role.[47]

Would not a more satisfactory explanation suggest that gambling differs qualitatively as well as quantitatively between the various types, that it means many things to many people, that within the situational context of the actor and participant it offers stimulations and gratifications for which an economic price is willingly and deliberately paid? Might it not be that moral disapproval—true to the motto 'I invest, you bet, he gambles'— far from being a positive functional necessity, is based on nothing other than malinformation, misconception or perceptive partiality?

As to our second category, concerned with sociological studies and explanations at the microscopic societal level, these allow themselves to be subdivided again into two separate schools of thought. On the one hand there are those who analyse gambling in terms of man's inherent nature and on the other hand those who seek to do so in terms of cultural factors.

The former viewpoint, most cogently argued in the works of Caillois and Huizinga, by and large perceives gambling as a form of 'secular divination'.[48] In this perspective gambling represents a modern survival of primitive animist society within which appeals to, and propitiation of, supernatural spirits exerted a powerful sway. Longing for intense emotional experience, believing in personal power to command one's destiny subject to proper performance of magic and ritual allied to the firm convictions of being able to divine the intentions of the supernatural deities, characterize contemporary gambling with its belief system of luck, magic and superstition no less than the religious system of primitive man. Caillois defines play activity as basic human experience. Play activity is characterized by isolation from real life, by uncertainty of outcome, and by being a non-productive voluntary activity from which the participant is at all times free to withdraw. He postulates the following distinctive categories of play: (a) *Agon*—competitive games resembling combat,

(b) *Mimicry*—games of illusion and delusion, (c) *Ilinx*—games of voluptuous panic and vertigo, and lastly, the one concerning us, (d) *Alea*—games of chance; activities in which the player is entirely passive, which are negations of work, discipline and labour. In his definition, *Alea*, apart from continuing to fulfil for modern man the functions of revelation of destiny, serves in modern social systems the additional and the now more significant purpose of providing a substitute world in which natural and individual differences are abolished, where social and economic equality, denied in real life, is artificially imposed. *Alea* accordingly assumes an especially significant role in societies in which there exists a sharp break between working time and leisure time, where perfect predictability and boredom prevail in the occupational sphere.

Concepts of man confronting his modern civilization, with his perceptual and psychological equipment basically unmodified since his emergence from the Stone Age, have, in the Social Sciences, been largely discarded with recognition of the infinite mutability of individual traits in response to differing social conditions. If gambling is defined as modern man's sublimation of magic and ritual, by what means do we account for primitive man's propensity to gamble, a propensity historically established as prevalent? Moreover, if the appeal to destiny by resort to magic and ritual is not only innate, but also demonstrably more effective in 'delivering the goods', why should modern man not have retained this habit, or at least have provided himself with a more efficient and normatively respectable instrument of sublimation? What, furthermore, happens to the non-sublimated impulses of those who do not gamble? Do they not experience the urge for divination, or do they sublimate their urges by different means—say rock-climbing or parachuting—and if so, what is it that predisposes them to choose this particular mode? Are such means effective to a lesser or greater extent and why should the one type of sublimation be socially neutral, while the other finds itself disenfranchised?

As to the theory of gambling being a reaction to boredom at the imposition of mechanical, routinized monotony in the occupational field, a definition also advanced by Bloch and Clinard,[49] does this provide us with answers to some of the questions raised? Though it would be fallacious to suggest Bloch's definition to be circumscribed by the concept expressed by 'Gambling is an escape from the routine and boredom characteristic of much of modern industrial life in which the sense of creation and the instinct of workmanship have been lost. Taking a chance destroys routine and is hence pleasurable', a direct causal relationship between (a) boredom and (b) gambling is proposed. But in what manner is the term 'boredom' to be defined? Do we take it to imply the powerful repugnance towards some activities allied to relative indifference to others; or is it a general attitude of indifference? Is it a dislike for some tasks, combined with a strong liking for others; or is it just a negative attitude towards the task at hand without awareness of possible orientation to alternative tasks? All these situations, as well as a variety of other possible hypothetical constructs, could be held to arouse boredom. Is gambling to be considered a reaction against any one particular type of 'boredom', against a combination of several types, or possibly against all of these added together? Does it occur in response to long or short, continuous or intermittent periods of exposure to boredom situations? Is it a spontaneous outburst against imposition of one particularly severe boredom-inducing ordeal, or does it arise as a result of the cumulative effects of exposure to a series of milder boredom-producing situations? Anyhow, what does induce individuals to adopt different means of adaptation to the experience of boredom? Why should one man, as a reaction to boredom, go into politics, while another goes into the betting shop? Why should one create the Mona Lisa while the other fills in his football coupon? Unfortunately, it seems that an explanation within the blanket terms of 'boredom' has not brought us any closer to the answers we seek. The assertion that boredom leads to gambling is of meagre analytical value, because the term 'boredom' itself is vague and unclear and further, even if a precise definition were possible, because boredom can lead to a multitude of actions and because the particular conditions which might lead to one type of action rather than another are not specified.*[50]

---

* The same criticism would apply to blanket explanation in unspecified terms of frustration, safety-valve, anomie or the one I would personally most incline to—alienation.

Nechama Tec in her book *Gambling in Sweden* attributes gambling propensity to the experience of status frustration.[51] According to her, regular gamblers are most heavily concentrated within the uppermost echelons of the working class, the regions of manual workers where income, descent and education most closely approximate the standards of the lower grades of the middle class. Postulating barriers between these two social strata to be surmountable only by those able to compensate for their lack of social and occupational skills by spectacular accretion of material wealth, she claims that members of the upper grades of the working class assuage their resultant status frustration through gambling in the hope of gaining mobility that would otherwise be unattainable. Although success is confined to the very few, latent anger, guilt and frustration is thus diverted into socially harmless channels. Indeed these drives, now rendered harmless, are frequently sublimated and directed towards effective action for advancement in their occupational and social careers. Neither the bottom layers of the working class nor the equivalent stratum of the middle class, by virtue of mobility facilities within their own social spheres, are beset by experience of status frustration and are thereby relatively less prone to participation in gambling activity.

Tec claims to have demonstrated this alleged association between status frustration at specific social levels and the propensity to gambling by analysis of the data of a large-scale Swedish multistage sample survey, designed to yield information on economic, political, familial, religious and recreational spheres of activity. While no objection can be raised to her recourse to secondary material itself, a number of severe methodological, as well as conceptual shortcomings render her hypothesis, at best, unproven. Questions on gambling* were only sent to one single group out of the six separate groups considered in the survey; varying numbers appear, for reasons undisclosed, as respondents throughout the various tables; a number of cells from which the data are derived are numerically too small to permit conclusions. Information as to response rates to the sample as a whole or to

* One must bear in mind that the sets of questions designated by Tec as signifying gambling were considered by the promoters of the Survey to indicate recreational preferences.

any set of questions is not provided. Above all, some of the correlations from which conclusions are drawn are of a statistically insufficient degree for relevant conclusions to be significant. Moreover, gambling finds itself defined as participation in football pools, an activity which, though widespread and extensive, is universally submerged, in outlay as well as intensity, relative to other forms of gambling activity and which for wide circles of the population has, subject to moderation in outlay, ceased to carry connotations of gambling at all. Gamblers are defined by the single criterion of being those who stake money on football pools once monthly or more often, without any attempt being made to relate the frequency of betting to the volume of betting, or the gambling on football pools to participation in other gambling activities. In fact, more than fifty per cent of all 'gamblers' staked less than the equivalent of $12\frac{1}{2}$p per week. Lastly, the criteria of differentiating those uppermost sections of the working class who were, as a result of their mobility aspiration blockage, considered to be status frustrated are unconvincing on the basis of the adduced evidence. Patently, the higher-paid workers' more frequent rate of participation in football pools is, even if general and real, probably due to possession of greater material resources with which to comply with subcultural gambling norms rather than greater intensity of social mobility drive.

Robert Herman in *Gambling as Work* postulates gambling as providing satisfaction of the urges towards decision-making, self-reliance and autonomy, present in all, but, in modern industrial societies, attainable by only a small select minority in real life.[52] Having, over a period, observed and recorded the gambling actions and behaviour of attenders at various American horserace tracks, Herman maintains that for large numbers of middle- and lower-class men, gambling—involving systematic study of form, sustained attention to fluctuations of market conditions, estimation of probabilities and ultimately the backing of personal judgment with real cash—contains all the essential elements of true and esteemed entrepreneurial roles and provides for the player who is denied exercise of such functions in his real-life occupational, familial, and conventional recreational roles, a substitute outlet that satisfies his otherwise unappeased drives. Furthermore, whereas gambling involves for all participants a rational, intellectual exercise in which money primarily fulfils the function of defining the decision-making process, differentiation needs to be made between the specific sets of needs satisfied for different categories of players. Whereas for lower-middle- and working-class men, decision-making is the principal attraction, women in the identical social groups—overwhelmingly inclined to place their bets on short-priced favourites—derive from their gambling the experience of frequent 'rewards', otherwise in short supply in their drab and humdrum daily life; while for the wealthy gamblers, gathered in the lush surrounds of the Private Enclosure, gambling provides yet a further reinforcing opportunity for experience of sociability, conviviality and above all conspicuous consumption.

While applauding Herman's classification of different categories of gamblers, the contribution, useful and original as it may be, lies open to the charge of unwarranted conclusions in face of the unsupported assumption that all lower price enclosure attenders are lower-middle and working class, and thereby *per se* automatically disqualified from participation in experiences offering opportunities for decision-making in their real-life world. Whatever may be the level of validity of the author's conclusions, the degree of relationship is unlikely to be as direct and as inextricably causally linked as is proposed.

The one and only sociological contribution seeking to study the gambler within his social gambling context and attempting to account for the satisfactions derived from gambling in inter-actional and transactional terms, which thorough research of bibliographical sources was able to reveal, is the brief but illuminating study presented by Zola under the title 'Observations on Gambling in a Lower-Class Setting'.[53] On the basis of extensive participant observation undertaken in a New England tavern—doing service as a sub-rosa betting shop—the author proclaims interpersonal factors and the dynamics of associations to be dominant in lower-class gambling action and activity. In his view the betting shop forms, for the occupationally, culturally and socially deprived, a common and self-contained refuge from the hostile and indifferent outside world. The betting shop provides for the defeated, dispossessed and despised a fantasy substitute universe where they are enabled to enact a charade transforming them into activists, victors and entrepreneurs; where—by 'beating the system' personified by the bookmaker's runner—they are able to experience the illusion of accomplishment, achievement and personal control, even if only in their brief and infrequent moments of triumph.* For these experiences the initial definition of insider and outsider and above all the associates' mutual fulfilment of their various functions and roles is considered to be vital and indispensable.

Although it is by no means established that the subcultural context of the American study would find itself essentially replicated within a different and divergent social milieu,† it would seem that systematic empirical investigations based upon observations of gambling within its social and interpersonal context and of gamblers inside their own natural environment, may well offer the best hope of elucidating causes accounting for the widespread persistence of gambling as well as disclosing some of the social functions gambling does serve.

V

The principal questions arising from above discussion may well be summarized as follows:

(1) Is gambling inevitably and inextricably bound up with lawbreaking and criminality, with illegalities and corruption, or can legislative codes and provisions compatible with dominant moral and social values be devised—and enforced—confining gambling within its legal barriers and restricting infringements to none other than a small and untypical minority? (This is the subject matter of Chapter I.)

(2) Does gambling make excessive claims upon national manpower and material resources? Does available evidence indicate a rate of expansion of volume of gambling expenditure disproportionate to the simultaneous rise in income, living standards and

* As one successful bettor is quoted as having exclaimed: 'What do you think I am—a nobody?' Op. cit. p. 30.

† Zola does not omit to point out that gambling is likely to mean 'many things to many people' and that the observations derived by him may well fail to hold true of different investigations carried out upon a different set of subjects within a different social context.

other comparable items of expenditure? (This is the subject matter of Chapter II.)

(3) Does gambling make excessive claims upon personal and household expenses? Is expenditure and participation in gambling generally or within specific social strata, excessive in terms of outlay and intensity? Does evidence, such as might be available, suggest that gambling is necessarily or predominantly habit-forming and addictive? (This is the subject matter of Chapter III.)

(4) Is gambling anti-redistributive, does it afflict the poorer sections of the community most severely? Is there a significant degree of association between the level of participation in gambling on the one hand and indices indicative of relative social privelege or deprivation on the other hand? (This is the subject matter of Chapter IV.)

(5) Is gambling a subversion of intelligence, enlightenment and education; does it imply an affront to the dignity of reason, an abandonment of the causal system? Is gambling disruptive to the personality, is it addictive and does it generally lead to increasing obsession?

(6) Does gambling fail to fulfil any socially productive function? Is gambling, based upon and leading to acquisitive greed and crassest materialism, anti-social in its effects, disruptive of fellowship, of mutuality and community? (Questions 5 and 6 are the subject matter of Chapters V and VI.)

Notes

1. Rubner, A. (1966) p. 98.
2. Ludovici, L. J. (1962) p. 1.
3. Ibid. pp. 218–19.
4. Perkins, E. B. (1962) p. 109.
5. Peterson, Virgil W. (1951) p. 3.
6. House of Commons, 17 April 1957.
7. *The Times*, London, 13 September 1966.
8. Perkins, E. B. Op. cit. p. 9.
9. Cotton, C. (1674).
10. Hobson, J. A. (1905).
11. Peterson, V. W. Op. cit. p. 49 and p. 150.
12. Lamb, C. (1832).

13. Quoted in Daniel Bell, *The End of Ideology* p. 135.
14. Trevelyan, M. M. *English Social History*, London (1951) p. 571; Rowntree, B. S. and Lavers, G. R. (1951) and Fowler, N. (1963).
15. *The Times*, London, 3 November 1959.
16. The *Daily Telegraph*, London, 3 November 1959 and the *Evening Standard*, London, 3 November 1959.
17. The *Yorkshire Post*, Leeds, 3 November 1959; *Eastern Evening News*, Norwich, 18 November 1959 and *Bath Chronicle and Herald*, Bath, 18 November 1959.
18. *The Times*, London, 23 December 1959.
19. *Catholic Herald*, London, 6 November 1959.
20. *Daily Express*, London, 22 December 1959.
21. *Evening News*, London, 22 February 1961.
22. *Socialist Leader*, Glasgow, 15 July 1961 and *Sheffield Telegraph*, 2 August 1961.
23. *Sunday Telegraph*, London, 9 September 1962.
24. *Evening Standard*, London, 8 January 1963.
25. *Sunday School Chronicle*, London, 25 April 1963.
26. See Millar, Robert (1966) pp. 257–8.
27. *Evening Argus*, Brighton, 27 May 1965; *Huddersfield Daily Examiner*, Huddersfield, 17 May 1966; the *Daily Mail*, London, 4 April 1963 and *Yorkshire Evening Press*, Leeds, 3 April 1963.
28. *Evening Standard*, London, 14 June 1965.
29. *Evening Times*, Glasgow, 17 May 1966.
30. *Nova*, London, August 1966, p. 17.
31. Weinberg, S. K. (1960) pp. 266–86.
32. Lundberg, G. A. *et al.* (1958) ch. 11, *Sociology*, Harper Bros., New York.
33. Brown, L. and Selznick, P. (1963) section 7, *Sociology*, Harper Row, New York.
34. Landis, P. (1964) ch. 22.
35. *The Nation*, New York, 22 October 1960, special issue: 'Gambling Inc; Treasure Chest of the Underworld'.
36. Peterson, Virgil W., *Journal of Criminal Law and Criminology* vol. XL, no. 3 (1959).
37. The *Daily Telegraph*, London, on 30 October 1967 quoted Mr Gordon Bagier, Member of Parliament for Sunderland (South) as follows: 'I am very disturbed about the American money being used for gaming operations in Britain. I am sure a lot of it is Mafia front-money, and it is more than we want.' See also *The Times*, London, 10 April 1967 (article by Norman Fowler), *Evening Standard*, London, 31 May 1967 (article by Lord Kilbracken); the *Sun*, London, 11 October 1967; and a series of articles in the *Sunday Telegraph*, London, of 16 February ('Close-up investigates the big clean-up. Crackdown on Britain's casinos'), 23 February and 2 March 1969.
38. An attempt at a comprehensive historical account of gambling would take us well beyond the scope af the present enquiry. It is enough to

mention in brief outline that the Chinese gambling game called Wei-ki (Japanese equivalent Go) is claimed to date back to 2300 B.C. The excavations at Ur (*c.* 2000 B.C.) unearthed an inlaid gaming board similar to the one found at Crete (*c.* 1800 B.C.). Dice—'Astragals'— carved from hind legs of sheep were found in Thebes (*c.* 1600 B.C.), Egypt (*c.* 1600 B.C.) and are also mentioned in Homer (1100–700 B.C.) Dice were also popular in India around the same time, while the Romans were charged with addiction to a game called 'Caput aut Navis' (similar to our game Heads or Tails). Tacitus claimed that 'The Germans will stake even liberty on the throw of the dice. He who loses submits to slavery, though younger and stronger than his adversary' (*De Moribus Germanorum*). The Roman Emperors Caligula and Nero were passionate gamblers. Claudius had his carriage arranged for dicing convenience. Horseracing with concomitant betting was common among the Hittites (*c.* 1400 B.C.) and to the present day the Pomo Indians hold the proficient professional gambler at a guessing game with bones in highest repute.

Dicing in England dates back to Saxon days (Saxon word for gambling is *Gamen*). Bishop Etheric is reported to have found King Canute and his courtiers gaming at dice on a midnight visit. An edict of King Richard I (1190) forbade members of the crusading army of ranks lower than Knight to gamble. A statute by King Henry VIII, himself an inveterate gambler, (1541) outlawed '. . . dicing, table or carding or any other manner of game prohibited by statute heretofore made . . .'. The first lottery to be held in England took place during the reign of Queen Elizabeth I; a lottery in 1612 proposed to raise money for the colonization of North America. Funds obtained from lotteries went a long way towards the establishment of the American Universities at Columbia, Harvard, Yale and Dartmouth.

See especially Ashton, J., *The History of Gambling in England* (1898); David, F. N., *Games, God and Gambling* (1962), and Ludovici, L. J., *The Itch for Play* (1962). Also Scarne, J., *Scarne's Complete Guide to Gambling* (1961).

39. Bergler, E. (1958); Lindner, R. M. (Annals) vol. 269 (May 1950) pp. 93–107 and Reik, T. (1942) p. 153. See also Freud, S. (1952) pp. 87–114.

40. Cohen, J. (1) 1960; (2) 1965; (3) 1958, vol. 13.

41. Devereux, E. C., Jr, unpublished Ph.D. thesis (1949).

42. Bloch, H. A. (1962) vol. 8 no. 4.

43. Rubner, A., *The Economics of Gambling* (London 1966) provides some information on the international legal and economic background to gambling and also quotes a number of further sources in the Bibliography.

44. See Thorner, I., 'Ascetic Protestantism, Gambling and One-Piece System', in *American Journal of Economics and Sociology* (New York January 1956) for a most interesting examination of this as well as of other related issues.

45. Aubert, Vilhelm in an article 'Chance in Social Affairs' (*Inquiry*, no. 1, Spring 1959; vol. 2, pp. 1–25) lists some of the areas in which reliance on chance decisions still prevails within modern societies.

46. See Adams, R. and Morgan J. (3 April 1964).

47. Apart from referring the reader to the works of Nietzsche, I would like to mention the book *Moral Indignation and Middle Class Psychology* by Svend Ranulf (1938) in connection with the subjects of the social origins and consequences of resentment, revenge and envy.

48. Caillois, R. (1962) and Huizinga, J. (1949).

49. Bloch, H. A, *American Journal of Sociology* vol. LVII, no. 3 (November 1951) pp. 215–21, *Crime and Delinquency* vol. 8, no. 4 (1962) and Clinard, M. B. (1963) pp. 276–81.

50. An unpublished German report on a research project undertaken by a team of sociologists at Cologne University (under the direction of Rene König, Karl-Dieter Opp and Fritz Sack), entitled *Das Spielen an Geldautomaten*, translated into English under the title of 'Gaming on Slot Machines' by the present author, failed to establish any connection between the frequency and intensity of gambling on slot machines on the one hand and the dimension of boredom, frustration, anomie, propensity to deviant behaviour on the other. The objections raised by them to the employment of the above terms without more precise and specific definition closely follow along the lines suggested in the text.

51. Tec, Nechama (1964).

52. Herman, R. D. in Herman, R. D. (ed.) (1967).

53. Zola, I. K, *Social Problems* vol. 10, no. 4 (Spring 1963) pp. 353–61 and reprinted in Herman, R. D. (ed.) op. cit.

CHAPTER I

Legislation and Present Major Forms of Gambling Activities

British Legislation

Gambling in Britain is conducted on the basis of the Betting and Gaming Act 1960, subsequently partly amended by the Betting, Gaming and Lotteries Act 1963 and the Gaming Act 1968.[1] It is overwhelmingly based on the recommendations of the 1949/51 Royal Commission on Betting, Lotteries and Gaming,[2] designed to remove existing anomalies. Prior to 1960, legal gambling was confined to circulation of football pools for credit betting, to betting on future events indirectly on credit terms as well as to cash betting at properly licensed horse- and dogracing venues. The use of any premises or loitering in the streets for betting and gambling, tendering or receiving ready-money in respect of bets or incitement by circulation of literature for cash betting were strictly prohibited.

As most of the prohibitions had, over the years, come increasingly to be disregarded, the Royal Commission took the view that a social habit as deeply ingrained as gambling could not efficiently be prevented by restrictive legislation; that by toleration of flagrantly illegal practices, progressive disrespect would be shown to the law and that, as a result of random enforcement and arbitrary interpretation due to ambiguity, the law officers, and in particular, the police, could be exposed to charges of overt favouritism and active participation in corruption.

The present main provisions are as follows:

OFF-COURSE BETTING

(1) The use of any public place, the loitering in streets for the purposes of betting continues to be strictly prohibited and transgressions are severely punished.

(2) The transmission of ready-money bets by post is no longer illegal.

(3) Licensed Betting Offices, colloquially referred to as 'betting shops', are now established for the first time in history. Members of the public, other than minors below the age of 18, may go there to place bets in cash.

(4) The use of any public place or premises, other than licensed betting offices, or racecourses and tracks, for the purposes of betting is strictly prohibited. This prohibition includes rooms or offices adjacent to betting shops and also applies to gaming in public houses.

(5) Licensed betting offices are legalized only subject to the grant or to renew a licence: (a) non-compliance with conditions granted to (a) the holder of a bookmaker's permit, (b) the Totalisator Board, (c) the accredited agent of a bookmaker of the Board. Planning permission will always be required before an application can be considered. Such application for the grant or renewal of a licence must be made in prescribed form to a Committee of the Justices in England and Wales and to the Licensing Court of Scotland.[3] There are several grounds for refusal to grant or to renew a licence: (a) non-compliance with conditions of access, such as entry through another place of business, (b) non-suitability of layout, character of location of premises, (c) inexpediency having regard to demand in the locality for betting offices and the existing number of betting offices in the locality, (d) in the case of application for renewal, improper conduct of offices, (e) reasonable doubt as to the applicant being holder of the necessary permits on the date when licence would come into force.

Betting offices must be closed between 6.30 p.m. and 7 a.m. the following morning; must neither advertise their location nor entice the public into their premises; must exclude persons below the age of eighteen from the premises and must not broadcast or televise racing transmissions. The use of the 'blower'—the telephone service set up by bookmakers to publicize runners, betting movement, commentary and results—is, however, permitted and the public are invariably kept informed by means of a loudspeaker relay.

In order to conduct business as credit bookmaker, a permit will have to be obtained in a manner closely similar to the one described above.[4] The bookmaker is then permitted to appoint agents as runners—such as factory and office agents, milkmen, etc—these must be issued with appropriate certificates and their registration must be noted.

POOL BETTING

The legality of registered Pool promoters—and one speaks in the context almost exclusively of Football Pools—was examined and confirmed by the Royal Commission, subject to certain safeguards. Pools are restricted to acceptance of bets on credit terms only, transmission of coupons is limited to dispatch by post alone, and advertisements other than those limited to factual information are prohibited. Registration of all Pool promoters is compulsory and they are responsible for regular supervision of conduct, of accounts, and of distribution by accredited accountants. The maximum amount of money to be retained after payment of all expenses, taxes and dividends is limited to 5 per cent of receipts and any promoter retaining more than 3 per cent as profit is required to publish in full an annual statement of accounts.*

The Royal Commission confirmed that the conduct of the Pool promoters in respect of observance of the law was unexceptionable but suggested that certain abuses, strongly suspected to be widespread and growing, should be eliminated by amended legislation.[5] They observed that promoters tended to inflate dividends by manipulation of expenses between the various pools as well as by charging costs at irregular intervals and they held anyhow that a maximum dividend in excess of say £10,000 would provide undesirable encouragement to betting and would, at the

* It has, in fact, been consistently regular practice of the Big Three—Littlewoods, Vernons and Sherman—to retain a profit margin of no more than 3 per cent and they have, as a result, escaped the necessity of publishing information beyond that contained in certified sets of accounts.

same time, be likely to prove deleterious and destructive to the recipient. It may, in passing, be noted that the Pool promoters were the one body of commercial organizers of betting who were adamant in their refusal to give evidence before the Royal Commission by responding to every invitation and enquiry with evasion and prevarication and that nevertheless, or possibly thanks to this tactic of stonewalling, they escaped all but the mildest criticism, and what is more to the point, were spared any encroachment upon their established rights and practices. Exhortation has apparently served the purpose of eliminating or, at least, of limiting the extent of artificially inflating dividends for selected pools or for critical single weeks, but it has failed to have any effect on the limitation of dividends—in fact the suggested maximum of ten thousand pounds does now almost sound as old-fashioned as cigarettes at 'twenty for a bob'—nor have the Royal Commission's recommendations as to compulsory publication of more informative accounts regardless of profit margin retained, had the least effect.* The 1963 Act does require the appointment of an independent qualified accountant and this has led not only, it is held, to more equitable distribution between the various pools, but further to minimization of any likelihood of insertion or of substitution of coupons after the results have been made known.

ON-COURSE BETTING

Betting on the course takes place almost exclusively as bets placed on horserace and dogtracks, although established periodic events such as coursing and other relative newcomers, such as donkey derbies, attract considerable crowds as well as bookmakers with their pitches, totalisators and all the other paraphernalia of the other major track forms. On-course betting takes two forms: firstly betting with bookmakers offering known odds, fluctuating from time to time in response to support, or otherwise, for certain runners and providing the punter with some certainty of the amount to be returned in the event of a win; and secondly, bets placed on the tote—the totalisator pool—in which

---

* Could this victory by withdrawal hold a lesson for others, suggesting that the most effective public relations may be absence of public relations?

all money staked on the various chances is accumulated and after the race, subject to predetermined rates of deduction, shared out amongst the winning tickets. In this form, although scoreboards indicate the flow of money on the various chances as betting develops, the punter is only able to guess at the final winning odds, as big money, generally placed at the very last moment will alter the odds reflected on the scoreboard.

(i) *Dogracing*

The proliferation of dogtracks, following their establishment in the 1920s, their growing pervasiveness and the lure they offered to the economically depressed urban proletariat, was one of the principal causes for which the 1933 Royal Commission was convened.[6] The Commission's recommendations, subsequently translated into legislation, provided for the compulsory licensing of tracks on which racing regularly takes place. It limited the annual racing days to a maximum of 104, restricted the betting days to identical days of the week within each licensing authority and the number of races to eight per meeting to take place within a continuous period of no more than four hours.

The 1949/51 Commission confirmed that in its most significant respects the 1934 Act had achieved its object, but it recommended various amendments. It considered the boundaries of the licensing authorities to be too narrowly confined, thus allowing the establishment of a large range of tracks situated within one single composite urban area but falling within the jurisdiction of several licensing authorities and providing betting facilities every evening and on most afternoons of each week contrary to the intention of legislation. Its recommendations, incorporated into the 1963 Act, now limit racing within a single wider urban area to two identical days in the week. The Commission also dealt with the question of unlicensed tracks being permitted, where racing does not take place on more than eight days per year subject to no more than prior notification to the police, who had no power to refuse permission. They achieved an amendment of legislation to the effect that applications for racing now had to be made for each single meeting on such tracks and such applications were capable of being refused on valid grounds.

Licensed dogtrack operators have the right, which is uniformly exercised by them, to install and to operate, on their tracks under their own management, totalisators confined to usage for races held at their tracks. Facilities must be provided for duly registered bookmakers, subject to charges not exceeding five times the amount of the highest charge made to members of the public for admission to the track. Bookmakers, in order to become registered, must pay a licence duty of excise, for the collection of which the management of the track is responsible.

(ii) *Horseracing*

Horserace courses, approved by the Horserace Betting Levy Board,* are exempt from the major provisions of the Betting and Lotteries Act 1934 and in particular do not require to be licensed or to observe restrictions as to the total number of days on which racing is permitted to take place. In practice, however, effective control on the number of days' racing at each course is exercised by the Jockey Club and the National Hunt Committee and such control was considered by the Royal Commission to be adequate as well as efficient. The management of horserace courses is prohibited from operating Totalisators and must allow enclosure space to bookmakers, whom they are allowed to charge fees not exceeding five times the maximum public admission charge. The management's financial interest is restricted to charges made to the bookmaker, charges made to the public for admission, rents paid by various enterprises providing services, such as refreshments on the tracks, and rent paid by the Horserace Totalisator Board for operating the Totalisator and to grants received by the H.B.L.B. which are confined to purposes conducive to the improvement of the sport of horseracing.

The H.B.L.B., established in accordance with recommendations made by the 1960 Pepiatt Committee,[7] has since its establishment in 1961 exercised a powerful and increasing control over horseracing. It is composed of a Chairman and seven other members and is charged with the duty of collecting a levy from all sides of the horserace betting industry, in line with the Pepiatt Commission's recommendation that 'there is almost unanimous opinion, on all sides of the racing industry (including

* Hereafter referred to as H.B.L.B.

the Bookmakers) that a Levy is required . . . The United Kingdom has for a long time been in the lead in horseracing, and we think the infusion of fresh money should be regarded not as serving to bolster a declining industry, but as an aid to improving it.'[8] Its principal recommendations were:

(a) Legislation should provide that detailed arrangements for the levy should be promulgated in a scheme.

(b) The Bookmakers' Levy Board should set up machinery for the collection of their share of the levy.

(c) The Levy Board and a Bookmakers' Levy Board should review arrangements for the levy year by year and should report to the Home Secretary.

These recommendations have been put into effect and an annual report is submitted to the Home Secretary.

GAMING

With the possible exception of the betting shops, the most fundamental changes in gambling legislation following the Royal Commission's report have been concerned with gaming in its various forms. Prior to 1960, the playing of games for stakes was not in itself unlawful. It was brought within the ambit of the criminal law either by reason of the game itself being unlawful, or by being carried out in a common gaming house or in a public place. Neither aspect allowed itself to be clearly defined, or to be efficiently and impartially administered. The proliferation of 'one-night gaming stands' in the early post-war years, the open toleration of bridge and whist clubs, both strictly speaking illegal, made mockery of the law and of the law's application. It was, in the words of the Chief Magistrate of London, 'practically impossible for the ordinary man to know what the law is'.[9]

The 1960 Gaming Act* repealed all statutes relating wholly or mainly to gaming and enacted that no longer was any game to be unlawful in itself, but that gaming would only become unlawful if it broke certain rules, namely that (a) the chances in the game are equally favourable to all the players (as they are, for instance, in whist or bridge); (b) the game is so conducted that the chances therein are equally favourable to all the players, i.e. if it is a game

* Now the Betting, Gaming and Lotteries Act 1963.

having a banker, all the players must have equal opportunity—of which, incidentally, they need not take advantage—of being bankers; (c) all the monies staked by the players must be returned in full as winnings and that the organizers must not benefit by a 'cut' of the stakes; (d) there should be no payment for the rights to take part in gaming, subject to certain modifications (i.e. table money) in respect of clubs; (e) gaming in a gaming house only is prohibited at any time when a person under the age of 19 is taking part in the game.[10] When infringement is held to have taken place, the burden of disproof devolves upon the defence.

The blatant failure of the 1963 Act to translate its intentions into actuality, inasmuch as it tolerated the unintended proliferation of gaming clubs without supervision and control as well as the exploitation of gaming by commercial and, as a rule, unidentifiable organizers and promoters, led to vociferous and determined agitation against existing legislation and finally to the introduction of the Gaming Act 1968, which was intended to prevent the uncontrolled exploitation of gaming by commercial interests and to provide a framework within which commercial gaming can be seen to be conducted in a proper, fair and orderly manner away from intrusion by undesirable elements; where expansion can be contained and where promoters' profits can be curtailed and controlled. The pivot of the Act is the setting up of the 'Gaming Board for Great Britain' charged to keep under review the extent and character of gaming throughout the country, empowered to exercise full control over all gaming activities and to make, whenever necessary and appropriate, recommendations to the Home Secretary for changes in legislation. The Board is supported by an Inspectorate whose duty it is to supervise the operation of the Act and to report any infringements or abuses to the Board for appropriate further action. Inspectors, as well as constables, are authorized to enter licensed gaming premises at any time without prior notification, to inspect the premises, machines or other equipment and to require production of such books or other documents as they may deem necessary. Promoters' failure to co-operate with Inspectors or to afford them access to such information as they may require will almost inevitably lead to revocation of their licence and possibly to eventual prosecution. The entire costs of the Board and the Inspectorate are to be defrayed by a levy upon all operators.

Proprietary clubs—clubs commercially organized for promoters' gain and profit—are only permitted to operate subject to the grant and annual renewal of a licence; application for a licence, costing initially £1,000 and a further £200 upon each annual renewal, to be ineffective unless supported by a current certificate issued to the applicant by the Gaming Board in advance. The Board, to whom all applications for all clubs intending to offer gaming of any type other than bingo must be made, is to consider the applicant's character, financial resources as well as general fitness to operate and to conduct gaming premises, whereas the Committee of Justices will only grant licences to such operators as are able to satisfy the committee that gaming facilities of the kind in question are not available in the locality, or that such facilities, if existing, are insufficient to meet demand. The onus of proof of demand or need lies entirely upon the applicant. By edict of the Gaming Board, gaming is now restricted to 40 areas of Britain and gaming clubs, numbering 1,200 in their heyday of the mid 1960s—the era when, according to Sir Stanley Raymond, chairman of the Gaming Board, Britain was 'an offshore island of Las Vegas'—have been reduced to about 120.[11]

Applications for a certificate of consent must disclose fully the identity of all persons to be concerned in the management, or such persons as are intended to derive any financial benefit from the activities of the club. The Board may revoke the certificate of consent on good grounds, such as irregular or improper conduct, the conviction of the holder for an offence under the Act, the habitual resort to the premises of undesirable elements, or evidence of the fact of the club being controlled by or run for the financial benefit of persons other than the holder of the certificate.

Furthermore, in addition to all executive members having to be considered fit and proper persons to be concerned in the management of a gaming club, all personnel and gaming operatives employed are to be personally certified by the Board as approved in respect of their fitness for such employment. Contravention of any of the provisions of the Gaming Act is likely to lead to revocation of certificate and to consequent debarment from employment in the gaming industry.

While clubs are permitted to cash cheques for immediate consideration, they are no longer allowed to extend gaming credit to clients, to accept post-dated cheques nor to make any deduction in respect of cheques tendered to them. All advertisements informing the public of the provision of gaming facilities, or inviting them to participate in gaming are prohibited under the Act.

A number of the provisions of the Gaming Act, in particular those ruling in respect of the authority to operate, are relaxed in the case of members' clubs in which the property belongs to all the members jointly.[12] Members' clubs do not require a certificate of consent from the Board, but only need a certificate of registration issued to them by the local Justices. The initial registration fee of a members' club amounts to no more than £20 and Justices are advised to be concerned solely with the club's credentials and freedom from commercial exploitation in consideration of the grant of registration.

The Gaming Act 1968 emphasizes the distinction between gaming clubs and other clubs in which gaming is limited to bingo.[13] The latter are exempt from almost all provisions of the Act, although clubs providing bingo also need to be licensed in order to operate legitimately. Bingo clubs are now authorized to provide linked bingo—the playing of the game at several premises simultaneously—subject to all players being present at the time at one or the other of the premises and subject to total prize money in any one week being limited to £1,000. All of the 1,500 clubs authorized to operate are now empowered to enrol members after a lapse of no more than twenty-four hours after application and the eventual granting of licences for liquor and cabaret-cum-dancing is officially foreshadowed.

GAMING MACHINES

Prior to the 1963 Act, gaming on any type of machine in a refreshment house or licensed premises was unlawful. In other places, e.g. fairs, amusement arcades, clubs, the legality of the machine depended on the degree of skill required to win a prize. When chance predominated, an offence under the Gaming Acts was held to have been committed, but even when skill could be said to be of greater significance, the Betting Act of 1853 might have come to be infringed and in public places the 1873 Vagrant Act could be used to establish an offence.

The 1963 Act allows gaming machines on premises to which the general public has no access, but only if the stake does not exceed 2½p and if all stakes are applied either in the payment of winnings or for purposes other than private gain. This permits the installation of gaming machines*—limited to a maximum of two—in duly registered clubs and allows retention of a proportion of the stake money for club purposes or for payment into club funds, but must not provide gain or benefit to any person as an individual.

Under the provisions of the Gaming Act 1968[14] the sale and supply of gaming machines, as well as their method of operation, are brought under the control of the Gaming Board. All persons concerned with the sale, supply as well as the maintenance of gaming machines are now required to apply and to obtain a certificate entitling them to perform their relevant functions. The issue of such certificates, costing £250 and lasting for five years is limited to persons considered by the Board to be fit and proper persons and offences against the Gaming Act are likely to result in revocation. Permanent use of gaming machines is restricted to premises licensed or registered as gaming clubs and to premises registered specially for gaming machines. The charge for playing the game is limited to a maximum of 5p at any one attempt, all prizes must be in cash, and the percentage of pay-out is now to be declared and to be prominently displayed on the machine.

LOTTERIES

The term 'lottery' applies to the distribution of prizes by chance and nothing but chance, that is by doing something which is equivalent to drawing of lots. If some degree of skill is involved, the activity is not a lottery. A typical example is the staking of money on football pools where, it is held, prizes depend on promoters' and punters' skill in selection. Likewise a newspaper competition, in which alternative word selections are offered, is not a lottery if skill or choice can truly be said to be an important

* These are generally referred to as 'one-armed bandits' or 'fruit machines'.

element. Subject to the following exceptions, all lotteries are considered to be unlawful:

(i) Small lotteries incidental to bazaars, sales of work and other entertainment of a similar character are not illegal if the entire proceeds after deduction of expenses other than a maximum of £10, used in the purchase of prizes, are devoted to purposes other than private gain. Tickets are to be sold only on premises in which entertainment takes place and the lottery must not be the intrinsic purpose of the function.

(ii) Private lotteries in respect of registered societies, established for purposes unconnected with gaming or wagering, are permitted under similar conditions with the additional prohibition of advertising of any kind.

(iii) Art Unions, operating under Royal Charter, are permitted to hold lotteries, again substantially subject to the same conditions.

Offences are committed by any person who prints, advertises, sells or distributes tickets in lotteries other than those exempted, who undertakes distribution of tickets in foreign lotteries, or who sends money in respect of such lotteries abroad, or who uses any premises for the purposes of illegal lotteries.

AMUSEMENTS AT COMMERCIAL ENTERTAINMENTS

Such places as amusement arcades require a permit from the Local Authority. Occasional fairs, such as the ones appearing on Bank Holidays, are permitted to provide amusements with prizes without being required to obtain a permit. Certain conditions are applicable to both types: entrance fee must not exceed 5p; total collection per single game must not be more than £2.50 and no money prize must be more than 5p. Where, however, such as in the case of darts, success is achieved by pure skill, none of the restrictions shall apply. Also amusement machines of a completely innocuous character, e.g. machines offering replay to successful players, are free from restriction.

REFRESHMENT HOUSES AND LICENSED PREMISES

Unrestricted gaming in refreshment houses or licensed premises is unlawful. All games of skill, such as darts or shove-ha'penny, are legal, and games such as dominoes and cribbage, although not games of skill, are considered to be traditional social amenities of a large number of such premises, hence are given exemption. Gaming is permitted in the private parts of an hotel. It is therefore lawful to play bridge, which was formerly illegal, in the lounge of a private hotel. Parts of licensed premises leased to clubs may be used for gaming, but members of the public at large must not be given access to these parts.

ENFORCEMENT OF WAGERING TRANSACTIONS

Under the 1845 Gaming Act[15] all contracts or agreements, verbal or written, in private or in public, made by way of wagering or betting were made null and unenforceable in a Court of Law. The Act only relates to the original transaction between the parties and any subsequent agreement for which fresh consideration has passed—such as withdrawal of a threat of blacklisting, or agreement to allow time to pay and acceptance of offer to allow reduction in the amount of the debt—is likely to be considered a valid and enforceable contract.[16] The Royal Commission (1949/51) gave careful consideration to the changed nature of such transactions once gaming ceased to be illegal. The various denominational delegations and the bookmakers' association stood in favour of changes in legislation, pointing to the likelihood of a decline in betting and diminution of dishonesty if gambling debts were to become legally enforceable.[17] The Royal Commission, nevertheless, decided to give weight to the following practical difficulties standing in the way of legislative reform: (i) the Courts might be unable to deal with a large volume of betting disputes in addition to the heavy demands already made upon their resources, (ii) a large number of troublesome cases might bring discredit upon the bookmaking and betting organizations and institutions, the overwhelming majority of which were above reproach in the conduct of their business, (iii) disputes are likely to arise as to whether (*a*) the alleged bet had in fact been made, (*b*) what were its terms, expressed or implied, (*c*) what was the outcome of the event on which the bet had been made. In respect of all these contingencies—such as off-course betting by telephone—conflicting evidence, absence of a written offer and acceptance, examination of a variety of witnesses of varying grades of competence and reliability, would make the work of the Courts unmanageable and judgment would impose excessive strain on the bench. Thus the Commission, although inclining towards the view that it would prefer transactions with registered bookmakers eventually to acquire the full status of contracts, recommended, in view of the practical difficulties, maintenance of the status quo. Under the 1968 Gaming Act, cheques cashed for means to gamble in gaming clubs constitute legal transactions enforceable at law.

Present Major Forms of Commercial Gambling Activities

BETTING OFFICES

In accordance with the requirements of Section 10 of the Betting and Gaming Act, annual reports on the number of bookmakers' permits, betting agency permits and betting office licences are presented to Parliament by the Home Secretary. Table I in the Appendix shows the number of betting office licences and the proportion to 10,000 population, in force at the 1st of June over the first eight years after the inception of the legislation.

In Wales, where there are almost 5 betting offices per 10,000 population, against fewer than 3 for England, the need is probably created by the shortage of registered bookmakers as well as the scattered nature of settlement and does not itself indicate any greater intensity of betting. Equally, in the case of Scotland the decline in betting shops reflects the immediate conversions upon changes in legislation of illegal betting shops, at that time much more prevalent in Scotland, against their gradual growth and extension in other parts in which, prior to legal sanction, they scarcely existed. The Table fails to reveal the considerable variations existing within the groups, ranging from a proportion of 1.2 per 10,000 population in Anglesey to 6.18 in Liverpool, displaying an increase from 0.85 to 1.86 between 1962 and 1965 in Plymouth together with a fall from 6.3 to 5.0 in the same period in York. This raises a number of interesting questions as to the social, economic and ecological factors involved, a subject to which the recent work by an L.S.E. research study-unit should make a most useful contribution.[18]

For purposes of illustration, it may be interesting to make reference to a survey of Public Library facilities made recently on three South London Boroughs, which shows in these areas the provision of one Public Library to each 14,677 inhabitants (with 1.5 books per inhabitant), so that the average Londoner with one betting shop to each 3,613 members of the population, has at his service roughly four betting shops for each Public Library.[19]

As will be seen from Table I, there has been virtually complete stability in the total number of betting shops for the past five years and, in fact, the proportion of betting shops per head of the population has actually declined. This may not be entirely due to a fall-off in demand, nor need it necessarily indicate attainment of saturation point, but it may well be largely attributable to the enactment and enforcement of rigorous safeguards and controls in the granting of new licences to operate betting shops. Opposition to a further increase has come from a number of sources— local residents objecting to the debasement of amenities and to increasing inducements to temptation; local shopkeepers fearing the decline in expenditure for their own commodities; Church authorities and social workers drawing attention to deviance, delinquency and decline in moral standards; and not least from established betting shop operators contending that saturation point has been reached and that further permits would introduce malpractices and even defaulting. It is, however, almost unanimously agreed that in the overwhelming majority of offices, business is conducted both within the letter as well as the spirit of existing laws, as is evident from the small number of refused renewal applications.[20]

By virtue of betting duty returns indicating a total off-course bookmakers' turnover of £969 million in 1967 and £946 million in 1968,[21] turnover of betting shops can now be estimated with some degree of accuracy. Although a proportion of the turnover is attributable to credit bookmakers, it would be legitimate to conjecture an annual average turnover of £50,000—or £1,000 per week—for each of Britain's 16,000 betting shops. With gross profit—the balance remaining after payment of successful bets—limited to around 10 per cent and weekly running costs for rent, rates, heating, lighting, wages and racecourse information making further sizeable inroads into takings, many bookmakers appear to exist on a precarious and marginal level of income, particularly in view of the capital at risk. The payment of betting duty, introduced at 2.5 per cent in 1966 and raised to 5 per cent of turnover in the 1968 Finance Bill, together with the newly-imposed betting levy designed to augment horseracing managements' waning resources, has widely been denounced as the final death knell to many of their enterprises. Although the bulk of additional burdens is traditionally recouped by manipulating the odds against the punter, there is a limit to what the market will bear and, indeed, turnover has dropped since the imposition of doubled taxation. Smaller bookmakers emphatically assert that illegal betting has greatly increased and the ability of large operators temporarily to absorb disadvantageous tax changes is driving many of them into liquidation. A number of betting office operators have indeed failed to apply for a renewal of licence. To what extent this indicates insufficient income, or whether their demise is due to inadequate initial capital, to untypical sustained runs of winning wagers, or to an infection with the bookmakers' occupational disease of themselves turning punter, is impossible to establish. Even prior to the introduction of a betting duty, there had been a noticeable trend towards the growth of chain-operators, as well as a marked tendency towards amalgamation and take-overs squeezing out the one-man business. This development, exacerbated by escalating levels of taxation, if tending towards a regional carve-up or a national monopoly control, may well have implications as yet undisclosed.

GAMING CLUBS

Although unofficial estimates of the extent of proliferation of gaming clubs, made in advance of the publication of the first official data upon the imposition of Gaming Duty,[22] were found to be grossly exaggerated,[23] there is little doubt that in the early 1960s, gaming clubs were one of the principal 'growth industries'. Shares of the C.H.T., the owners of London's smartest gaming club Crockfords, rocketed seventy-fold in a span of two years on the evidence of a weekly net profit of £5,000,[24] while some provincial clubs expanded their premises four-fold in less than two years. Casino-type gaming which had, beyond the annual flutter of summer visitors to the continent, as a rule been confined to a hard core, spread to ever-widening circles as a regular, even if infrequent habit. Attempts to attract a middle-class, artisan and latterly even a bingo-type public had introduced gaming to circles where previous knowledge of roulette, chemin-de-fer, and baccarat had been limited to the pursuits of fictional heroes. As succinctly put by the director of the Golden Nugget casino, 'Not exactly the betting shop types, but the idea is that Dad and his family can have a bit of a flutter for a fiver.'[25]

According to the earliest Gaming Licence Duty returns a total of 1,058 gaming clubs had established themselves by 1967, altogether offering the entire gamut of casino games from the 'hoi aristoi' types such as roulette, chemin-de-fer, and baccarat to the 'hoi polloi' games of blackjack, dice,* poker, and kalookie.[26] Such games were affording the management a margin of advantage ranging from 1.35 per cent at roulette to 7.75 per cent at dice. At some of the less reputable twilight establishments the management were still, according to reliable reports, levying a fixed-rate deduction, in some cases as high as 5 per cent, from every single spin of the wheel.

Despite the fact that indications were then suggesting that the bonanza years for the clubs had drawn to an end,† pressures for thoroughgoing revision of legislation, in the direction of curtailment and strictest control, were beginning to mount. Although casino gaming, as it had evolved, had clearly not been envisaged or intended, inadequate initial definition and case-law interpretation in favour of operators had allowed a situation to develop in which promoters were deriving a considerable profit

---

* Chemin-de-fer and dice are in popular parlance referred to as 'chemy' and 'craps' respectively. 'Blackjack' is a smartened-up version of pontoon or twenty-one.

† From the evidence of reliable observers, the pool of wealthy, large-scale bettors had, as their money kept running out, progressively diminished. Competition was compelling the clubs to reduce their margin of profit from the games and to offer ever-more costly gratuitous inducements in the way of drinks, food and entertainment and finally, the Gaming Duty was beginning to exercise its impact.

by continuously operating the bank, affording them an assured recurrent margin of profit. At some of the larger clubs, by announcement made at intervals in French, or by the display of inconspicuous notices, the bank was made, at least in theory, available to all clients. The surreptitious manner in which these acts were proffered and, above all, the immense risk involved to any individual bold enough to bid for the bank when in the short run losses can be very heavy, inhibited all response from the players. Additionally, a series of acts of violence exhibiting the characteristic, if for Britain overtly unfamiliar, hallmarks of enforced protection, extortion, and gang warfare,* gave rise to a considerable degree of public unease and indignation and to determined demands to put an end to underworld infiltration. Furthermore, the alleged escalation of submission to the gaming habit, as well as the widespread assumption that casino life produced, as well as attracted, delinquents, racketeers and criminals, were also considered as intolerable. It was against this background that the Gaming Act 1968 was introduced, the principal regulations of which have already been referred to in an earlier section. By the time of the deadline for applications in April 1969 only 630 applications for gaming licences had reached the Board. By January 1970, no more than 477 gaming clubs were left in operation and by the end of that year, the level was being reduced to the statutory 165. It is now confidently expected that the Gaming Board will be able to ensure the fulfilment of the principal objectives of the Gaming Act, namely:

(i) that gaming should be free from all infiltration by the underworld,

(ii) that organizers should deal honestly with their clients and with the public at large,

(iii) that promoters' profits should be limited and controlled, and

(iv) that the gaming industry should make its appropriate financial contribution to the Exchequer. An annual contribution

* A grim battle involving several deaths had occurred in a South London club in 1966 in which it was said intimidation of eye-witnesses was hindering the work of the police. In June 1967 a certain John Buggy, a notorious associate of gamblers, had been shot and a few months later there occurred the murder of Enrico Girado, a gambler and part-time croupier. George Wynberg, the manager of one of London's leading clubs, was reported to have said that, in his view, fewer than 20 per cent of all gaming clubs were not paying protection money.

of £4.5 million in place of the previous £1.5 million is now envisaged.

The one unresolved outstanding issue now concerns the source of promoters' income and the gaming clubs' legal authority to derive direct gain from the games they provide. The original set of proposals circulated by the Home Secretary early in 1966 was designed to deprive promoters of any recourse to profits from the games offered by them in their clubs.[27] It was then intended for clubs to have no other access to income than the charge of an annual membership fee plus an additional charge representing players' attendance at various gaming sessions. However, early and determined representation made by casino promoters succeeded in persuading the Home Secretary that the operators' right to direct profit from the tables was legitimate as well as indispensable. They confronted the Home Office with the assertion that casino gaming had firmly established itself as a social habit*— widespread, ingrained and, in respect of the overwhelming majority, entirely harmless—which, if not legally provided, would be driven underground with all the concomitant evils and ramifications. Supporting their submissions with statistical evidence of the 'Theorem of Ultimate Ruin', proposed on their behalf by no lesser an authority than Professor M. G. Kendall, past president of the Royal Statistical Society†, they prevailed in their main line of attack and were, by the provisions of the initial draft of the Gaming Bill itself, intended to be allowed to derive a direct profit from the conduct of the games which they were providing.

Ironically, a ruling of the House of Lords, made on the very day on which the Gaming Bill was first published, to the effect

* The 931 gaming clubs registered for purposes of collection of Gaming Duty in 1968 had then a reputed membership of 1 million.

† The 'Theorem of Ultimate Ruin' as submitted by Dr Kendall argues that severance of direct connection between stakes and profits, the abolition of the differential advantage accruing to the promoters thanks to the imposition of the zero, and the requirement that chances between the bank and players should be absolutely equal would lead to a situation in which the player with funds unlimited (in this case the public *en masse*) would inevitably annihilate the opponent with limited means (in this case the promoter). Consequently the promoter would, in the absence of revenue deriving to him from the tables, face inescapable final bankruptcy. Session charges at fixed amounts would, furthermore, fall unequally and inequitably upon players staking different sums of money.

that the playing of roulette with a zero constituting a game of unequal chance, hence was illegal, rendered casinos providing such games liable to prosecution and conviction.[28] This reopened the issue and gave to the large and influential body of opinion demanding total abolition of promoters' profit, fresh heart as well as a superior arsenal of ammunition.[29] Their confidence was further bolstered by several subsequent Court decisions, of which the most significant was the case brought by Raymond Blackburn M.P., under an order of Mandamus concerning the Golden Nugget Club, Piccadilly. When this case, having been awarded a differing verdict in the lower Courts, finally reached the Court of Appeal in January 1968, Lord Denning, Master of the Rolls, pronounced as follows: 'The law has not been enforced as it should. This has discouraged the police from keeping observation and taking action. But it does not, I think, exempt them from their share of responsibility. The proprietors of gaming houses have taken advantage of the situation. By one device after another they have kept ahead of the law. As soon as one device has been held unlawful, they have started another. But the day of reckoning is at hand. No longer will we tolerate these devices. The law must be sensibly interpreted so as to give effect to the intention of Parliament, and the police must see that it is enforced. The rule of law must prevail.'[30]

By mid-1970 the situation had not finally crystallized. The majority of clubs had ceased to operate a zero; some were levying session charges and others were 'inviting' voluntary offerings from participants. A number of operators, while awaiting events, claimed to be losing money at rates which, in the absence of relief, would put them either at the mercy of the underworld or into the Bankruptcy Court. With adequate safeguards of control existing for the remaining clubs, with distinction between 'hard' and 'soft' gaming now firmly established and with live entertainment statutorily banned from club premises, the Board felt confident that the re-establishment of operators' profitability by the restoration of a differential advantage would not impair the effective operation of the Act. The first report published in April 1970 accordingly recommended such a course of action.[31]

Meanwhile doubts were already being voiced as to whether the small force of twenty-six inspectors would be sufficient to ensure supervision and control of this notoriously volatile fraternity. Finally, the eternal problem of *'quis custodiet ipsos custodes'* (who will control the controllers?) still had to be resolved.

BINGO

This form of gambling—prior to the 1960 Act banned as an illegal lottery—was the first to hit the headlines in the early period following the new legislation. The 'Bingo craze' was a new form of compulsion. Excessive loss of money by the poorly paid, pensioners and housewives, neglect of young children, and subjection to mindless, passive distraction were charges variously invoked against this activity, being, as a rule, accompanied by gloomy prophecies of ever-growing ensnarement and proliferation.[32] But even on the evidence of the C.C.G., initially one of the most vociferous anti-bingo spokesmen, the craze was showing signs of waning by 1962, although in that year, an estimated total of £30 million was being staked by an unknown number of bettors. The Top-Rank Bingo Club had at that time 60 centres with a total of half a million members. In 1963, the newly-formed National Association of Bingo Clubs, representing seventy proprietors, 1,000 halls and six million members, charged to 'promote and encourage in any and every possible legal manner the game as a popular and reputable pastime', instituted new incentives, such as a 'national' game of bingo, with top prizes of up to £8,000 against a previous maximum of £200, in an effort to consolidate and perpetuate Bingo as a way of life. Attempts made to introduce a refined version of 'postal bingo', in which cards costing $17\frac{1}{2}$p were distributed by post and results announced over Radio Luxemburg proved abortive, on being pronounced a Lottery.

Although there are few indications of a radical decline in the popularity of this game, strictures and outright condemnations have, on the whole, over the years faded from the pages of publications originally so intent on highlighting this new form of evil and enslavement to triviality. Even the C.C.G. in its latest reports refers to bingo in a manner almost benign, commenting upon the social needs of togetherness, group activity, an antidote to loneliness and so on, but, at the same time, stressing that the absence of a preference for more spiritual or self-fulfilling alternatives is a pathetic index of isolation, drift, and of a lack of purpose of modern society. Indeed, few observers, however contemptuously they may themselves refer to the vacuity of the game itself, fail to note the evidence of social satisfaction, communication and the relative absence of overt avidity which typically exist.[33]

FOOTBALL POOLS AND FIXED ODDS

The strong tendency for institutions, at first marginal and semi-deviant, to gain establishment and gradually acquire status and respectability, until they finally emerge as pillars of the social framework, may be perceived in the case of Football Pools, certainly, in their 1920 infancy, the *bête-noire* of the anti-gambling lobby. The Football Pools have in their days faced and weathered all the usual charges of wastefulness, extravagance, particularly as form of subversion to which the poorer sections of the population are vastly more prone, gateways to delinquency and mindlessness now being laid against emergent activities such as bingo and casino-type gambling.[34] They had to face, in addition, the further charges peculiar to them, of the high relative operating costs of promoters and consequent low ratio of return to bettors,[35] as well as of nett outlay being almost certainly equal to nett loss where odds against single bets being successful in some pools amounted to 25 million to 1. There was also the charge that each single jubilant winner of a £250,000 dividend achieved his win out of the lost stakes of around 3 million bettors, and that for one punter to win £70, the remaining 29 out of 30 had to subscribe £180 (apart from the cost of postage). One would suggest that the displacement of Football Pools as target number one of the anti-gambling spokesmen is not entirely due to the emergence of new and more immediately 'pernicious' forms of gambling but, to no small measure, to the adroitness with which promoters have learned to shun the limelight, other than for occasions of publicizing a new 'world-record' win. Little of it could be attributed to any decline in the participation and popularity of this form of gambling. Nor are all promoters—of which the two largest, Littlewoods and Vernons alone account for some 75 per cent of the total turnover—as immaculate in the conduct of their affairs as their integration into the élite of commercial giants might make one assume. Whilst, no doubt, the evasion of tax obligation or the falsification of entries are as a deliberate method unimaginable, the Royal Commission pointed to a number of subterfuges regularly resorted to in order to inflate particular dividends or pools for the purposes of publicity; their immunity to public accounting also presents them with opportunities to inflate administrative expenses and directors' remuneration to an unknowable extent. The approximate split-up of takings for the latest published period is: Tax 33 per cent, Expenses 30 per cent, Prizes 37 per cent, so that out of each pound staked less than $37\frac{1}{2}$p is returned to the punter in the form of winnings. In recent years the Pools have staged a recovery *vis-à-vis* the competitive method of Fixed Odds. Whilst, in the former, the entire stake money, after the usual deductions, is divided and shared amongst the winning bets in the manner of the totalisator, in the case of the latter the punter confronts the bookmaker who, on selected fixtures, offers firm terms, so that bettors will know in advance the amount to be returned to them on winning bets. Fixed Odds, allowing for the choice and study of form to a much larger degree, but furthermore benefiting at the time from tax immunity, gained considerable popularity in the first years of the 1960s and accounted for an annual turnover of £65 million, against £70 million on the Pools, in 1963. Partly in an effort to bring it into line with tax regulations on Pools, but chiefly, it is being held, in order to nip in the bud emergent manifestations of bribery and of corruption (ten footballers had been charged in that year with deliberately having 'thrown' matches for betting purposes and the press was full of allegations of widespread organized practices of corruption) the Chancellor of the Exchequer imposed a 25 per cent tax on Fixed Odds, as from August 1964. Immediately odds, previously not ungenerous to the true initiate, were reduced and the leading firms were announcing withdrawal from this form of betting. Tax revenue, expected to produce an annual £15 million, fell short of this target by £4 million. Many observers were predicting the 'quicksilver' reaction, so familiar in the case of alcohol and tobacco, when, after the imposition of a new and higher level of tax, the shock effect can be observed as an instant, violent fall in consumption, but where, after a short interval, consumption finds itself restored to its former 'natural' level. This however did not happen to Fixed Odds betting. Turnover fell from an estimated total of £65 million in 1963 to no more than £15 million in 1965, a fall of 80 per cent. If any lesson in strategy may be learned from this operation, so successful in the achievement of its objective, it may well lie in the direction of the vastly greater effectiveness of shock treatment and in the far greater efficacy of one single heavy blow upon a single limited target in preference to dispersion over a wider diffuse area.

GAMING MACHINES

The student of gambling is, at an early stage, struck by the extent to which British policy follows the traditional patterns well established in the more prominent and respectable spheres of politics, social welfare and economics. It displays the same balance between idealism and commonsense pragmatism, between conservatism as a normal orientation and a simultaneous preparedness to undertake radical innovations, which used to characterize British grand policy in the past. Other countries operate totalisators, betting shops, football pools but none display the unique blend between private enterprise and central control, *laissez-faire* and corporate planning, liberalism and philistinism, which confronted the Royal Commission in all the varied aspects they were charged to consider. However, in their consideration of gaming machines they had before them the live example of the United States and of the effects of various kinds of legislation on 'one-armed bandits' within a similar social climate of moral disapproval and practical recognition of inevitability.[36] On the basis of information before them, probably largely swayed by the evidence of the intense infiltration by gangster elements and mobsters ruling by absolute terror where fruit machines had been allowed to flourish, the Royal Commission recommended that gaming machines should be made entirely illegal.[37] Nevertheless, when the Act was put in front of Parliament, a limited use of gaming machines was permitted, providing that on club premises to which the public at large had no access, a maximum of two machines, with stakes limited to $2\frac{1}{2}$ pence per game and with all stakes to be applied either as winnings or for purposes other than private gain, would be allowed to be installed. This provision, permitting appropriation of profits at the rate of approximately 15 per cent of the taking —possibly an average nett annual sum of £350 per machine—for club benefit and club functions, had by the end of 1963 led to the installation of 25,700 machines into 14,870 club premises registered with the Commissioner of Customs and Excise.[38] The virtual impossibility of the framing of Bills to provide for every contingency in advance of the ingenious methods which wealthy and powerful commercial interests will employ on top-level legal advice to drive a horse and cart through every puny loophole (a situation not unknown to domestic law-makers in other spheres), is well illustrated by the history of gaming machines in premises other than registered clubs. Gaming machine manufacturers and particularly distributors, a great many of whom had American background and experience, undertook an intensive sales campaign directed at cafes and coffee bars, providing owners with completed application forms and illustrating methods of straining the Act to conform with the letter of the law by being able to offer prizes in kind of up to £2.50 in value by insertion of discs rather than coins. Local Authorities, refusing applications in face of the proliferation not only in coffee bars but also into licensed premises, found themselves overruled with costs awarded against them by Quarter Sessions and it was largely their representations that impelled the Home Secretary to introduce an amendment to the Act in 1964. Directed in his words 'against what I hope I may legitimately describe as the almost limitless ingenuity not so much of the gaming public as of the people who exploit gambling for their own benefit',[39] he confined the installation of gaming machines to amusement arcades, wholly or mainly used for the provision of amusements by means of machines, and increased the discretionary powers of local authorities to refuse permits to applications they consider beyond the spirit of the Act. To date, suppliers have not yet found a way to circumvent the Act as amended, and with installation confined to registered clubs, where saturation point must be very close, rumours of outbreaks of violence and warfare between organized groups acting as distributors over profitable territorial rights may not be far off the mark—again, a feature of gaming-machine by-products not unfamiliar to United States authorities.

The provisions of the Gaming Act 1968, requiring all persons concerned with the sale, supply and maintenance of gaming machines to obtain a licence to carry out their functions from the Gaming Board and insisting upon the percentage of pay-out to be prominently displayed on all gaming machines, should go a long way towards the elimination of any infringements and abuses which may, at present, exist and may well succeed in eradicating any intrusion which criminal elements may hitherto have achieved.

PREMIUM BONDS

These are a product of pre-1960 Betting Act Legislation, brought into being with the passing of the Small Lotteries and Gaming Act in 1956.[40] It has been observed that it may well have been the adoption of income from lotteries as a way of financing national expenditure, which, by conferring respectability on betting as a way of life (caricatured in 'Opportunity Mac'), created the backdrop against which the Royal Commission deliberated and paved the way to the permissive, 'wide-open' legislation which was soon to follow. The scheme is based on National Savings units of £1 bearing interest of 4 per cent (now 4.5 per cent), the whole of which goes into the lottery draws for prizes. Although Premium Bonds strictly differ from other types of gambling in as much as the original stake money does not stand hazard, it cannot validly escape definition as a gambling activity when the investor stakes his right to interest on a betting pool, with a chance of winning, in any single draw, of the order of 125,000 to 1 against himself. Although the maximum prize was increased in 1965 to £25,000,* the sale of bonds has, for the past years, been on a decreased scale, falling short of the £72 million subscription records level set up in 1961.

* £50,000 in 1971.

Notes

1. 1960 Betting and Gaming Act (8 & 9 Eliz. 2 C 60); 1963 Betting, Gaming and Lotteries Act (Eliz. 2.1 C 2); 1968 Gaming Act (Eliz. 2 C 65).
2. Royal Commission on Betting, Lotteries and Gaming 1949–1951.
3. See Betting (Licensing) Regulations, 1960 and Betting (Licensing) Scotland Regulations, 1960.
4. 'To be a bookmaker a person must carry on, or be held out as carrying on, the business of receiving or negotiating bets.' Betting, Gaming and Lotteries Act, 1963, S.4 (2).
5. Royal Commission on Betting, Lotteries and Gaming 1949–51, par. 289, 290, pp. 88–9.
6. Royal Commission on Lotteries and Betting, 1933.
7. Report of the Departmental Commission on a Levy on Betting on Horse Races, H.M.S.O., Cmd. 1003, April 1960.
8. Ibid. par. 17, p. 7.
9. Sir Lawrence Dunne, M.C., in evidence before the Royal Commission, 1949–51. Ibid. par 17, p. 6 (Dunne Q.2417).
10. Part II of the Betting, Gaming and Lotteries Act, 1963.
11. Report of the Gaming Board for Great Britain, 1970, House of Commons Paper 344, H.M.S.O. (London 1971).
12. Gaming Act 1968, Sched. III.
13. Gaming Act 1968, s. 20.
14. Gaming Act 1968, ss. 27, 28, 29, Sched. VI.
15. 1845 Gaming Act (8 & 9 Vict. C 109).
16. To refrain from reporting a person as a defaulter, for instance, was sufficient consideration to support an action on a subsequent promise to pay betting losses (Hyams v. Stuart Ving (1908) 2 K.B. 696), but forbearance to sue for the amount of a bet was not good consideration since the winner did not in fact have a good case of action (Poteliakoff v. Teakle (1938) 2 K.B. 816). The House of Lords decision in 1949 in the case of Tom Hill v. William Hill Ltd (1949 A.C. 530) held that any consideration inherent in the original bargain—the bet—such as for instance withdrawal of threat to report to the Jockey Club, would not pass as fresh consideration.
17. The Chief Magistrate of London suggested in evidence before the Royal Commission that if gambling debts were to be made to be recoverable by law it would 'tend to diminish the volume of betting generally and to diminish a great deal of the present rascality in betting'. Royal Commission, 1949–51 Report (Q.2429–2441).
18. A research project charged with the task of enquiring into Gambling in Great Britain was launched in 1963 at the London School of Economics by Professor Titmuss under the personal direction of two L.S.E. lecturers—Dr David Downes and Dr Bletwyn Davies—whose

initial project was an ecological study of the distribution of betting shops in England, Scotland and Wales.

19. *Counterwise.* The Magazine of the Blackheath & District Consumer Group, no. 1, 1966.

20. In no more than the astonishingly small number of nine cases was renewal application for betting offices denied in 1969. Betting, Gaming and Lotteries Act 1963: Permits and Licences; H.M.S.O., London, 17 December 1968.

21. Churches' Council on Gambling, 'Gambling . . . a bad risk for Britain', Annual Review for the year ended 31 December 1968, Churches' Council on Gambling (London 1969).

22. With effect from 1 October 1966 annual Gaming Licence Duties became chargeable on all premises where bingo and casino-type gaming takes place. The original rates in respect of casino premises varied from £500 per annum on premises whose rateable value was below £1,000 to £50,000 per annum on premises whose rateable value exceeded £3,000. The rates have since been increased on two separate occasions and were last raised to rates varying from £750 per annum to £75,000 per annum in the budget announced on 25 March 1969.

23. A private survey undertaken in 1965 by a German television company put the figure of gaming clubs in the United Kingdom in the region of 5,000.

24. The *Daily Telegraph*, London, 8 February 1964.

25. 'Gambling: a nation's responsibility', Annual Review of the Churches' Council on Gambling (London 1966), p. 4.

26. Betting and Gaming Duties—Revenue Statistics, H.M. Customs & Excise, Press Information Office, London, 18 December 1967, table 56, p. 117. 842 clubs registered at the lowest annual Gaming Duty rate of £500 (signifying a rateable value below £1,000), 128 clubs registered at the medium annual rate of £5,000 (rateable value £1,000–£3,000) and 9 clubs registered at the highest annual rate of £50,000 (rateable value £3,000 and above).

27. Section 12d of the Home Secretary's draft proposals, confidentially circulated to interested parties on 31 August 1966 stated: 'There shall be no odds in favour of the bank in any game in which the bank does not pass in turn among the players or is not won or lost in the course of play.' The Home Secretary's, Mr Roy Jenkins', personal viewpoint of that time might well be guessed from remarks made by him in the course of a speech to a Labour Conference at Hounslow Town Hall, as quoted in *The Times* on 13 September 1966: 'This country has become a gamblers' paradise, more wide-open in this respect than any other comparable country.'

28. Crickitt v. Kursall Casino Ltd and others heard before Viscount Dilhorne, Lord MacDermott, Lord Guest, Lord Wilberforce and Lord Pearson; House of Lords, 19 December 1967.

29. 'All that is required is for the Home Secretary to state that he will

seek to amend the Bill in committee so as to retain the prohibition on games of unequal chance. In all probability this would cream much of the profits off gaming—which would be harsh but desirable, because it is the attraction of large, easy profits for criminal intervention which has caused so much worry . . . and it is now the duty of the police to see that all the clubs keep within the letter of the law.' *The Times*, London, 2 January 1968.

30. Lord Denning, Master of the Rolls, Court of Appeal, 29 January 1968.

31. House of Commons Paper 208, 8 April 1970.

32. 'Gambling—Why', Annual Review of the Churches' Council on Gambling (1964), p. 29.

33. 'Everyone still hopes to win . . . But most women now go for the company and for the break . . . To the uninitiated bingo seems utterly dull and pointless; yet people still flock to it in thousands . . . in some cases the only way of filling a huge vacuum in their lives.' *South Wales Argus*, Swansea, 26 May 1965 in an article entitled 'Gambling to buy Companionship'.

34. 'The alleged study of form is sheer waste of time, as far as the pools are concerned. The tragic consequence is not only the waste of time, but the debilitating effect upon the mutuality and social outlook of those who follow the pools.' E. Benson Perkins, *Gambling in English Life* (London 1958), p. 66.

35. 'I have long been interested in the laws of chance, and their deductive verification. In 1949 I began to investigate the football pools. It did not take me long to discover that in these competitions the study of "form" and the exercise of judgment have no bearing at all upon success. I played the pools (on paper) for some months, and came to the conclusion that they are lotteries. I found them, moreover, to be lotteries in which those who take part get a singularly poor return for their money.' Hubert Phillips, *Pools and the Punter* (London 1955), Foreword, p. vii.

36. See *The Annals* vol. 269, May 1950, special issue: 'Gambling', particularly the article, 'Anonymous: Slot Machines and Pinball Games'.

37. 'There is one type of machine, of which the best known example is the bell-fruit machine which is actuated by the insertion of a coin or disc, and which automatically delivers the prize to the successful operator. The particular danger we see in this type of machine is that, since it does not require the intervention of an attendant in order to give the prize, it is capable of a rapidity of turnover which would render the element of gambling, even within the strict limits which we have set, no longer trivial. We, therefore, recommend that the provision of machines of this type should be illegal.' Royal Commission, 1949–51 Report, pp. 130–1.

38. Report on Enquiry into Gaming under Section 2 of Finance Act, 1963, H.M.S.O., Cmd. 2275.

39. C. M. Woodhouse, M.P., Joint Under-Secretary of State for the Home Department in his speech in the Second Reading Debate on the 1964 Act (28 February 1964).

40. Small Lotteries and Gaming Act, 1956 (4 & 5 Eliz. 2 C 45).

CHAPTER II

Gambling and Economic Resources

Use of Manpower

Table II provides particulars of the total number of persons employed in the provision of betting facilities for each of the years from 1959 to 1968, together with particulars of the total national labour force for each of the years as well as annual rates of growth for both items.

Whereas in 1959 a total of 36,400 persons were employed in the betting industry, the number had risen by 20,900 employees to a total of 57,300 in 1968, a rate of increase of 57.4 per cent in only 10 years. Within the same period the total number of employed persons in Britain rose by only 83,000, an increase of no more than 0.37 per cent.

The highest rate of growth of manpower in the betting industry occurred in the 2 years 1963-4 (10.8 per cent) and 1964-5 (12.1 per cent), the years which—according to whatever scant evidence may be available—witnessed the peak point of the post-legislation gambling expansion boom. Both the annual Home Office 'Betting, Gaming and Lotteries Act 1963' reports[1] as well as the annual reports of the Horserace Betting Levy Board[2] indicate the maximum rate of expansion within these two years. According to the former, these were the years of firmest betting shop consolidation and according to the latter, a considerable proportion of registered bookmakers were, for the purposes of levy collection, transferred into a higher profit category. Since 1965 the rate of increase of employment in the betting industry has noticeably levelled off and the employment totals for the years 1967 and 1968 are identical at 57,300 persons.

Despite the fact that in the 10 years under review the total manpower employed in the betting industry has risen by as much as 57.4 per cent—compared to a simultaneous increase in the total national labour force of a mere 0.37 per cent—it is true to say that the betting industry makes no more than a very minor claim upon the national manpower resources. No more than 1 employee out of 400 (1959 totals: 1 person in 600 employed) was in 1968 concerned with the provision of gambling facilities.

National Turnover

THE PRESENT

The questions concerned with the volume of gambling have in Britain, in common with all other countries, engendered a considerable amount of speculation as well as controversy. The Churches' Council on Gambling—the only permanent unofficial body which has in this, or any other country, devoted itself to research on the subject of gambling—has in each of the years since 1945 published annual estimates of the presumed volume of gambling in this country. Of necessity, these were bound to be to a very large extent a compound of sparse reliable data plus an admixture of inspired guesswork and wishful thinking; it has now been recognized by the Council that their estimates in the past have failed to reflect the volume of gambling realistically.[3]

However, thanks to the imposition of taxation upon all commercially promoted forms of gambling as from October 1966 we are in Britain uniquely in a position to assess the volume of gambling, commencing with the year 1967, with a considerable degree of accuracy and confidence. Tables III–VII attempt to reproduce some of the major quantitative information collated from the available official sources for the years 1967 and 1968. The following principal conclusions emerge from these Tables:

(1) Table III establishes that the total outlay on gambling in Britain in 1967 amounted to £1,497 million. This seemingly staggering sum represents an average annual individual outlay of £27.20, or 52p per week, for each man, woman and child in this country, more than £1 per week for each member of the national employed labour force, closely corresponding to the total national

expenditure on meat and bacon (£1,503 million). Before giving way to the temptation of drawing any conclusions from this total, it would however be advisable to await the outcome of the data discussed in the final section of this chapter.

(2) Gambling turnover fell by £61 million between 1967 and 1968, a decline of 4.2 per cent, which, taking account of the factor of inflation amounting to 4.4 per cent within that period, represents a decrease in real money terms of 8.6 per cent within one year; a period within which national outlay on virtually the entire range of consumer expenditure items expanded at varying rates of increase.

(3) The March 1968 Budget imposed new and increased taxes upon all gambling activities with the exception of Premium Bonds and gaming machines. Promoters of all the affected activities reimbursed themselves by passing on the full burden of increased taxes directly to their clients by way of reduced pay-out and inferior odds. The decrease in turnover from 1967 to 1968 would suggest that bettors reacted against this imposition of inferior odds by curtailment of their betting activities, thereby indicating that:

(a) higher rates of taxation produce a lower volume of outlay and that therefore gambling expansion allows itself to be curbed by fiscal controls,

(b) bettors in general respond to increased taxation—i.e. inferior transactional terms—by curtailment of outlay. This would seem to provide strong indication that bettors as a whole, although indulging in an allegedly irrational activity, react to changes in the market situation in a rational manner, suggesting that for the bettor gambling is not a compulsion but a freely entered into, self-regulative activity.

(4) With the exception of football pools where outlay fluctuates only very slightly from year to year and in which stakes—representing an activity in which bettors place their stakes almost entirely on pools where prizes are few and spectacular, but odds against winning almost astronomical—are highly inelastic to variation of odds, the lowest rates of negative reaction to increased taxation occurred for bingo and off-course betting with bookmakers—i.e. the placing of bets in betting shops. Although needing to guard against unwarranted ascription of significance

to fluctuations that are possibly largely fortuitous, it may well be plausible to suggest that gambling activities involving the greatest degree of associational and interpersonal content will be the least liable to contraction when odds against bettors change adversely. Whilst bingo, which together with Premium Bonds was unaffected by higher rates of taxation, showed an absolute rise —the extent of which may, however, in the absence of firm data be subject to error—the placement of bets with bookmakers off-course, though experiencing a tax surcharge of 100 per cent (from 2.5 to 5 per cent), fell by only 3.2 per cent, while the volume of on-course betting, subject to the same rise in tax, declined by as much as 22 per cent.

(5) As shown in Table IV, horseracing is outstandingly the major gambling activity. More than one half of all the money staked is laid out on horseracing, largely and increasingly in bets made off the course. Although the proportion of adults who bet on football pools is twice that of those who bet on horseracing, the outlay on the latter is seven times as great as that on the former, indicating a far greater frequency of betting and of volume per bet in respect of horseracing. Dogracing, though steadily declining in appeal over the past twenty years, does still occupy second place behind horseracing and does still account for a higher share of the total volume than the combined totals of the creations of the 1960 Act—gaming machines, bingo and casino gaming (combined total: 14 per cent). Trends, such as can be detected, suggest that the internal distribution, as shown in Table IV, has largely stabilized.

(6) Betting on horses is not necessarily linked with interest in horseracing as a sport. More than 90 per cent of all monies are placed with bookmakers off the course, suggesting that the intrinsic attraction lies not in the love of the contest itself, but rather in the wager or possibly the social environment and atmosphere in which the activity of betting takes place.

(7) Table V furnishes evidence of the fact that more than one half of the entire stakes are placed with bookmakers in betting shops: 56.5 per cent of the 1967 total of £845 million and 57.1 per cent of the total in 1968 of £820 million were placed in bets with bookmakers in betting shops. As, therefore, the staking of money in betting shops, accounting for more than 50 per cent of all

national stakes, is by far the largest single gambling activity, it would seem evident that empirical research into the actions and interactions in betting shops is not merely a legitimate, but in all probability the primary object of study.

THE PAST

We will in the present section attempt to subject the widely held and propagated assumption that 'the only trend in expenditure on gambling which remains constant is that more money is devoted to it by more people each year'[4] to examination on the basis of existing available sources. We shall pose the question as to whether such evidence as is attainable does indicate that inflation in gambling outlay has in the last two decades—or alternatively in the years subsequent to the introduction of the 1960 Betting and Gaming Act—been inordinate and excessive and whether the increase in outlay on gambling has been at a rate exorbitant or otherwise, relative to other items of expenditure during the same period.

The first natural source for information is the Churches' Council on Gambling who have been collecting and publishing annual estimates of the volume in this country for the past 20 years and whose estimate of an apparent volume of gambling, amounting to £795 million, was submitted to the Royal Commission in 1949 (see Table VI). Unfortunately their subsequent estimates are vitiated by the fact that, in response to the Royal Commission's criticisms of the Council's estimates as being exaggerated and excessive, the Churches' Council adopted a policy of deliberately tending towards underestimation in their subsequent submissions. In their own words 'The Council has been conscious that in an area where little more than guesswork is possible, it could easily be accused of taking the biased view by presenting inflated estimates. It has therefore deliberately under-stated what is thought to be a true picture and there is now evidence that indicates that, in its effort to avoid appearing biased, it has provided a figure far below the true value.'[5] We are there-fore compelled to disregard their post-1947 estimates, since these err unrealistically towards underestimation, and are limited to the Council's 1947 estimate, suggesting, on the basis of scrupulously and objectively assembled material, a turnover of £795 million for that year, as the initial basis of our discussion.

The only other well-documented estimate of the past volume of gambling in Britain available to us, is the one prepared by the New York State Legislature in respect of the year 1962.[6] This report, containing sixty pages of facts, figures and reasoned argument, submitting an estimate of gambling turnover in Britain of £1,290 million for 1962 (see Table VII) was, in the view of a considerable body of informed opinion, considered to reflect the outlay on gambling at the time with a reasonable degree of accuracy. The British economist Alex Rubner in his book *The Economics of Gambling*[7] fully associated himself with this estimate. Ruth Adams in a separate investigation arrived at a similar total outlay[8] and the Liberal M.P. Peter Bessell, in a House of Commons debate in 1965,[9] adopted a figure of £1,300 million as the likely volume of gambling turnover in Britain at the time. We therefore feel justified, subject to the reservations stated at the foot of Table VII, in regarding the figure of £1,290 million as reflecting the outlay on gambling in Britain in 1962 with a reasonable degree of accuracy.

Table VIII lists the total amount of national income and personal income as well as annual outlay on several selected representative items of personal expenditure for the years 1947, 1962 and 1967 and further includes for each of these years the estimates of gambling turnover proposed by us as valid within a considerable degree of accuracy. The items nos. 1–6 were chosen as reflecting some of the major items of personal expenditure and are, in their rates of increase, representative of the larger bulk of items making up total personal expenditure. In view of the fact that full statistical information on national and personal income, on total consumer expenditure and on all the other various items of personal expenditure does not, at present, extend beyond the year 1967, this year rather than 1968 will be used as a basis of comparison in respect of gambling for the remainder of the present chapter. As even the most cursory inspection of the Table will reveal, outlay on gambling, though being on an increased scale, has been far outstripped by each of the other items included in the Table. Whether viewed in a twenty-year perspective, from 1947 to 1967, or in the briefer span of the five-year

period from 1962 to 1967, rates of increase in outlay on gambling
have been below those of the other items. For example, outlay on
gambling rose by 88.5 per cent (from £795 million to £1,497
million) between 1947 and 1967, while total personal income
increased by as much as 252.7 per cent (from £9,476 million to
£33,435 million) in the same period. Gambling pre-empted at the
latter date less than one-half the proportion of total personal
income claimed by it in 1947. Equally, while total personal
income in the years from 1962 to 1967 grew by 30.5 per cent
(from £25,624 million to £33,435 million), the rate of increase in
the outlay on gambling amounted to no more than just over one
half, namely 16 per cent (from £1,290 million to £1,497 million).

The highest rate of increase in expenditure for both periods
occurred in respect of outlay on housing and on books—both of
these items being almost universally regarded as social priorities
—while the lowest rates of increase applied to outlay on gambling, tobacco and to a lesser extent alcohol, the items of
expenditure generally considered as indulgences, even if not
profligacies or compulsions. There is thus every indication that
advances in the standard of living will bring with them increased
personal self-direction, judgment and discrimination, and that
the volume of participation in gambling is likely, under conditions
of increasing and more widely-pervasive affluence, to decline
relatively—in all probability irrespective of legal provisions—
rather than to expand.

Without seeking to claim, in respect of the annual gambling
outlay figures presented by us, a degree of accuracy they may not
possess, it can be asserted with confidence that national gambling
outlay—and with it, manifestly, national participation—has in
the past twenty years, despite the far-reaching measures of
liberalization in recent years, grown at a more moderate rate than
either gross national income or any of the other comparable items
of personal expenditure.

NATIONAL EXPENDITURE

The statement that, in respect of gambling, turnover is not
analogous to expenditure is, once postulated, powerfully persuasive and, to most, almost self-evident. Although its truth is

still denied by many commentators, it has for long been recognized by most observers that gambling differs from other forms of expenditure, inasmuch that the overwhelming bulk of money staked (*en masse*) is returned to the investors (*en masse*) in the form of winnings and that only the amounts retained before distribution—in the form of taxation, administrative expenses and overheads and promoters' profits—represent money expended. Official records and publications—such as the Royal Commission on Betting, Lotteries and Gaming, the White Papers on National Income and Expenditure and the annual Family Expenditure Surveys—have for many years now differentiated between Gambling Turnover and Gambling Expenditure, considering the latter to be equivalent to the total amount of money lost to bettors, while the former respresents the total amounts of monies staked. Indeed the Royal Commission maintained that turnover figures alone give a false and misleading impression, as they were not only responsible for vastly inflating the amount of money actually gambled and lost, but that they further failed to differentiate between the way in which different types of gambling redistribute the amounts staked.[10] While turnover figures are limited to indicating the degree of total participation and examining the changes in popularity of different types of gambling, the economic significance—national as well as personal—can only be determined by a method which seeks to elucidate in what manner and to what extent money is returned to the investor in the different types of gambling under consideration. While in football-pool betting, for instance, a large proportion of the total stakes is distributed in the form of a few large prizes to a minute proportion of total investors, in horserace betting or dogracing the regular bettor will, over a period, have a number of successful bets which will return to him a substantial proportion of his stakes. Undeniably, gambling thus differs from other forms of expenditure, such as say expenditure on a packet of cigarettes or on a joint of meat, in which, post-consumption, none of the outlay returns in a tangible form to the purchaser while in gambling no habitual bettor will, over a period, not have at least some of his stakes returned. Granted that some—in particular the professionals or semi-professionals—win more than others, that manipulation, inside information, and at times probably even fraud, keeps some of the stake money within an inner ring; granted that winnings are not always allocated towards mitigation of losses past or future, and are not even then always prudently spent— frequently got rid of in treats, indulgences and extravagances— while stake monies lost will have to be drawn from the household budget. Even when all these factors are taken into account, national gambling expenditure does still exhibit unique features which may possibly best emerge by considering play on a 5p slot-machine, where an initial stake of 50p, with the almost certain intermittent draws, is likely to afford the bettor not the 10 plays one might expect, but in all likelihood, as many as 55–60 single plays and where a total final loss of 50p—net expenditure— will equal a turnover of £3.

The aim must therefore be to elucidate the amount of national expenditure on gambling in relation to total consumption as well as to other forms of personal expenditure by consumers, an undertaking which, thanks to the introduction of taxation on all the various forms of gambling, is relatively uncomplicated and trustworthy owing to the fact that the total amount deducted by organizers is either known or can be accurately assessed. Responsible officials concerned with the collection of taxes and the supervision of records are firmly of the opinion that the amount of evasion or falsification is likely to be on no more than the most minimal scale.

Tables IX and X are devoted to the task of converting total turnover into net expenditure. Table IX seeks to translate turnover for each of the various forms of gambling previously enumerated into net expenditure for the two years 1967 and 1968 (see particularly Table IXA) and Table X lists total net expenditure for 1967 against firstly, total consumer expenditure, and then, against eight other items of personal expenditure as obtained from the 1968 Central Statistical Office report on National Income and Expenditure for the same year. The principal conclusions emerging from these two Tables allow themselves to be summarized as follows:

(1) Gambling expenditure amounts to a sum much lower than gambling turnover. In 1967 expenditure at £268.3 million was no more than 17.9 per cent of total turnover (= outlay) at £1,497 million, while in 1968 expenditure rose slightly to £277.2 million,

19.3 per cent of the total turnover of £1,436 million for the year. A large proportion of money retained from the bettors, accruing to the Exchequer by way of taxation, can be said to be redistributive, inasmuch as it reallocates cash resources from the body of bettors to the total population at large. As much as 25.6 per cent (£68.6 million) of total expenditure in 1967 and 34.7 per cent (£96.4 million) in 1968 was claimed by the Exchequer in the way of taxation.

(2) While the overall rate of return to the bettor in 1967 stood at 82p for each £1 invested (81p in 1968), the rate of return differed widely between different gambling activities. Whereas those who bet on horseracing received 85 per cent of their stake monies back as winnings, only 55 per cent of all stake monies returned to those who staked money on football pools. Premium Bonds, now the one and only untaxed gambling activity—suffering no more than a deduction of 10 per cent and therefore achieving a pay-back rate of 90 per cent—now represent the 'best buy' for the investor.

(3) Recognition of net expenditure, rather than total turnover, as being the true yardstick for assessing the economic significance and implications of gambling, implies that the average *per capita* annual cost of gambling for 1967 is not the staggering sum of £27.20 (52p per week) as suggested at the beginning of this chapter, but £4.85, no more than 9p per week. Each member of the adult population of 18 years or above would spend an average amount of £6.70 per year (13p per week) on gambling, or adopting an alternative perspective, by relating total expenditure on gambling to the total number of employees in all Industries and Services (22,828,000 persons), it appears that the average person employed spent a weekly sum of 22½p (£11.75 per year) on gambling in 1967, which is less than the cost of one single packet of cigarettes.

(4) While, even at £268 million per year the cost of gambling still represents a formidable total, Table X reveals that as compared to other items, expenditure on gambling is relatively modest and not by any means inordinate. For each £1 expended on tobacco, no more than 17½p is spent on gambling, and for each £1 spent on gambling as much as £5.90 is laid out on alcohol. For a nation as notoriously ill-housed and as hostile to the printed

word as commentators would frequently have us believe, to spend on gambling no more than 9p for each £1 spent on housing and 70p for each £1 spent on books, is a record considerably less shaming and dismal than initial consideration of the subject would suggest.

(5) For each £1 spent on gambling the average member of the population would in 1967 have spent as much as £90.45 on all other items of consumer expenditure.

Gambling in 1967, absorbing no more than 0.25 per cent of the total national labour force and laying claim to no more than 1.1 per cent of total personal expenditure (1.1p in each £1) and to 0.78 per cent of total national economic resources (0.78p in each £1)[11] cannot on a national scale, by even the most rigorous standards, be considered as constituting any other than the most minor problem in present-day Britain.

Notes

1. Home Office, Betting, Gaming and Lotteries Act, Permits and Licences, annual reports laid before Parliament in accordance with the requirements of Schedule 1 of the Betting, Gaming and Lotteries Act 1963, H.M.S.O., London.
2. Horserace Betting Levy Board and Horserace Totalisator Board, annual reports and statements of accounts, 1963–8, London.
3. Churches' Council on Gambling, *Gambling: time to think again* (1967).
4. Smith, L., 'The Gambling Boom', *New Society*, London, 17 January 1963.
5. Churches' Council on Gambling, *Gambling: time to think again* (1967), p. 4.
6. Roman, S. and Paley, H. D., 'Report to the New York State Legislature' (New York December 1962).
7. Rubner, A. (1966) pp. 116–18.
8. Adams, R., 'The Gamers and the Games', *New Statesman*, London, 3 April 1964.
9. Hansard, H.M.S.O., London, 27 May 1965.
10. Report of the Royal Commission on Betting, Lotteries and Gaming 1949–51, pp. 16–17, paras. 63, 64, 65 and 66. See, for instance, par. 66, p. 17: '. . . The only purposes for which turnover figures have a certain limited value is in examining changes in the popularity of particular forms of Gambling; for example, the figures of the annual amounts staked on dogtrack and horserace course totalisators indicate the rise and fall in the popularity of these forms of betting and

may conveniently be used for this purpose provided that it is borne in mind that they do not represent actual expenditure.'

11. Gross National Product in 1967 amounted to £34,292 million. Central Statistical Office, National Income and Expenditure, 1968, table 1, p. 3.

CHAPTER III

Patterns of Gambling

We will, in course of this chapter, seek to find answers to the following sets of questions:

(1) How many people within the adult population gamble?
(2) How many people gamble on the various gambling activities,
    (*a*) Dogracing
    (*b*) Horseracing
    (*c*) Football Pools
    (*d*) Bingo
    (*e*) Casinos and Gaming Clubs?
(3) How often do bettors gamble?
(4) How much money do bettors stake?
(5) What are the major divergences between:
    (*a*) Men and Women
    (*b*) Members of different age groups and of different marital status
    (*c*) Members of different social classes
    (*d*) Bettors as compared to non-bettors and occasional bettors
    (*e*) Habitual bettors as compared to regular non-habitual bettors?
(6) What are some of the public attitudes towards gambling?

These questions we will, in turn, attempt to answer, on the basis of the following survey material available:

(1) Government Social Survey, 1950, entitled *Betting in Britain* (M.S. 710/4). Subjects: 1,350 men and 1,562 women, total 2,912 adults aged 16 and above. (Abbreviated to GSS in subsequent text.)[1]

(2) Statistical data obtained by Research Services Ltd on behalf of B. S. Rowntree and R. S. Lavers and published in

English Life and Leisure (London, 1951). (Abbreviated to R & L in subsequent text.)[2]

(3) National Opinion Polls Ltd; surveys conducted:
(*a*) January 1963 (Special Supplement: Gambling) and
(*b*) May 1966 (NOP Bulletin, p. 8).
(Abbreviated to NOP in subsequent text.)[3]

(4) The Gallup Poll Ltd; surveys based on quota samples on approximately 1,000 adults aged 21 and above and in part stratified by sex, age group, social class and occupation.
(*a*) July 1964 and March 1965
(*b*) January, February, April, May and June 1966
(*c*) May and October 1967
(*d*) February, July and December 1968
(Abbreviated to GP in subsequent text.)[4]

(5) A specially commissioned survey carried out by Research Services Ltd entitled *Betting Habits and Attitudes*, August 1968, upon:
(*a*) A national quota sample of 1,114 men aged 18 and over, stratified by age, marital status, social class, region and betting habits (National Sample)
(*b*) Interviews conducted outside selected betting offices with 206 off-course bettors (Off-course Sample)
(*c*) Interviews with 219 race-meeting attenders at racecourses (On-course Sample)
(*d*) A short list of questions added to a subscription survey upon a quasi-random sample of 1,025 women aged 18 and over, stratified by age, marital status, social class, region and betting habits.
Findings reported in 2 volumes containing 75 tables and extensive commentary, plus 18 additional tables on off-course bettors. (Abbreviated to RS in subsequent text.)*[5]

(6) A Household Survey conducted by the author, Winter 1967, in the Bow South Ward of the London Borough of Tower Hamlets, London, on 54 subjects (37 men and 17 women) aged 18 and above by way of informal intensive interview and distributed as follows:
(*a*) 18 interviews (12 men, 5 women and 1 refusal) in a local authority two-storey block of flats, built in 1963

* Surveys nos. 3, 4 and 5 were supplied privately to the author by kind courtesy of promoters.

(*b*) 18 interviews (12 men, 6 women) in a street composed partly of privately-rented and partly of owner-occupied houses, the majority lacking in full range of standard domestic amenities
(*c*) 18 interviews (13 men, 5 women) in a street almost entirely classified as slum property scheduled for clearance.

Subjects were exclusively active or retired workers within the lower-skilled and unskilled manual grades, corresponding to social grade DE classification. (Abbreviated to HHS in subsequent text.)[6]

How Many People Gamble?

The GSS (1950) declared that 4 out of 5 adults had taken part in some form of gambling at some part of their lives and that between 10–13 per cent of the adult population (approximately 4 million people) could, by virtue of their placing bets at least once per week, be classified as regular bettors.

In 1963, 68 per cent of men and 45 per cent of women—55 per cent of the entire poll—answered 'Yes' to the question: 'Do you ever gamble?' put to them by the National Opinion Poll. There was, surprisingly, for both men and women virtually no social class difference in participation in gambling and almost exactly 50 per cent of all men as well as women, regardless of social class, above the age of 45 declared themselves as taking part in gambling. The survey did, however, reveal a striking sex differentiation for subjects below the age of 45. Whereas 60 per cent of males under 45 gambled, only 40 per cent of women in the same age group did so.

The HHS (1967) revealed that as many as 84 per cent of men and no fewer than 70 per cent of women amongst the sample entirely composed of manual workers—more than 75 per cent of the entire sample—gambled either on horses, dogs, football pools, gaming clubs, or bingo with a fair degree of regularity.

These data should, however, be looked upon with a considerable degree of reservation. Different answers will be obtained according to the manner in which the question is phrased. Fewer people will admit to gambling than to betting and more will answer positively to the question 'Have you ever laid out money on gambling?' than to 'Do you gamble?' This response is likely to be determined by social class towards a higher positive response rate for members of the middle class. For instance, whereas some people will consider the annual '10p each way' on the Derby or the Grand National, or even the buying of a few raffle tickets as taking part in gambling, others will look upon a modest weekly stake on the football pools in the winter season as a diversion rather than gambling.

A more meaningful indication of gambling participation will be derived by asking how many people stake how much money, how often at one or the other of the various activities which are conventionally regarded as constituting gambling. These are the questions we will seek to consider in the sections to follow.

How Many People Gamble On:

DOGRACING?

The GSS declared that 4 per cent of the adult population (approximately 1.5 million people) regularly gambled on dogs, a finding completely confirmed by R & L one year later in 1951.

By 1963, the proportion of the adult population betting on dogracing had, according to NOP, altered only very slightly to 5 per cent and although, according to two separate surveys carried out by GP in 1964 and 1966, the percentage of bettors stood at 8 per cent for both years, the findings of the RS survey in 1968, once more, confirmed the percentage of dograce bettors at around 5 per cent. All surveys agree that males outnumber females in the ratio of about 5:1 and that the younger age group (below 45 years) is slightly more likely to bet on dogs than those above that age (ratio 1.4:1).

Dogracing has since its inception been regarded as an over-whelmingly proletarian pastime both in respect of attendance as well as the placing of stakes off the course. Ferdynand Zweig declared in 1949, on the basis of numerous interviews carried out by him, that as many as 20 per cent of all male adult manual workers were regular attenders at dogtracks. The 1967 HHS indicated that little change had taken place in that respect. Slightly more than 20 per cent of all males—entirely belonging to the semi- and unskilled manual worker category—declared themselves as regular attenders at dogtracks and a further 20 per cent (combined total: 41.3 per cent) were in the habit of placing bets on dogracing in betting shops. The relative female incidence, in respect of both attendance as well as off-course betting, was considerably in excess of that for the total population which showed a male preponderance to the extent of 5:1. The HHS, in contrast, indicated that within the lower-grade manual wage group the ratio would be no higher than just above 2.6:1. The HHS confirmed a slightly higher incidence of both attendance as well as off-course betting amongst the below-45-years age group.

In summary it might be said that betting on dogracing is, and always has been, a male-dominated minority activity, declining in popularity of attendance since the early post-war period, but gaining in support off the course since the introduction of the betting shops. It remains a predominantly proletarian pursuit in betting off-course even more than in on-course attendance (Social grade AB:DE—attendance 1:2.5, off-course betting 1:5). While, however, betting off the course is, for a large section of bettors, likely to be an irregular and spasmodic habit, attendance is, for the majority of those who frequent dogtracks, a regular and frequently routinized activity, in which a certain track will be visited on a certain day of the week with outlay per visit varying only slightly in response to success or otherwise.

HORSERACING?

(i) *Attendance at Horserace meetings*

Racecourse organizers and promoters have over the years, despite improved on-course facilities, deplored the fact of falling attendances. Their plaint is confirmed by the data at our disposal. Total annual attendance which had, in 1950, been estimated to be between 10 and 15 million per year had by 1967, according to the reports of the H.B.L.B. fallen to 4.6 million. Whereas in 1950 7 per cent of the total adult population (approximately 2.5 million people) attended horserace meetings, the percentage had fallen to 5 per cent by 1968; 8 per cent of the total male population and no more than 2 per cent of the female.

The Research Survey 1968 showed significant differences

between age groups as well as social grade. Whereas 10 per cent of the sample in the age group 55+ attended race meetings, only 5 per cent of the age group, 18–34 did so. Attendance was, at 4 per cent, lowest for social grade C1—lower non-manual middle-class subjects—and, at 11 per cent, highest for social grades DE—semi- and unskilled manual workers.

No more than one quarter of attenders visited the race tracks more often than 10 times per year, the majority of these visits taking place at weekends and no more than 10 per cent evening meetings. Frequency of attendance was, again, highest in the 55+ age group, but in contrast to likelihood of attendance, most frequent for the AB social grade group—members of the upper-middle and middle class and lowest for manual workers (ratio 2:1). Only two of the men (5.5 per cent) and none of the women in the HHS had visited a racecourse within the twelve months preceding the interview.

(ii) *Betting off-course*

The GSS estimated that, although as many as 50 per cent of the total adult population were in the habit of placing bets on one or other or several of the major classic events, no more than 10–13 per cent of the total adult population (4 million people) could be considered as regular horserace bettors, using as their criterion a minimum of one bet per week. Within the following 15 years—whether as a result of the liberalization of legislation, or whether due to other factors such as growing national prosperity or increased amount of personal leisure—the proportion of regular bettors on horseracing had doubled. All three independent surveys available to us—NOP, GP and RS—suggest that no fewer than 25 per cent of the entire adult population now bet on horseracing off the course with a reasonable degree of regularity.

The preponderance of male to female bettors had, according to the NOP, remained stable at 1.5:1 between 1950 and 1963, but had according to the RS, shrunk to almost negligible proportions by 1968 (men: 28 per cent, women: 26 per cent), possibly the outcome of increased female financial and social independence.

The GSS considered that gambling on horses off-course was relatively heaviest amongst the lower income groups of manual workers earning a weekly wage of £5–£10 in 1950, equivalent to approximately £15–£20 in the present day. It also suggested that it was most heavily concentrated among men in the middle age group. The RS data deny that the middle age group is more prone to betting on horses, but reveal that single men between the ages of 18–34 were far less likely to bet on horses than their married counterparts or members of the other two older age groups (20 per cent single men 18–34 years; 30 per cent of all other groups). The disparity, in respect of women, was even greater. Whereas a mere 14 per cent of single women between the ages of 18–34 gambled on horses, as many as 34 per cent of married women in the same age group did so, while for the two groups above that age (35–54 and 55+ years) the proportion fell to 25 per cent. These data furnish further evidence of the financial independence of young married women and of the convergence of consumption patterns between young husbands and wives.

Social class differentiation is far less pronounced than in the case of betting on dogs. According to RS, the difference between the two extreme groups—AB on the one hand and DE on the other—is 20:37 per cent for men (ratio of 1:1.85) and 22:33 per cent for women (ratio 1:1.5). The HHS, confined to members of social class DE, indicates a far heavier incidence of participation in this activity. The proportion of regular bettors on horseracing in the HHS was found to be as high as two adults in three. Three quarters of all men and 45 per cent of women interviewed placed bets on horseracing with bookmakers in betting shops at least once per week.

Credit accounts—the placing of bets on horses with bookmakers other than in betting offices—are limited to no more than 5 per cent of all bettors almost exclusively confined to the non-manual social groups. All off-course bettors in the HHS placed their bets in betting shops. Most of the money staked, as well as the bigger stakes, is wagered at bookmakers' odds rather than on the tote.

FOOTBALL POOLS?

The proportion of the adult population betting on football pools appears to have slightly declined in the course of the past twenty years. The GSS claimed that 44 per cent of adults of both sexes took part in the football pools. By 1963 (NOP) the percentage had fallen to 40 per cent and it had further declined to 38.5 per cent (RS) by 1968. At the same time the sex differential had extended. While in 1950 for each 100 men who staked money on football pools as many as 75 women did so, by 1968 no more than 50 women to each 100 men took part. The present-day social class differential (RS) appears to be relatively slight as well as contracting. Forty-two per cent of men in social class AB as against 57 per cent of those in social class DE—a differential ratio of 1:1.36 as compared to a ratio of 1:2.41 in 1950—declared themselves as bettors on football pools. There is, however, a striking difference between single and married men. While 55 per cent of all married men staked money, a mere 29 per cent of unmarried men took part in this activity.

The HHS seemed largely to bear out the findings of the RS survey. Sixty-two per cent of the subjects interviewed (75 per cent of men and 35 per cent of women) placed bets on football pools throughout the British football season. In the off-season when promoters run pools on Australian fixtures, the percentage fell to below 40 per cent (men: 50 per cent, women 18 per cent), while in the RS sample the percentage of off-season participants declined to below 20 per cent.

Ninety-four per cent of all bettors on football pools invest all, or at least the major part, of their stakes on the treble chance pool where, in return for near certain loss of total stake, the minute fraction of successful competitors receive prizes not infrequently exceeding sums of £100,000. Twenty-five per cent of all bettors do, in addition to betting on the treble chance, complete at least one of the other pools such as '4 Aways' or '3 Draws', while only one bettor in twenty will gamble on a fixed-odds coupon where odds on various selections are named in advance and where, although prizes are very much smaller, the likelihood of winning is far greater than in pool betting.

Seventy-five per cent of all football pool bettors make use of readymade permutations copied entirely from newspapers or even from pools' promoters rosters and no more than 10 per cent of bettors devise their own plan in selection. Thus it appears that for the overwhelming majority the football pools are a purely mechanical activity implying no personal skill or initiative whatsoever, where, in pursuit of a major once-and-for-all windfall, they are willing to sacrifice fully their entire customary stake.

BINGO?

This activity owes its existence to the provisions of the Betting and Gaming Act 1960, and soon after its introduction, the first sets of premises started to appear with astounding, and, to many observers, highly alarming rapidity. NOP estimated in 1963 that 12 per cent of the adult population took part in commercially organized bingo activities. In January 1966, 24 per cent of all subjects interviewed in the GP survey answered 'yes' to the question: 'Have you played bingo in the last twelve months?' though, it must be borne in mind, not thereby indicating regularity by their positive reply. According to the RS 15.2 per cent of the total adult population took part in commercial bingo games.

It is widely taken for granted that gambling on bingo is predominantly attractive to women and to members of the working class and these assumptions are borne out by the various surveys. NOP reports that there were more than three female to each one male bettor on bingo in 1963, while RS found in 1968 that while the percentages for both sexes combined had more than doubled in the five years since the NOP survey—from 10 to 21 per cent for women and from 3 to 11 per cent for men—the ratio now stood at less than 2:1 in favour of women. The entire increase however seems to be attributable to additional participation of members of the working class. The percentage of upper- and upper-middle-class members playing bingo remained stable at 4 per cent within that period, while the percentage of manual workers betting on this activity had grown from 8 per cent to 21 per cent. As many as 16 per cent of men in social class DE, compared with a mere 4 per cent in social class AB, were regular attenders at bingo sessions.

In respect of all male social classes, bingo betting was found to be most heavily concentrated within the middle-age group. While single men between the ages of 18 and 34 scorned this activity (only 3 per cent took part), 14 per cent of married men in the age group 35–54 were regular bingo bettors.

These particulars appear to indicate that:

(a) there was in the five years 1963–8 a considerable growth for both sexes, but a much higher rate of growth for men than for women;

(b) participation in bingo had remained stable for members of the upper and middle class within that period, but that as regards members of the lower and unskilled manual worker grades it has expanded significantly in respect of women but even more remarkably in respect of men, and

(c) regular visits to Bingo Halls had become a joint activity for married working-class couples, particularly within the 35–44 years age group, for whom visits to the Bingo Hall and its attendant betting had assumed the character of a social outing and a family occasion, and had ceased to bear connotations of being a gambling activity.

These assumptions are very largely confirmed by the findings of the HHS survey. Out of a total of 53 subjects interviewed, as many as 17 per cent of all the men and 34 per cent of all the women—a combined total of 21 per cent—were in the habit of attending commercially organized bingo games. None of the men admitted to doing so, other than in the company of their wives ('Give the missus a bit of an outing' as suggested by one), and the habit of joint visits to Bingo Halls—although it must be admitted that the sample did not include any age stratification—appeared to be most prevalent in the age group from 35 to 50 years. Incidentally, two young married women (8 per cent of total female sample) whose husbands disapproved of and did not indulge in gambling, regularly went with their 'mates' to bingo sessions, without thereby incurring their husbands' wrath or even disapproval, suggesting once more that betting on bingo has, at least for the lower-skilled manual workers, ceased to be regarded, if conducted with restraint, as gambling at all.

Finally, bingo is the one and only gambling activity in which any significant regional difference was shown to exist. Its incidence, according to the RS survey, is most heavily concentrated in the Midlands where 15 per cent of all males, compared to only 9 per cent in Scotland and the North and only 10 per cent in

London and the South (national total: 11 per cent) indulged in this activity.

CASINOS AND GAMING CLUBS?

Although taking part in casino gaming constituted a legal offence prior to 1960, a considerable amount was known to persist illicitly in the years following the Second World War. It must be assumed that the category of 'other'—then affecting 4 per cent of the adult population—to which the GSS refers would represent casino type gaming. This figure of 4 per cent appears to have remained stable until 1963 (NOP) but had, according to RS, grown to 6.5 per cent by 1968.

There had, furthermore, in addition to overall growth by over 50 per cent, been a number of internal changes as regards participants in casino gaming between the years 1950 and 1968. Whereas, in the earlier period, participation had been most heavily concentrated within the working-class group (ratio 1.66:1), it is now considered that members of the upper and upper-middle social classes are more than twice as likely to gamble in casinos than are lower-skilled manual wage earners.

One feature, however, which has remained unchanged is that casino gambling continues to be a young man's or woman's game. The GSS found in 1950 that while as many as 6 per cent of their subjects below the age of 45 belonged to their 'other' category, a mere 2 per cent of the subjects above that age did so. The 1968 RS survey claimed that, while a startling 20 per cent of single men below the age of 34 frequented casinos, no more than 2 per cent of men in the age group 55 and above did likewise (Ratio 10:1). It now appears likely that virtually 40 per cent of young unmarried men in the upper and upper-middle class gamble in casinos. Casino betting, in fact, is most frequent among the groups least likely to indulge in other forms of betting—young unmarried people and those in the non-manual social grades.

The habit of casino gambling, in common with all the other forms of gambling discussed in the present section, appeared more widespread among the subjects of the HHS than according to other surveys, either for the population as a whole or even for the corresponding social class. Eleven per cent of the men and

6 per cent of the women interviewed (sex ratio 1.83 : 1) frequented gaming clubs with some regularity, in most cases for games such as 'chemmy' or blackjack rather than table games. Attenders were relatively more heavily concentrated in the 30–45 age group and neither of the two single men interviewed admitted to casino gaming.

How Often do Bettors Gamble?

The GSS declared in 1950 that for those who gambled on horses or dogs off the course, the average number of bets would be 3 per week. Although this information does go some way towards enlightening us as to gaming patterns and outlay, it fails to tell us whether it would have been more typical for the average bettor to lay three bets on only one day per week, or to have one single bet on three separate days in a week. The post-legislation surveys are more illuminating in that respect.

The NOP estimated that 75 per cent of those who had admitted to gambling were in the habit of doing so at least once per week. The GP in answer to the question 'When was the last time you had a bet on a horse or a dog', put in June 1966 elicited the information that:

57 per cent of their respondents declared themselves to be total non-participants in this activity.

Of the 43 per cent who declared themselves as bettors on horses and dogs, 12 per cent had placed a bet on the previous day (5.16 per cent of total adult population).

A further 30 per cent had last placed a bet once or more within the previous week (12.90 per cent of total adult population).

For 25 per cent, at least one month had elapsed since their last bet (10.75 per cent of total adult population),

and an equal percentage—25 per cent—had not staked any money within the previous six months (10.75 per cent of total adult population).

A final 12 per cent (5.16 per cent of total adult population) disclaimed any bets in the period of between 6 months and 1 year preceding the interview.

More than 30 per cent of the sample of regular bettors, defined by placement of bets at least once per week, were in the habit of placing bets no more often than one day per week, 16 per cent each bet two and three days per week respectively and 20 per cent of regular bettors gambled five days a week or more often. On the basis of this survey it would appear that more than one third of the total 43 per cent, who rank themselves as bettors, are likely to confine their betting activities to one or more of the major classic races and that, within the most commonly used criteria, they resemble the non-bettor more closely than they do the regular bettor.

The RS survey asked all those subjects who admitted to betting with bookmakers off the course (21 per cent of the total), as well as the 206 off-course bettors interviewed by them outside betting offices, how often they were in the habit of placing bets. As many as 40 per cent declared that they placed bets either every day or almost every day and 70 per cent declared themselves to be doing so at least once a week. Although the GP finding would suggest a lower proportion, the weight of evidence would seem to suggest, (a) there has been little change in the frequency of betting off-course in the years from 1963 to 1968 and (b) that of those who do bet on horses and dogs off-course no fewer than 70 per cent do so at least once per week and that for probably no fewer than 20 per cent the daily bet is virtually a matter of routine.

Not unexpectedly, a number of differentials were shown to exist. Twice as many men as women place bets twice a week or more often (NOP: 19 per cent: 10 per cent) and while 25 per cent of female bettors placed bets no more often than 2–3 times a year, the proportion of male bettors placing bets with equal infrequency was fewer than 14 per cent. For an identical 56 per cent of both sexes, the norm seemed to be the placing of a bet once per week.

While 25 per cent of male working-class bettors placed bets at least twice a week, the proportion of upper- and middle-class members doing so was no more than 10 per cent. Twenty-nine per cent of bettors of both sexes in the upper- and middle-class group did not bet any more frequently than 2–3 times per year, whereas the equivalent percentage for members of the working class was no more than 15 per cent. Age for both sexes and all classes appeared to be a factor of irrelevance in respect of frequency of betting. More than one half in each of the two age groups in the sample (under 45 years and 45 and over) declared that they placed bets on one occasion per week, and for all age groups, all social classes and both sexes the modal frequency of betting was exactly once per week.

As to frequency of betting on football pools, RS found that while virtually 50 per cent of their subjects gambled on football pools regularly in the course of the winter season—the fixture period of the British Football Association—only 20 per cent did so during the off-season period when promoters circulate Australian fixture coupons. Only 11 per cent of those in social class AB gambled on football pools in the off-season, compared to 21 per cent of manual workers (ratio 1:1.92), while the ratio of single men to married men of all ages was 1:1.66, suggesting that the filling-in and betting on football pools as a regular all the year habit is considerably more likely to be particular to married manual wage-earners of middle age and above, while both the younger age groups as well as non-manual workers tend to associate betting on football pools with the British football season.

The question of frequency of gambling was not systematically polled in the HHS. Paradoxically, such information as is available does suggest that it is the young married women in the age group below 35 years and the male old-age pensioners who, among the bettors, are the more likely to indulge in this activity as a regular daily habit. The former, inclining to long-odds bets of the accumulator type,* tended to look upon their daily '5p each way' stake in a manner similar to the purchase of a ticket in a lottery and the latter, equally restricting the amount of their stake, tended to prolong their stay in the betting shop, frequently for several hours, pleading that interest in horseracing 'keeps my mind occupied, gives me something to do'. The balance of regulars—the majority group of active males—are rather more diverse. For most of them selection is a matter of deliberation undertaken with some degree of gravity. They will tend to wait

---

* Accumulator bets depend for their success upon the contingency of several separate selections being successful. The winnings of each successful runner are added to the following selection.

until 'something I fancy', 'a horse that owes me money' or alternatively 'a horse that has won me money' appears on the race card. They are likely to display awareness of the interactional processes and functions of their favourite betting shop in which, when resources, leisure or time sneaked-off from work will allow, they will spend their time. The majority, I would suggest on the basis of available material, bet no more often than 2–3 times per week, but will when betting be likely to place at least 3–4 separate bets.

How Much do Bettors Stake?

The National Opinion Poll obtained the following sets of answers to their question: 'How much would you say you spend each week on gambling?'

Sixty-six per cent of bettors claimed to be spending less than 25p per week (males: 56 per cent, females: 81 per cent; upper and middle class: 70 per cent, working class: 65 per cent), a further 20 per cent were spending between 25p and 50p per week (males: 24 per cent, females: 14 per cent; upper and middle class: 20 per cent, working class: 19 per cent). Ten per cent of bettors spent between 50p and £1 weekly (males: 12 per cent, females: 3 per cent; upper and middle class: 6 per cent, working class: 9 per cent) and no more than 5 per cent admitted to spending £1 per week or more (males: 8 per cent, females: 2 per cent; upper and middle class: 4 per cent, working class: 7 per cent).

While tempted to remark upon the modesty of average weekly outlay, it must be borne in mind that the question is likely to have been interpreted by a majority of subjects as seeking to elicit the average amount of weekly losses (the term used was '. . . spend each week on gambling') and that it will therefore do little to indicate the average weekly outlay (total amount of stakes) which, assuming on the basis of above information an average weekly net loss of 50p, would suggest a total individual outlay (stake) of perhaps £3 per week.

Although these data, while failing to distinguish between outlay and expenditure (stakes and losses), therefore only throw meagre light on the question of stakes, they give us nevertheless very useful information on relative patterns of outlay by various groups of the population. There is not, according to these tables, any difference in amount of outlay between the different age groups, but considerable divergence between men and women on the one hand and the different social classes on the other. The data reveal that men are four times as likely as women to spend (lose?) 50p and above on gambling per week and furthermore that the ratio of those belonging to the working class as against those of the upper and middle class who will spend 50p and above is 1.6:1. The major conclusions therefore emerging from these tables is that heavy gamblers are much more likely to be men rather than women and that, despite their considerably lower income and fewer financial resources, the majority will be members of the manual working class.

In order to acquaint ourselves with amounts of money staked, we will need to turn to those surveys which have sought to determine in unambiguous terms how much money bettors lay out on the various betting activities. Looking, in the first place, at the football pools, we have at our disposal two separate surveys, the first conducted by Research Services Ltd in 1950 and the latter carried out by the same firm in 1968. The earlier report arrives at the following conclusions as to the average weekly amounts staked (the figures in brackets represent the equivalent current value of stakes in terms of 1968 patterns of expenditure).

Average weekly stake per bettor on football pools
men 19p (51½p), women 10p (26½p)
upper-middle class: men 38p (£1.01), women 10½p (27½p),
   combined: 30p (72½p)
working class: men 18p (48p), women 10p (26½p),
   combined: 15½p (41p)
all bettors: 16p (42½p) per week

The 1968 report—not, in this instance, stratified by either sex or social class—reveals the following data in respect of average football pool expenditure:
20 per cent of bettors stake 12½p per week or less,
the largest single group of 45 per cent of bettors stake between 12½p and 25p per week,
25 per cent of bettors stake between 25p and 50p per week

and no more than 10 per cent of bettors stake 50p per week and above.

Twenty-five per cent of bettors stake exactly 25p per week and within none of the above outlay categories is there any other than the most minimal difference between the regular all-year and the regular winter-only bettor. According to the RS 1968 report the average stake per bettor is 21½p per week and this, in terms of current expenditure patterns, is no more than one-half the average individual outlay of 20 years previously.

As regards the betting on horseracing, plus the relatively subsidiary activity of betting on dogs, we can, once more, refer to two reports separated by the same length of time. The GSS, carried out in 1950, asserted that the average on-course attender staked £2.50 per meeting and that the average off-course bettor would place three weekly bets of 28½p each bet, constituting a total weekly stake of 84½p. In terms of current expenditure patterns these correspond to an outlay of £6.50 per meeting for on-course attenders and an average outlay per bettor of £2.25 per week off-course.

The 1968 RS survey supplies us with comparative data for the present day. Turning, firstly, to those who attend at race courses, we are given the following information:
25 per cent of attenders stake less than 30p per race,
a further 30 per cent of attenders stake between 30p and 50p per race,
an insignificant proportion, 3 per cent of attenders stake between 50p and £1 per race.
the largest single group, 22 per cent of attenders stake precisely £1 per race,
a further 18 per cent of attenders stake between £2 and £5 per race
and a final 2 per cent of attenders stake £10 per race and more.

The proportions of those who stake below 50p per race and those who stake above 50p per race are virtually identical and the average bettor will wager around 62½p per race which, assuming that he will bet on 5 races out of the total of 6, suggests an average outlay per attendance of £3.25. Reference has been made earlier to the small and dwindling number of attenders (5 per cent of all adults—7 per cent in 1950—of whom no more than 25 per cent attend more than 10 race meetings per year) and above figures strongly suggest, comparing 1950 with 1968, that fewer attenders stake almost exactly one-half their individual 1950 stake in terms of current values per head of the racetrack attendance.

As regards the more widespread and significant activity of betting off-course, the following data on stakes are for 1968: 45 per cent of off-course bettors stake less than 30p per race, a further 30 per cent of off-course bettors stake between 30p and 50p per race,

only 5 per cent of off-course bettors stake between 50p and £1, the largest single group, 13 per cent of off-course bettors stake precisely £1 per race,

a further 6 per cent of off-course bettors stake between £2 and £5 per race

and a final 1 per cent of off-course bettors stake £10 per race and more.

Seventy-five per cent of all off-course bettors (of whom 95 per cent will place their stakes in betting shops), compared to only 50 per cent of on-course attenders, stake less than 50p per race and only 7 per cent compared to on-course 20 per cent, bet £2 per race and above. The average bettor will stake approximately 27½p per race which, assuming an average total number of 8 bets per week—3 betting days with 2–3 bets per day—will imply a total weekly outlay of £2.20, almost exactly corresponding to the £2.25 (in current expenditure terms) of the average bettor 20 years ago.

Having, in the course of participant observation in several betting shops, noted the wide disparity between actuality and virtually instantaneous recall in respect of stakes, as well as winnings and losses not merely towards the outsider, but also towards the closest associates and even oneself, the questions concerning amounts staked were deliberately omitted from the Household sample. Such tendencies as did emerge suggest that women, within the social group concerned, generally tending towards ingrained self-denigration and inclined to look upon their activity as a form of self-indulgence, recall their stakes and net expenditure with a reasonable degree of faithfulness, while men display a strong tendency towards inflation of stakes and minimization of losses in recall.

Major Divergencies between:

(*a*) Men and women;
(*b*) Members of different social classes;
(*c*) Members of different age groups and different marital status;
(*d*) Bettors as compared to non-bettors and occasional bettors;
(*e*) Habitual bettors as compared to regular, non-habitual bettors.

The data contained in this section are derived and combined from the various surveys described at the beginning of the chapter and wherever one or another of the various surveys conflict with the main data presented, such differences will be indicated where-ever appropriate. A number of differentials, with regard to the above categories *a*, *b* and *c*—some of which have already been briefly referred to earlier in the text—are summarized in Table XI.

(*a*) *Men and Women*

Women are considerably less likely than men ever to gamble at all, are far less likely to bet on dogracing and relatively more inclined to bet on horseracing, on football pools or to visit casinos. However, they are over three times as likely as men to take part in bingo games. Their stakes are much more limited than those of their male counterparts, there are far fewer heavy female gamblers and they are also much less likely than men to gamble habitually. Single women are relatively much less inclined to gamble than married women in the comparable age groups—for each 10 single female bettors there will be 15 married female bettors—but other than that, there is no appreciable difference between different age groups, social classes or the various geographic regions. There is evidence of only the slightest, if any, change in relative gambling patterns between the sexes in the years since 1950 and there exists altogether a remarkable degree of coincidence between the different surveys related to gambling conducted over a number of years.

The findings of the HHS survey, exclusively concerned with lower-grade manual wage earners, suggest a wider sex differential in respect of horseracing (Men 17:Women 10), football pools

(22 : 10) and gaming clubs (18 : 10), but a lower sex differential for betting on dogs (26 : 10) than appears in Table XI.

(b) Social Classes

The 1950 Social Survey declared gambling to have been more popular among the mass of wage-earners and to have been highest in the income group of £5–£10 per week, equivalent to roughly £15–£20 in the present day. This statement has substantially been confirmed by the various surveys carried out since that date. Whilst there is no more than the most minimal difference in gambling patterns between the middle class and the lower-middle class and further, only very slight difference between, on the one hand, these classes combined and, on the other hand, the upper and upper-middle class, the manual wage-earners as a whole, and in particular their subsection consisting of semi- and unskilled workers, stand out. With the single exception of casino gaming, a higher proportion of this group gamble on each of the various gambling activities. They are likely to gamble more often, more regularly and despite their lower income and their more meagre financial resources they will, even in absolute terms, spend more money than the other social groups on the various gambling activities, particularly on the major gambling activity—the gambling on horses and on dogs in betting shops. It can be stated with confidence that gambling is predominantly a proletarian predilection.

(c) Age Groups

With the single exception of casino gaming, in which unmarried men predominate relative to their married contemporaries, married men are more likely to gamble than single men of the same age. While, for instance, 30 per cent of married men aged 18–34 years bet on horses, no more than 20 per cent of single men in the same age group do so. The marital-status discrepancy is even more pronounced in respect of women. No more than 14 per cent of unmarried women aged 18–34 bet on horses, while as many as 34 per cent (ratio 1 : 2.43) of married women—a percentage higher even than for same-age men—admit to betting on horses.

Whereas, irrespective of marital status, betting on horses and on dogs possesses an almost identical appeal to all age groups, betting on football pools and playing of bingo are forms of betting which are markedly more attractive to the older as against the younger men. While as many as 57 per cent of men aged 34 and above bet on football pools, and as many as 13 per cent play bingo, the percentages of men aged 18–34 who take part in these activities is no more than 43 per cent and 5 per cent respectively (ratios 1.33:1 and 2.14:1). In respect of casino gaming, however, the tendency is reversed. Fourteen per cent of men aged 18–34 as against no more than 5 per cent of men aged 35 and above (ratio 1.8:1) admit to gaming in casinos or gaming clubs.

The HHS sample contained two unmarried men and no single women at all and consequently it would be unacceptable to draw any inferences from their divergencies, if any, from the main group. There did, however, appear a manifest difference between the gambling pattern of a clearly distinguishable group of young married men below the age of 25 and the rest of the sample, a difference affirmed and underlined when, in addition to the Household sample, account is taken of observation, conversation and self-reporting extending over a far wider group within the same social setting. Suffice it to state in the present context that a firm and resolute rejection of gambling, based neither on conscientious nor on moral grounds but founded entirely on their emphasis on the wastefulness of the vicious circle of irrational hopes and inevitable despair, was found to be present within a significant proportion of young married men. Closer attention to this phenomenon will be given in a later section.

(d) Bettors as compared to non-bettors and occasional bettors

In respect of gambling, the adult population of Great Britain is divisible into three near-equal parts. One third do not place any bets at all on any gambling activity, a further one third—indulging in either one single form of gambling only with some regularity, or more frequently being in the habit of placing moderate stakes, from time to time, on one or another gambling activity—can best be termed as occasional gamblers, while a final one third allow themselves to be classified as regular gamblers—those to whom gambling constitutes a distinctive feature of their way of life. The available evidence powerfully suggests that the dividing line between the regulars and the occasionals runs almost entirely along the axis separating those who bet on horses from those who do not do so. Regular bettors can, as Table XII illustrates, with confidence be defined as participants in gambling on horses.

People who bet on horses—women as well as men—are much more likely than others, the occasionals, to indulge in other forms of betting. They are overwhelmingly more likely to visit gaming clubs and to bet on greyhound racing, and are considerably more likely to take part in all the other various gambling activities, to gamble more frequently and to place higher stakes when they do so.

Among women, no betting activity is as popular as any of the four other activities asked about—playing or watching sport, going to the cinema, a public house or a dance. Among men, however, a larger proportion do the football pools than go to dances or to the cinema. Women who bet on horses are more likely to take part in all four other activities than non-bettors— particularly the playing or watching of sport and visiting public houses. Men horse-bettors are more likely than other men to go to a public house and to play or watch sport, but are less likely to dance or to go to a cinema.

None of the surveys forming the basis of the present chapter attempt to specify any of the characteristics of the betting abstainer. Within the HHS, as well as the much larger range of additional contacts made in the identical social environment, an attempt was made to distinguish some of the major personality differentiations between the regular gambler, on the one hand, and the non-gambler on the other hand, and such material as was assembled will be discussed in a subsequent section.

(e) Habitual bettors as compared to regular, non-habitual bettors

The basis of distinction between the above two categories will be the data acquired on those 219 subjects who were, in the course of the survey conducted by Research Services Ltd in 1968, interviewed as on-course bettors at racecourses, together with the 206 off-course bettors interviewed outside selected betting offices, on the one hand, and on the other hand, those other subjects who neither attended racecourses nor were found to frequent betting shops at the time of the interview, but who admitted to betting on horses. The former two groups can be considered to form the hard-core of habitual gamblers, while the latter groups, though regulars, are devoted to participation in gambling activities to a lesser extent in terms of frequency, stakes and, in all probability, emotional and psychic involvement.

The habitual gambler is considerably more likely than the regular to expand his range of bets, such as betting on Fixed Odds as well as Four Aways—Pools which call for greater selectivity and are likely to be the outcome of greater familiarity with the activity itself—in addition to the Treble Chance, the coupon made use of by 94 per cent of all football pools investors. The Treble Chance, though offering from time to time prizes running well into six figures but at the same time involving near-certainty of total loss of stake, requires no more than the most minimal knowledge and skill.

Equally, the habitual gambler is, in the approximate ratio of 2:1, more likely to avail himself of the facilities of the Tote as well as the bookmaker in off-course betting, and more likely to base his choice of one or the other on the differential scale of advantages offered in terms of odds in the particular event; he will also scan the race card more systematically for the races or runners which he considers to be the most favourable. He will be more aware of the organizational and managerial arrangements of the activity in question—such as possessing superior knowledge of special horserace pools such as the Jackpot*—as well as of the identity of the promoters of the Tote. As is implied by the term by which he is defined, he will gamble more frequently and will consequently, on the whole, stake higher sums of money, but will, by virtue of his superior skill, expertise and critical judgment, be unlikely to suffer absolute losses higher than those of the regular bettor whose losses, proportionate to stake, are almost certain to be greater.

Apart from these distinguishing features, the habitual and the regular bettor display several interesting common characteristics, such as their shared desire for the introduction of more horserace

---

* The Jackpot is a horserace pool in which the successful bettor is required to forecast correctly the winners of six nominated races out of six. A consolation prize is given for five winners.

betting on longer odds,* as well as their moral approval of the bookmaker with whom they transact and who is, after all, the beneficiary of their almost inevitable long-term losses. Twenty per cent of bettors consider the bookmaker to be preferable to other alternative facilities, being generally more personal; an equal proportion consider that bookmakers offer better odds and almost unanimously they express the view that bookmakers are no less trustworthy than the Tote.

Public Attitudes

Gambling as an interest or pastime, even if not as an addiction, carries the moral approval of the bulk of the British population. Seventy-seven per cent of subjects—a percentage higher than those who take part in commercial gambling—answered the question 'Do you think gambling is wrong in principle?', put to them by National Opinion Polls in 1963, in the negative, revealing only the very slightest divergence between the sexes, social classes and age groups (men: 81 per cent, women: 74 per cent; upper and middle class: 80 per cent, working class: 76 per cent; under 45 years: 83 per cent, 45 and over: 72 per cent negative answers).

At the same time, a large majority take the view that promoters, benefiting from commercial gambling, ought to be required to contribute a share of their profits to the National Exchequer and that the country, as a whole, should benefit from the prosperity of the gambling profession. Furthermore, a majority advocate that the State ought actively to enter the gambling arena and, either as monopolist or as competitor, ought to act as promoter of gambling activities. A large and increasing proportion of the population approves of the imposition of taxes on gambling (from 51 per cent in 1963 to 84 per cent in 1968) and 66 per cent in February 1966 were in favour of an increase in the rate of taxation upon betting and gambling activities. While, incidentally, 51 per cent of the entire NOP 1963 sample were favourably disposed towards the introduction of gambling taxes prior to their imposition, the

---

* Three quarters of all bettors are in favour of a larger number of Jackpot races, involving a much reduced probability of winning and the near-certain loss of their entire stake in return for the prospect of a large-scale win.

proportion differed only slightly between two of the categories—men: 48 per cent, women: 54 per cent; under 45 years: 49 per cent, over 45 years: 54 per cent—but diverged significantly in respect of the third category, social classes. While as many as 63 per cent of members of the upper and middle class expressed themselves in favour of imposition of tax on gambling, no more than 39 per cent of members of the working class did so (ratio 1.6:1).

Seventy-five per cent of the popultaion polled in February 1968 declared themselves in favour of a State Lottery—a mere 23 per cent approved of the House of Commons rejection of the proposal in July 1968—and almost one-half were in favour of Government-run football pools (47 per cent), Government-run betting shops (42 per cent) as well as casinos run by Local Authorities (41 per cent). The tendency towards Government promotional participation appears to have increased considerably in the course of the twelve months preceding the survey. No more than 61 per cent of the subjects expressed approval of Government organized State Lotteries in March 1967. Whilst favouring State participation, three quarters of the population approve of stricter Government control over gambling activities. Seventy-seven per cent of those polled in May 1966 wanted stricter control of gaming clubs and 72 per cent were in favour of similar action towards betting shops. Yet only a minority of the population, as shown in Table XIII, consider gambling to be a serious social problem in present-day Britain.

The following conclusions may be drawn from Table XIII.

(1) The data provide powerful evidence of a growing public preoccupation with social problems in the period from March 1965 to December 1968. While, in respect of the 11 items polled in the earlier period a total of 498 mentions are recorded, the total recording for the same 11 items had risen to 537 by May 1967 and to 595 by December 1968, a total rise of 20 per cent within the two and three quarter years under review. With the single exception of prostitution, 10 items out of 11 displayed growth of concern, at varying rates, over the period.

(2) Together with the general tendency of positive mention of all items to rise, there is, at the same time, a noticeable trend towards relative stability of rank order of the various items. The

rank order for gambling has remained virtually stationary in the course of this period and has, throughout the period, featured within the lower half of subjects considered to be of major public concern, ranking 7th out of 11 at the time of the first survey and 8th out of 13 on the occasion of the third survey.

All items ranked initially as the 5 major subjects of public concern were still within that sector in 1968 and the same is true of the items at the lower end of the scale. Drug taking had, as a subject of public concern, climbed from 4th to 1st place in the period from March 1965–May 1967 (growth rate: 52 per cent) and prostitution had declined from 8th to final place between the 1st and 3rd survey.

(3) The range of growth of public concern between the first and the final survey was highest for the subject central to our discussion, namely gambling, which rose from 31 per cent to 47 per cent, a growth rate of 51 per cent; a rate approximated only by drug-taking as an item of major public concern within the period. It seems likely that a spectacular change in the magnitude of public concern is strongly related to publicity given to a particular subject in the various mass media at any given time. The prevalence and evil effects apparently associated with drug-taking featured strongly as an item of public debate around the time of the second survey, and the infiltration of gangster elements into gambling, as well as the diverse ramifications of link-up between casinos and the underworld, were widely discussed within the public media in the months preceding the submission of the new Gaming Act, 1968. The rate of increase of public concern with gambling, which had been only 16 per cent between March 1965 and May 1967, rose a further 31 per cent (from 36 to 47 per cent) between May 1967 and December 1968. Equally, prostitution which in recent years, with the widespread toleration of a more permissive sexual morality, had faded as an item of public debate, declined in absolute as well as in relative terms.

(4) Despite the spectacular rate of growth of public concern with gambling in the period under discussion, it will be noted that the percentage of mentions given to it as a major social problem does not widely differ between Great Britain and France. In the latter country, all casino gambling having traditionally come

under skilful and expert government control is widely and authoritatively held to be entirely free of infiltration by gangsters and racketeers and, furthermore, the rate of outlay and involvement relative to total population is considered to be on a very much narrower scale than it is in Britain. It may not be fanciful to suggest that within all highly-industrialized nations, gambling is an activity in which a majority of the population participate, but of which a sizeable, and proportionately similar, minority strongly disapprove.

The December 1968 survey provides a number of additional data in respect of all items. As regards gambling, which 47 per cent of the entire sample considered to constitute a serious social problem, there appeared a total absence of social class differentiation (Class AB: 47, C1: 48, C2: 46, DE: 47 per cent); the differences between the sexes was only slight (women: 50, men: 44 per cent; ratio 1.13:1) and while there was virtually a total absence of differentiation between the 3 major regions of England and Wales (South: 46, Midlands & Wales: 47, North: 42 per cent; combined: 45 per cent), there emerged a clear difference between the three combined regions of England and Wales, on the one hand, and Scotland, where 60 per cent of all subjects polled named gambling as a major social problem (ratio England & Wales: Scotland 1:1.33). Equally, there existed a sharp divergence between the different age groups within which the following percentages nominated gambling as a major social problem: 16–24 years: 37 per cent; 25–34 years: 41 per cent; 35–44 years: 37 per cent; 45–64 years: 53 per cent, and 65 years and above: 61 per cent. Therefore, for each 10 persons aged 16–24 years who responded positively to the question put to them concerning gambling, 17 persons in the age group 65-and-above did so, a degree of age differentiation surpassing that for any of the other items. For the majority of all the items, there appeared a general slight tendency for women, older age groups and inhabitants of Scotland to give a higher rate of positive nominations.

Finally, those who consider gambling as a major social problem are 50 per cent more likely than others also to consider— in rank order of preponderance—heavy smoking, drunkenness, prostitution, homosexuality and rape to fall within the same definition, while, equally, those who perceive heavy smoking, prostitution and drunkness as social problems are also inclined to regard gambling in a similar manner. Those who declare gambling to be a serious social problem are relatively most lenient towards immigrants, bad housing and crimes of violence.

The following conclusions may now be postulated:

(1) In respect of gambling, the adult population of Britain* can be split into three near-equal sections. One third of the population do not gamble at all, a further third may be classified as casual gamblers—those who will, in all probability, for most weeks of the season stake money on football pools and who will, for the most part, bet on the major classic events in the horserace calendar, predominantly with stakes only moderate relative to income—and finally an equal section of regular bettors, almost entirely composed of those who will bet at least once a week on horses or, possibly, on dogs.

The final category of regulars may be subdivided into two further sections. Sixty-six per cent of this group—approximately 20 per cent of the adult population (8 million people)—will bet no less often than once or twice per week as a matter of routine, and the other 33 per cent of the group, approximately 10 per cent of adults (3 million people), can be described as the hard core of habitual bettors to whom gambling is an integral part of their way of life. The habitual bettor will not only bet more often and more heavily, but, furthermore, gambling is almost certain to represent for him an important—if not *the*— central component of his existence. He will regularly and intensively peruse the racing news, he will eagerly and frequently enter into conversations devoted to discussion of racing and gambling matters with his friends and associates, considering himself possessed of expert knowledge and critical judgment in this area and, in all likelihood, he will congregate with his associates in the betting shop—the principal arena of his gambling activity. Of the 4 million people of both sexes belonging to this category, no fewer than 2.5 million (approximately 60 per cent of the total) are likely to be male members of the medium, lower and unskilled manual working class.

* Adult in this context is taken to be the age of legal betting consent, namely 18 years and above, and is estimated to embrace approximately 40 million people in Britain in 1967/8.

One is, on the basis of available material, unable to guess, let alone state, whether the quarter of the population (10 million people) who morally disapprove of gambling is largely, or entirely, made up of those who do not gamble, or how many of those who gamble do at the same time consider gambling to constitute one of the major contemporary social problems. Nevertheless, it is safe to assert that, among those condemning gambling, there will be a disproportionate element of middle-aged or elderly females.

(2) From a combination of the statistical data of Chapters II and III, we are able to summarize the rate of participation, as well as the average *per capita* outlay and expenditure, per member of the adult British population on the various gambling activities in the following manner:

(a) 5 per cent (2 million) adults stake a total amount of £234 million* per year on dogracing, of which £34 million represents net expenditure. Average outlay per bettor on dogracing on and off the course is therefore £117 per year (£2.22½ per week) and the average net cost per bettor is consequently £17 per year, or 32½p per week.

(b) An equal percentage attend and bet on horses directly on the course, laying out a total of £86 million per year, of which £13 million is net expenditure. Average annual stakes per horse-race attender are therefore £43 (82½p per week) and net individual costs are £7 (13p per week).

(c) 25 per cent of the adult population (10 million people) can be considered as reasonably regular bettors on horseracing off the course. The turnover in this activity is £790 million per year and net outlay totals £115 million. Average annual outlay per off-course bettor will be £79 (£1.56 per week) and net individual cost therefore amounts to £12.50 (24p per week). Of these totals, together with roughly one half of the total sum attributable to dogracing, more than 90 per cent will be staked in betting shops.

(d) The largest single numerical group—40 per cent of the population (16 million people)—consists of bettors on football pools, together with the very minor subsidiary activity of fixed odds, whose total outlay is £135 million per year, representing a

* For the sake of conciseness all figures in the present subsection have, wherever appropriate, been rounded-off.

total net loss of £61 million. Average individual outlay is £7.50 per year (14½p per week) of which £3.80 (7½p per week) represents loss to bettors as a whole.

(e) Bingo is supported by 6.5 million people (16 per cent of the population) whose annual outlay of £65 million and net cost of £7 million suggests reasonably infrequent and moderate *per capita* participation, as total personal net outlay is no more than £10 per year (19p per week), of which no more than £1 (2p per week) is total individual net expenditure.

(f) The outlay, however, of the much smaller sector of those who take part in casino games—2.5 million people (6.5 per cent of the adult population) is at £57 million as great as the turnover on bingo, while the total net expenditure at £13 million is considerably greater. In consequence, average personal outlay will be £23 per year (44p per week) and average individual cost will amount to £5.20 (19p per week) per bettor.

In each of these activities, with the single exception of the minority activity of bingo, men will outnumber women both in extent of participation as well as *per capita* outlay in a ratio ranging from 5:1 in dogracing to no more than 1.5:1 in betting on horses off the course, while, at the same time, members of the lower and unskilled ranges of manual working class will, with the single exception of casino gaming, predominate over members of the non-manual classes in both respects—volume of participation as well as level of individual outlay—in the approximate ratio of 2:1.

(3) As is confirmed in Table XII, betting on horses is, other than for the numerically very insignificant minority of casino-gaming-only addicts, the criterion of distinction between regular and non-regular bettors. While, for instance, twice as many men as gamble on horses will gamble on football pools, those who gamble on horses are, at the same time, much more likely than any other group to gamble on dogs, bingo, casinos, and even on football pools. In addition, horseracing is far and away, in terms of outlay, the major gambling activity. In 1967, 58.7 per cent of all money staked, a total of £876 million, was laid out on betting on horses.

(4) There exists every likelihood that members of the manual working class, in addition to being beset by a supposedly less

effective level of conceptualization,[8] will be predisposed to interpret questions such as 'Do you gamble?' differently from members of the middle class. Whereas the latter will almost uniformly perceive the question as being designed to elicit a negative answer only from those who do not gamble at all, the former are much more likely to answer positively only when indulging in gambling as a regular and recurrent habit. Members of the working class are not unlikely to redefine infrequent participation and modest outlay, or possibly even regular indulgence at moderate stakes, as not being gambling at all. Subject to a restraint in financial as well as psychic investment, participation in activities such as football pools or bingo may be sub-culturally classified as constituting 'non-gambling'. This assumption, apart from being reasonable and well-founded on the basis of material already discussed, is further borne out in the light of the data assembled from the annual Family Expenditure Survey,[9] which suggests a considerably higher measure of positive falsification and minimization in recall among members of the lower-income manual wage groups.[10]

(5) Young married women belonging to the manual wage-earning class have in the course of the past twenty years displayed a noticeable tendency towards relative, as well as absolute, expansion in gambling participation. As traditionally the majority of these women have been in full-time gainful employment as a matter of necessity rather than choice, this tendency is unlikely to indicate a change in female working-class consumption patterns consequent upon the attainment of independent income and resources. It does, however, suggest a convergence between the sexes in patterns of consumption and in leisure pursuits, a phenomenon hitherto considered to be peculiar to the middle classes alone in respect of other patterns of outlay, activity, and interest.[11]

There has, at the same time, been a withdrawal of a small, but nevertheless significant, section of married men in the same age and social group from gambling as a result of their deliberate refusal to become enmeshed in the traditional working-class style of life, involving, in their view, a hand-to-mouth pattern of existence which they firmly reject and feel confident of being able to transcend.[12]

(6) Although numerically the proportion of members of the middle class indulging in all forms of gambling is not significantly lower than the corresponding proportion of the working class, their frequency of participation and volume of outlay, both per single act as well as over a given period, is certain to be lower not merely in terms relative to their income, but also in absolute pound for pound terms. For example, the level of attendance and outlay in betting shops, which accounts for an annual outlay of almost £850 million—57 per cent of the entire gambling outlay —and which amounts, in terms of placement of bets, to 95 per cent of all off-course betting, will be proportionately six times as high for the member of the lower and unskilled manual working class as it is likely to be for the average member of the upper and upper-middle class.

Notes

1. See Kemsley, W. F. F. and Ginsberg, D., Government Social Survey M.S. 710/4 (London 1950); in consultation with the Royal Commission on Betting, Lotteries and Gaming, 1945–51.
2. See Rowntree, B. S. and Lavers, R. S. (1951).
3. National Opinion Polls Ltd, London.
4. The Gallup Poll, London.
5. Research Services Ltd, London. It is necessary to point out that all the commercially operated opinion polls whose findings are made reference to in the present Chapter—the National Opinion Poll, The Gallup Poll and Research Services—in common with other large-scale national and international market and opinion polls, employ the method known as 'quota sampling'.

   In quota sampling, once the general breakdown of the sample has taken place by means of standard sampling procedure—e.g. stratification by sex, marital status, age groups, social classes—the interviewers, having been allocated a certain number of interview schedules, are then free to choose their own subjects fitting into the relevant categories. Thus, the chances of unequal selection—such as fortuitous absence or presence at a certain place at a certain time, appearance, availability—which do not exist in a fully randomized sampling procedure, are one of the features of quota sampling.

   For this reason it has often been alleged that the method of quota sampling, subject to error and personal bias, is of lesser reliability and validity than random sampling. Account must, however, be taken of the fact that the major national opinion polls, now well-established and

98 PATTERNS OF GAMBLING

highly experienced, employ the most refined methods of safeguards and controls in order to obviate error or bias. The considerable degree of correspondence of findings between the various market and opinion polls and above all their very considerable degree of success in prediction over a wide field of political, economic and social activity have largely stilled the objections raised against their methods, subject to sampling on a sufficiently large scale.

6. London Borough of Tower Hamlets; Parliamentary Constituency: Poplar; Ward: Bow South; Postal District: London E.3.

7. The Gallup Poll: Social Surveys (Gallup Poll) Ltd, March 1965, May 1967 and December 1968.

8. See Hyman, H. H. (1955) pp. 138–70, and Goode, W. J. and Hatt, P. K. (1952) pp. 186 et seq.

9. Department of Employment and Productivity (previously: Ministry of Labour), Family Expenditure Survey, H.M.S.O. (London 1960–8).

10. According to the five most recent annual reports of the Family Expenditure Survey, members of the lower-income groups spend a much lower percentage of their income on gambling than the higher-income groups (from 0.6 per cent for the lowest to 1.3 per cent to the highest of total income in 1968). However, compared with other items of expenditure, such a relationship appears to be suspect. According to the findings of the Family Expenditure Survey, gambling accounts for no more than 0.7 per cent of the total consumer expenditure, whilst, according to Table XI, it accounts for 1.1 per cent. It must be assumed that the lower-income groups—i.e. largely the lower- and unskilled manual wage-earners—systematically understate the amount of money spent by them on gambling.

This view is shared by the compilers of the Family Expenditure Survey who consider that subjects tend to understate expenditure on items which they assume public morality would consider as wasteful and even as 'sinful'. An identical level of understatement, once again applicable in particular to the lowest income groups, arises regularly also in respect of declaration of expenditure outlay on alcoholic drinks. See particularly Family Expenditure Survey, Ministry of Labour (London 1965).

11. See Gans, H. L. (1967) *The Levittowners*, London: Allen Lane.

12. See Lockwood, D., (1960) 'The "new working class"', *European Journal of Sociology*, vol. 1, 2.

CHAPTER IV

Distribution of Betting Shops

So far we have established in Chapters II and III that betting shops are by far the principal arenas of gambling activity in contemporary Britain. Close on £850 million are staked in Britain in betting shops each year; this represents more than one half of all the money staked on gambling. As many as 95 per cent of all wagers and as much as 90 per cent of all the money staked on horse- or dogracing—overwhelmingly the largest gambling activities—is placed in one or the other betting shops set up in Britain since the passing of the 1960 Betting and Gaming Act.

The data included there, support the view that gambling is an activity involving the lower grades of manual wage-earners to a disproportionately significant extent and it may be claimed that the presence and participation of this group is particularly prevalent in betting shops. It ought to follow therefore that betting shops, rather than being randomly distributed throughout a given area, should be found to be concentrated at a relatively greater density in districts inhabited mostly by people belonging to the lower-grade manual classes

In this chapter, cognizant of the fact that the empirical study of the modes of transaction within betting shops suggests itself as a subject for a study of primary importance, we seek to determine how betting shops are dispersed throughout a given area of settlement, and if there is correlation between their degree of concentration and the characteristics indicative of the socio-economic status of the area in question. In other words, to what extent is the degree of density of betting shops within a given area itself a yardstick of socio-economic status, and to what extent does this allow observations, peculiar to one particular set of betting shops within an area, to be generalized in respect of other betting shops in areas found to be closely similar as regards a number of representative socio-economic characteristics?

As the only set of officially published data relating to location of betting shops[1] does not provide any breakdown beyond the limits of Counties and County Boroughs, and in view of the fact that resources limited examination to one single representative unit, it was decided to subject the area of Greater London to critical discussion, in order to establish the degree of association between a given set of socio-economic variables on the one hand, and the density of betting shops on the other. For this purpose, information relating to the number of betting shops registered and licensed within each of the thirty-three boroughs comprising the total urban area of Greater London in 1966 was obtained and the density of betting shops per 10,000 members of population was computed.[2] These particulars were then enumerated and matched in Tables XIV and XV against a number of representative categories indicative of socio-economic status, as derived and compiled from data contained in the 1966 Sample Census tables.

However, before turning to these tables, it must be stated that, although, in addition to the data pertaining to Greater London as a whole, full data for each of the 33 London boroughs are provided in both Tables, we shall confine the discussion to only 31 of the 33 boroughs, excluding, for these purposes, the Cities of London and Westminster since both are unrepresentative. These boroughs constitute London's principal commercial, financial, business and amusement centre, have a small permanent population and are subject to a daily inflow of more than one million workers of all grades during the working day.

In the case of the City of London the minimal registered population amounts to no more than 4,850 people* (7.2 persons per acre) but, as a result of the daily 'working-day' flow, this becomes inflated by 7,450 per cent to 361,040 people, a daytime density of 531.8 persons per acre, more than six times a high as

---

* All figures quoted henceforth in the present chapter relate, unless otherwise stated, to the year 1966.

any of the other London boroughs.[3] The 40 registered betting shops represent a density as high as 8.26 per 10,000 members of the registered population,* but this density is reduced to only 0.11 when related to the total number of people present in the borough in the course of the working day.

The City of Westminster does not experience such a wide daily fluctuation of population since it houses a registered population of 254,210 persons (47.7 per acre) in an area extending over 5,333 acres (compared to the City of London's 677 acres). Therefore its divergence between daytime and night-time population, between weekday and weekend occupation, and between density of betting shops, is less extreme relative to the permanent population on the one hand, and the working-day population on the other. Nevertheless, it does experience a daily increase of 610,620 people—much larger than that of the City of London—at a day-time density of 162.1 persons per acre. The 150 registered betting shops providing a density of 5.91 in respect of the registered population, have to cater in the daytime for a population inflated by 240.2 per cent, at a betting shop density of no more than 1.73.

All other London boroughs suffer a daytime working day net population loss, ranging from only 16.5 per cent in the case of Camden to 72 per cent for Lewisham. While generally the outer dormitory boroughs—which also are uniformly those belonging to the upper social class ranges[4]—decant proportionately the largest quantity of their registered population towards the centre while, at the same time, the inner boroughs—which also tend to be those falling within the lower social class ranges—are, apart from the City of London and the City of Westminster, the main recipients of the daily working-day influx, no firm or even significant relationship between socio-economic status of a borough and degree of daily inflow was found to exist. Five of the 10 boroughs in which the number of people who are employed in the area exceeds those resident in the area by 50 per cent (Barking, Ealing, Hounslow, Hillingdon and Kensington and Chelsea), display a relatively low density of betting shops for registered population, indicating that there is only a very slight

* Density of betting shops is henceforth taken to indicate the number of betting shops per 10,000 members of population.

degree of association between daytime employment in the area and density of betting shops. This would imply that:

(a) people are likely to bet where they live rather than where they work, and

(b) those who travel to work from the outer boroughs towards the central boroughs are, as members of the non-manual middle and upper classes, less likely to bet in betting shops than those who, belonging to the manual wage-earning classes, earn their living inside their boroughs of residence.

With this in mind, we will next turn to the data assembled in Tables XIV and XV listing the number and density of betting shops for the various Greater London boroughs in conjunction with a number of demographic and socio-economic characteristics for the same areas, and concern ourselves in the first place with the number of betting shops within the various boroughs of Greater London and the density of betting shops per 10,000 members of population. In 1966 there was a total of 2,249 betting shops in operation within the urban area designated as Greater London, at a density of 2.83 per 10,000 members of population. This rating was lower than that ruling for the United Kingdom as a whole (amounting to 2.97) and very slightly below that for England only (2.84). Although, in view of the changes in the boundaries of the Greater London area enacted in 1965, comparative figures for preceding years do not exist, there is, on the basis of such data as are available, every reason to assume that the ratio for the area now defined as Greater London varied only slightly in the course of the years following the establishment of betting shops. Between the years 1966 and 1968 for Greater London it rose very slightly from 2.83 to 2.89 while, at the same time the national ratio declined slightly to 2.94.[5] The overall stability of density however gives no clue as to any internal changes which might have occurred meanwhile. Local Licensing Authorities tend to diverge in their policy toward the granting of licences for new and additional betting shops, but in observance of the guidelines provided for them by the Home Office, they tend to restrict the grant of such permits only to cases where, by virtue of population growth and significant, attested change in demand or the demise of previous operators, good grounds for such action can be shown to prevail.[6] It is therefore safe to assume that the expansion of the numbers of betting shops will have been accompanied by regional expansion of population, or that it will have been limited to those areas where existing supply could be shown to be inadequate to meet existing demand.

In 1966 the highest number of betting shops in one borough stood at 138 for the Borough of Islington, while the Borough of Kingston-upon-Thames possessed no more than 11 betting shops (see Table XIV, col. 1). As, however, Islington contained a total of 235,340 people while Kingston-upon-Thames, being numerically the smallest borough, consisted of 142,010 people, these figures by themselves, fail to reflect the existing situation realistically. Density of betting shops—the ratio of betting shops per 10,000 members of the population—does, while removing the factor of inequality of size and volume, still exhibit a considerable, degree of disparity between the different boroughs in Greater London.

Nineteen out of the thirty-one boroughs under consideration fell below the municipal average of 2.83, while only twelve exceeded the average (Table XIV, col. 1 and Table XV, col. 2). Density ranged from 0.77 for Kingston-upon-Thames at the lowest end of the scale (28 per cent of the average for Greater London) to 6.17 for Tower Hamlets at the highest end of the scale (218.3 per cent of the average). The six lowest-density boroughs all had densities of 1.75 or below, while the six highest had densities of 4.16 and above. The lower-density quartile (the boroughs listed under numbers 1–8 in Tables XIV and XV and hereafter referred to as 'Upper Quartile') are all situated at the periphery of Greater London, while the upper-density quartile (the eight boroughs listed as 24–31 and hereafter referred to as 'Bottom Quartile') do, with the single exception of Newham, all lie within the confines of the boundary line designated as Inner London.

Boroughs of superior social standing would be those exhibiting a sparse population density, with only few households suffering occupation in excess of one person per room, few lacking the provision of an internal hot water tap and the large majority possessing the domestic amenities of hot water, bath, and inside w.c. A high proportion of owner-occupation of households as well as a high ratio of ownership of cars are further indices of upper- and middle-class communities. Modern up-to-date residences are universally provided with internal garages and the price of property and rentals in these areas would inhibit all but the most marginal immigrant infiltration. By the terms of its own definition, superior social class districts would be those in which a relatively high proportion of residents belong to the uppermost social classes and would contain only a meagre proportion of those who, by virtue of following semi- and unskilled occupations, would also, on financial as well as social grounds, be excluded from well-to-do, middle-class communities.* All these characteristics should be associated with a relatively low density of betting shops, while the reverse characteristics in each and all combined categories should, if our assumptions are justified, be related to a high density of betting shops in the area.

Neither of the two demographic categories provide discernible consistent patterns indicative of social grade, nor do they relate to a very significant degree with density of betting shops. Boroughs deviate from the mean population volume—amounting to approximately one-quarter million—to a considerable extent, varying from the least populated borough of Kingston-upon-Thames (population 142,100 persons) to the most populated borough of Croydon (population 322,570 persons). As however the boundary lines revised and redrawn in 1965 followed, wherever possible, the outlines of natural historical development and, as in course of the revision of boundary lines and nomenclature of the Greater London boroughs, the policy of retaining and amalgamating natural units was strictly adhered to, population size of a borough by itself is unrelated to social class characteristics and to density of betting shops. The least populated borough of Kingston-upon-Thames does also happen to be the one of lowest betting shop density. However, at the same time, the borough with the highest degree of betting shop density, Tower Hamlets, is the fifth lowest of all Greater London boroughs in respect of volume of population. Five out of the eight boroughs falling into the Upper Quartile, in respect of density of betting shops, and an identical proportion of those

* Members of social class I and II are professional workers, employers and managers, while those of social classes IV and V are service workers and semi-skilled and unskilled manual workers.

in the Bottom Quartile are below the Greater London median, in respect of population volume and the remaining three in each group are above. There is therefore no apparent association between volume of population and density of betting shops.

The degree of density of persons per acre does, in spite of deviating characteristics of certain areas, provide a much better measure of social class grade and betting shop density. Salubrious exclusive neighbourhoods are generally those containing a high proportion of detached houses standing in spacious grounds, while crowded terraced back-to-back housing and densely populated tenements have, throughout the period of industrialization, provided the habitat of the urban underprivileged and poor. However, a high density of persons per acre does, to an increasing degree, no longer inevitably denote low status and social deprivation; it may equally well indicate the socially mixed neighbourhoods of multiple occupation or a profusion of single unit flats and bedsitters, while low population-density areas may well derive their status by virtue of a mixture of high-density low-grade housing together with large tracts of occupation by industrial premises, warehouses or waterside docks. Within these reservations it is generally true to say that despite the fact that not all upper social class, low-density betting shop boroughs display a low density of persons per acre, there is a definite correlation between inferior social grade boroughs and a high degree of betting shop density on the one hand and population density on the other. Hackney, Islington and Tower Hamlets, shown to have easily the highest density of betting shops per 10,000 of the population, are also those which have—other than for the single exception of Kensington and Chelsea to which reference will be made at a later stage—the highest population density per acre.

As regards the quality of domestic facilities and arrangements, whereas once more the three boroughs with the highest density of betting shops per population—Hackney, Islington and Tower Hamlets—are those three which display the highest percentage of households with more than one person per room (12.9, 16.4 and 13.1 per cent respectively), as many as seven out of eight of the boroughs within the Upper Quartile have fewer than 4 per cent of their households with occupation exceeding one person per room. (Average for Greater London: 7.1 per cent.)

Out of the five boroughs in which still more than 33 per cent of households lack exclusive use of a hot water tap, four once more belong to the Lower Quartile (= highest betting shop density), while in all those with a lower density of betting shops less than 10 per cent of households lack this amenity. (Average for Greater London: 20.5 per cent.)

There are six Greater London boroughs, all falling within the category of high density of betting shops, in which fewer than 50 per cent of all households have access to the services of hot water, bath and internal w.c., whereas in the majority of the Upper Quartile boroughs more than 90 per cent of households possess the entire range of such amenities. (Average for Greater London: 65.6 per cent.)[7]

Property ownership, or absence of it, is the category exhibiting the most extreme degree of internal differentiation. It is further the criterion most closely associated with social class status and is also the one in which association between the social grade of the borough and betting shop density is the most apparent. The extent of owner occupation ranges from the low level of 3.7 per cent for the Tower Hamlets, the borough with the highest density of betting shops, to the highest level of 71.1 per cent for Harrow, a ratio amounting to a figure of one to nineteen. While in six out of the eight boroughs ranking within the Upper Quartile in respect of betting shops, more than 66 per cent of householders owned or were buying their own homes, fewer than 25 per cent of householders in seven out of the eight boroughs in the Bottom Quartile were buying or had bought their own home.[8] (Average for Greater London: 44.8 per cent).

While per hundred households in Bromley and Brent there existed ownership of seventy-one cars, no more than twenty-five cars per one hundred households were owned in the highest betting shop density borough of Tower Hamlets (twenty-six in Islington and twenty-eight in Hackney). While in seven out of eight boroughs in the Upper Quartile, more than 66 per cent of householders owned one or more cars, no more than 33 per cent throughout the boroughs in the Bottom Quartile did so. (Average for Greater London: 48 cars per 100 households).

In Bexley, 61.3 per cent of all cars, compared to no more than 7.1 per cent in Islington, were housed in an internal garage within their owners' dwelling curtilage. In all the eight boroughs within the Upper Quartile more than 50 per cent have internal garages, while in seven out of eight of the Bottom Quartile, fewer than 15 per cent of all cars are housed in internal garages. (Average for Greater London: 37.4 per cent).

The relationship between density of betting shops and immigrants stemming from the Commonwealth, Colonies and Protectorates is less direct and clear-cut. This category not only includes the majority of coloured low-status immigrants originating from the Caribbean, Africa, India and Pakistan, but also the minority of white immigrants coming from the Old Commonwealth, Australia and New Zealand in particular. Furthermore, some boroughs (of which Kensington and Chelsea is the prime example) which, by virtue of general criteria, belong to the upper-status boroughs, house both a relatively high proportion of white immigrants from the Old Commonwealth, as well as tight enclaves of disproportionately high coloured immigrant occupation;[9] while other boroughs, such as the Bottom Quartile borough of Newham, on other criteria ranking as low status communities, have by virtue of the absence of the provision of local employment requirements for other than a minority of coloured workers, a relatively low density of coloured immigrants among their residents. Thus Kensington and Chelsea has a proportion of Commonwealth immigrants amounting to 11.6 per cent, while in Newham no more than 4.3 per cent of the population are registered as having originated in the Commonwealth. Nevertheless, in seven out of the eight Upper Quartile betting shop density boroughs, the Commonwealth immigrant population was lower than 2.5 per cent, while in only one out of the eight Bottom Quartile boroughs—the exception is Newham—the proportion amounted to no less than 8.5 per cent. (Average for Greater London: 5.2 per cent).

The proportion of residents belonging to social classes I and II differed from 29.8 per cent for Kensington and Chelsea to 5.6 per cent in respect of the borough with the highest betting shop density of all, namely Tower Hamlets. In six out of the Upper Quartile boroughs over one quarter of the population ranked as members of social classes I and II, whereas in five out of eight of the Bottom Quartile boroughs, fewer than 10 per cent belonged to the upper social grades. (Average for Greater London: 17 per cent). Conversely, while only 13.9 per cent of residents in Harrow followed occupations classifying them as members of social classes IV and V, as many as 37.3 per cent of the population of Tower Hamlets belonged to these categories. In five out of eight of the Upper Quartile boroughs fewer than 15 per cent of residents were members of social classes IV and V, whereas in one-half of the Bottom Quartile boroughs, the proportion of those belonging to these social grades exceeded 30 per cent.[10] (Average for Greater London: 22.4 per cent).

While, as has been shown, the degree of inter-borough disparity varies between the different categories—from 1:1.8 in respect of the percentage of residents belonging to social classes I and II to a ratio of disparity of 1:19 concerning the proportion of owner occupation—we have, for each of the categories (in Tables XIV and XV), witnessed a considerable extent of differentiation between the highest and the lowest ranking groups of boroughs and have, at the same time, established a very significant degree of consistent association between the density of betting shops and a variety of other characteristics indicative of social class, rank and status. A low degree of betting shop density is overwhelmingly associated with upper- and middle-class socio-economic characteristics of a district, while a high degree of density of betting shops is almost invariably a hallmark of lower grade characteristics of an area.

It would seem, on the basis of this material, that not only are betting shops not randomly distributed throughout the various districts of Greater London, but that their degree of concentration strongly reflects social class divisions and follows very closely upon the outlines of social privilege, on the one hand, and social deprivation on the other. Boroughs of superior social status are likely to have a relatively moderate density of betting shops, while boroughs of inferior social status and composition appear, to contain a higher density of betting shops.

All the Upper Quartile boroughs are sited at the periphery of London and three (Sutton, Kingston-upon-Thames and Richmond-upon-Thames) are situated in the extreme south-west, one

(Bromley) lies in the south-east, two (Havering and Redbridge) in the north-east, one (Harrow) in the north-west and one (Hillingdon) in the west. All of the boroughs in the Bottom Quartile, with the single exception of Newham, lie within the confines of the Inner London area. Hackney, Newham and, in particular, Tower Hamlets represent the area widely-known as London's East End, while the remaining five boroughs (Camden, Hammersmith, Islington, Lambeth and Southwark) have for the past century provided homes for those who have done the mass of menial, lower-grade and low-paid manual jobs in London.[11] Apart from Bromley and Richmond which very marginally touch upon Southwark and Hammersmith, only Redbridge and New-ham are contiguous to the extent of approximately one quarter of their total boundary lines. Elsewhere, the boroughs containing the lowest and the highest density of betting shops are every-where geographically segregated.

Six of the eight boroughs with the lowest density of betting shops and an equal number of those characterized by the highest density of betting shops are within identical categories in respect of the degree of ownership of house property as well as the propor-tion of residents classified as members of social clasess IV and V by virtue of their occupations. All of the four divergent boroughs at the top end of the scale—Enfield and Bexley in respect of owner occupation and Croydon and Richmond with regard to membership of social classes IV and V—are, in common with their rank associates, situated on the fringes of the Greater Lon-don area. At the opposite end of the scale, the boroughs ranking highest as regards density of betting shops and not falling into the identical category in respect of the above named variables, diverge to no more than a very limited extent. With regard to owner occupation, Lambeth ranks twenty-first and Newham twenty-third, and in respect of social class composition, Camden ranks twentieth and Newham twenty-second. Six of the Upper Quartile boroughs and seven of those in the Bottom Quartile, appear in the identical category in respect of domestic amenities, implying independent access to hot water, bath and internal w.c. Barnet and Bexley deviate at the upper end of the scale, while at the lower end, Lambeth ranks twenty-second. The relationship between car-ownership and density of betting shops is even more pronounced. Six of the Upper Quartile boroughs are among the eight most highly ranked in car-ownership and in the case of the Bottom Quartile, correspondence is total. All the eight boroughs occupying the terminal positions in regard to car-ownership, are also those boroughs with the highest betting shop density.

We are, therefore, on the basis of a considerable body of conforming data, able to construct a profile of Greater London in which a number of socio-economic variables indicative of social status and class overlap, and overwhelmingly coincide with the relative density of betting shops.

The two innermost boroughs—the Cities of London and Westminster—exhibit a high level of density of betting shops which, once account is taken of the vast influx into this zone of the daily commuter traffic, becomes comparatively low in relation to the workday population. Their incidence of betting shops is untypical and their various social characteristics disparate and diverse. Some of the other inner boroughs—such as Kensington and Chelsea, Lewisham and Greenwich—overwhelmingly serving as short-range dormitories for the central parts and, housing a heterogeneously composed admixture of residents, are, though closely alike in their incidence of betting shops, slightly assorted with regard to social characteristics. They are uniformly densely populated, housing a high ratio of persons per room, poorly provided with modern domestic amenities and lowly placed in respect of owner occupation, ownership of cars per household and extent of internal garages. They are likely to contain a relatively high proportion of immigrants—coloured and otherwise—as well as to comprise a wider range of social classes and occupational grades. Their degree of density of betting shops is very similar (2.17 for Lewisham, 2.22 for Kensington and Chelsea, and 2.33 for Greenwich), ranking in all cases somewhat below the municipal average.

In all other boroughs, as is most clearly demonstrated by those at the extreme ends, density of betting shops is very closely linked with the possession or the lack of social privilege and material possessions; it is lowest in areas where privilege and possessions are widely attained and highest in districts in which indices of social deprivation and lack of material possessions are most widespread and apparent. At the upper end of the scale—

indicating low level of betting shop density—one borough (Bromley) features among the leading boroughs in each of the ten categories representing possession of privilege; one appears nine times, another eight times and only one (Richmond-upon-Thames) appears fewer than five times. Although this group displays a greater assortment and diversity of characteristics than the non-privileged group at the opposite end of the scale, none of the eight boroughs in the Upper Quartile appear below the rank of the uppermost one-third in any of the ten social grade categories. The weight of evidence strongly suggests that wherever middle-class occupation predominates, there gambling in betting shops is least likely to prosper and prevail.

At the opposite, lower end of the scale, the degree of positive association between density of betting shops and, in this instance, lack of social privilege and material possessions is even more total and consistent. All of the eight boroughs ranking within the Bottom Quartile with regard to the density of betting shops, are placed within the same sector with respect to the ten combined categories indicative of social grade. Two (Hackney and Islington) figure within the lowest sector in each of the ten categories, two further boroughs (Tower Hamlets and Hammersmith) feature in nine, a further two (Camden and Southwark) in eight. Only one single borough (Camden with respect to proportion of residents being members of social classes I and II) ranks other than within the lowest one third in any of the ten social grade categories and of the eighty possible social grade placements within the lowest quartile, this group achieves the unenviable distinction of attaining a total of sixty-six. All boroughs within this group are situated in the inner regions of Greater London, either directly within the innermost circle—widely documented as the poor quality domicile of the low grade and poorly paid manual urban supply force[12]—or in the three boroughs spanning London's East End, traditionally associated with poverty, deprivation and social neglect.[13] Universally these boroughs are characterized by high population density, lack of domestic space, inferior and inadequate level of domestic amenities, low incidence of home ownership as well as of possession of capital goods such as cars, also by the presence of a large proportion of those belonging to the semi- and unskilled manual wage-earning groups, as well as by a high density of betting shops.[14]

While the eight boroughs with the lowest level of betting shop density, and containing 23.5 per cent of the total population, possess no more than 12.7 per cent of the total number of betting shops, the eight boroughs at the opposite end of the scale with 25.6 per cent of the total population, contain 41.9 per cent of all the Greater London betting shops.[15]

In view of the internal social similarity of these boroughs and their overwhelming degree of association between the large range of categories, indicative of social deprivation and density of betting shops, we feel justified in suggesting that such modes of transaction and interaction as might be found to exist within betting shops within a representative sample would not merely be valid and accurate for the, perforce, limited area to which the study would be confined, but would furthermore be equally valid and accurate for other districts distinguished by closely resembling social characteristics, as well as by a similar density of betting shops. Thus, observations conducted on modes of transaction and interaction in a district, characterized as lower-grade working class, would not merely be specific to the limited number of betting shops to which such observations might be confined but would, by virtue of the above data allowing themselves to be generalized, be descriptive of modes of conduct particular to a much wider range, extending to possibly more than one third of all betting shops in the entire Greater London area.

Apart from the basic ecological similarity of large-scale modern industrial cities throughout the world,[16] as well as the virtually total absence of inter-regional differentiation with regard to patterns of gambling found to be prevailing in Britain,[17] London has traditionally served as prototype not merely for other British conurbations but equally, other than for minor regional modifications, for other large scale British urban centres.[18] It would thus seem valid to maintain that conditions found to prevail within Greater London would, *ipso facto*, be almost totally replicated in other large British industrial centres. Wherever, therefore, within any such city, one were to find the phenomenon of a high degree of concentration of betting shops, one would be safe in postulating the coexistence of characteristics indicative of social deprivation and wherever one were to discern a cluster of indices reflecting relative social deprivation, one would be justified in presuming a high level of concentration of betting shops.

Notes

1. Betting Gaming and Lotteries Act 1963: Permits and Licences. Presented annually by order of the House of Commons pursuant to Act Eliz. II 1963 c2, sch 1. H.M.S.O. (London December 1963–8).
2. The sources responsible for information relating to the total number of licensed and registered betting shops within the various Greater London boroughs were: (a) Home Office, Statistical Data Branch, Statistical Division, (b) Town Clerks of the various Greater London boroughs, (c) Clerks to the Justices of the various betting licences divisions and (d) finally, in respect of the 5 boroughs for which this information was still outstanding, personal inspection of the files relating to betting shops was undertaken.
3. For the extent of daily inflow and outflow of population into and out of the various Greater London boroughs see General Register Office, Sample Census 1966; Economic Activity Leaflet, Greater London, H.M.S.O. (London 1968); table 2: Persons in Employment by area of workplace: Occupations by sex; pp. 49–84.
4. Donnison, D. V. (1967) ch. 10.
5. Betting, Gaming and Lotteries Act 1963: Permits and Licences, H.M.S.O. (London, 17 December 1968).
6. Betting Licensing Authorities areas of competence do not coincide with the boundaries of the Greater London boroughs. In a number of cases boroughs are split into 2 or 3 licensing areas and in other cases licensing areas and borough boundaries intersect.

    The 13 Inner Boroughs of Greater London are: City of London, Camden, Greenwich, Hackney, Hammersmith, Islington, Kensington and Chelsea, Lambeth, Lewisham, Southwark, Tower Hamlets, Wandsworth and Westminster.

    General Register Office, Sample Census 1966, England and Wales; County Report, Greater London; H.M.S.O. (London 1967); tables 1, 7A, 8, 9, 11, 12, 13 and 14.
7. According to a survey carried out in 1963, 68 per cent of all households in Great Britain possessed a separate bathroom in that year. (Reader's Digest European Surveys, 1963; Reader's Digest Association Ltd.) The 1961 Census declared that 73 per cent of all households in the United Kingdom had access to a fixed bath or shower in that year. (General Register Office: Census 1961.)
8. According to the data provided by the Sample Census 1966, 46.3 per cent of all households in Great Britain were owner-occupied, 27.6 per cent rented their accommodation from local authorities or new town

corporations, 18.7 per cent rented private unfurnished accommodation, 2 per cent rented private furnished accommodation and 5.4 per cent belonged to the category 'other or not stated'.

9. See Glass, R. and Westergaard, J., 'London's Housing Needs', Centre for Urban Studies, Report no. 5, University College, London (1965), and London, Report of the Committee on Housing in Greater London (Milner Holland Committee), Cmd. 2605 (London 1965).

10. Of those born in the New Commonwealth and resident in Greater London, 10.4 per cent belonged to social classes I and II and 38.7 per cent belonged to social classes IV and V. General Register Office, Sample Census 1966; Commonwealth Immigrants Tables, H.M.S.O. (London 1969).

12. Freeman, T. W. (1959); Pahl, R. E. (1970) *Patterns of Urban Life*, London: Longmans. See also Hatt, P. K. and Reiss, A. J., Jr, *Cities and Society*, chapter 4: Duncan, O. D. and Duncan, B., 'Residential Distribution and Occupational Stratification', pp. 283–96, as well as Mays, J. B., *Growing Up in the City*.

13. Mayhew, H. (1851) vol. 2; Booth, C. (1902); Spinley, B. M. (1953); Robb, J. H. (1954) ch. III.

14. Reference has, within the present context, been confined to those social grade categories as were able to be documented and discussed on the basis of comprehensive data in the present chapter. There is little doubt that a host of further indices of social deprivation—low and irregular income, occupational injuries, chronic illnesses, outdated educational institutions, early school-leaving etc.—as well as indices of social pathology—crime and delinquency, alcoholism, prostitution, illegitimacy and others—would exhibit a similar pattern of regional distribution and a disproportionate concentration within the same areas. A recent report on Mental Illness, for instance, confirms that the East End has a startlingly high rate of mental illness and neighbouring affluent boroughs a significantly lower rate. Comparing discharge rates for patients from psychiatric hospitals in Tower Hamlets, Hackney, Greenwich and Bexley, researchers found an overall difference of 52 per cent between the two East London boroughs and the two South London boroughs, proving, in their view, a direct relationship between schizophrenia and poor socio-economic conditions.

See *Mental Illness in Four London Boroughs*, Psychiatric Rehabilitation Association (London 1969).

15. The 40 betting shops within the City of London and the 150 betting shops in Westminster have, for the purposes of these computations, for reasons stated previously, been omitted making the number of betting shops within Greater London, in this instance, a total of 2,059.

It is, of course, appreciated that numbers and density of betting shops when taken by themselves do not automatically provide any clue as to support, turnover or profitability. It may well be possible that fewer large-scale betting shops within a given area attract a higher total volume of bettors as well as bets than a much larger number of small-scale units elsewhere. It is an empirical fact that a number of betting shops in areas of greater affluence are smarter and more amply appointed than the average, generally sordid and bare betting shop. Such superior establishments are likely to require much higher outlay and running costs and may therefore have to rely on much higher turnover than the average betting shop. This may, however, at least theoretically, be counterbalanced by superior expertise and, in consequence, wagering skill of the habitual working-class bettor and thus larger size and superior appointments may well mean higher ratio of profit per amount staked. In the absence of any confirmatory data, particularly in view of the fact that a fair proportion of working-class neighbourhood betting shops are organised on a large scale, it has been assumed that betting shops throughout the Greater London area achieve a very similar ratio of profitability.

16. Gans, H. J. (1967) *The Levittowners*, London: Allen Lane.
17. The findings derived by the surveys of Research Services Ltd in particulars widely made use of in Chapter III, are almost entirely stratified by geographic region and show throughout virtually total homogeneity in betting patterns in respect of the major regions of Britain.
18. Freeman, T. W. (1959).

CHAPTER V

The Sociology of the Betting Shop

Methodology and Description

The research described in this and the following chapter was carried out throughout the year 1967 and for part of 1968 in the borough of Tower Hamlets in the East End of London. The reasons for which empirical study of betting shops appeared to be of prime importance have already been alluded to in the foregoing sections, where it was indicated that a major portion of all monies expended in gambling are staked on horseracing in gambling premises situated away from horserace courses; that more than one half of the total national gambling outlay—amounting to not much less than £1,000 million per year—is disbursed via betting shops; that as much as 10 million people —25 per cent of the total adult population—were in the habit of frequenting betting shops, and that, although statistical data on gambling patterns did exist, empirical observations of modes of action and interaction within betting shops had not yet been undertaken. It has been, furthermore, shown that, within Greater London, betting shops are found to be disproportionately concentrated in areas in which manual wage-earner occupation traditionally abounds and that, in such areas, a large range of common socio-economic characteristics, as well as their powerful degree of association with density of betting shops, is of a sufficient degree of correspondence to suggest that empirical study, if true and relevant of one area, may be generalized to be applicable not merely for a variety of similarly composed London districts, but furthermore for socially conforming areas of occupation, existing throughout the various large-scale British towns and conurbations.

The methods of investigation, all based upon research into gambling and gamblers within their natural environment, took the following forms:

(a) direct observation of gamblers as they gambled
(b) participant observation of gamblers as observer, associate, and co-gambler
(c) interviews with householders in the district,* informal and unstructured in character and principally designed at establishing confidence and rapport
(d) informal talks—initiated in all manner of localities such as betting shops, dogtracks, gaming clubs as well as pubs, cafés and street corners—some relatively brief and others many hours long; some confined to gamblers within the arenas of their gambling activities and others reaching out for a cross-section of the local population, in situations in which gambling activity and participation were of no relevance.

For a variety of reasons, the East End in general and Bethnal Green in particular were chosen as the subject of empirical research. In the first place, it was found that they conformed closely with respect to the various social characteristics among which betting shops, as has been established, are wont to thrive. I had, furthermore, in course of previous experience in that area, learned to respect and to value its virtues of vitality, humanity, humour and realism. It also afforded me not too inconvenient regular access to and from my home in South-East London—a not inconsiderable asset when having to travel back and forth, at times twice in the course of one day—and last but not least, being one of the centre-points of urban social enquiry, it offered a wide, varied and versatile bibliographical choice.[1]

Shortly after my arrival in the area I was, by the kind intervention of a friend, introduced to two bookmakers who in partnership owned and managed a single-unit betting shop in Bethnal Green. At our very first meeting they offered me the full use of their premises, subject only to compatibility with the conduct of

---

* These interviews constitute the Household Survey, previously referred to and discussed in Chapter III.

their business, for any empirical work I might seek to undertake. It was agreed that I should initially install myself on the management's side of the counter, from there to observe the conduct of the public within the betting shop, their actions and reactions towards each other and to the management within the betting situation, as well as such other factors as I might consider relevant to my studies. I was, furthermore, to be allowed within discretion to ask the clientele, as well as the management, any question connected with my research and was also to be given full and free access to any of the books of account which I might choose to consult.

I gratefully accepted the offer and soon after began stationing myself daily behind the counter, usually from the time the premises opened at ten o'clock in the morning until they closed again at six in the afternoon. My presence was on entry explained by one of the owners as: 'A friend of ours who wants to learn all about gambling'. This vague and ambiguous formula assured for me initial acceptance and I found myself within a few days in a position in which my presence had ceased to arouse curiosity and comment, where remarks were beginning to be addressed to me and where I could, at an early stage, without ceremony, transfer to the 'public enclosure', declare my intent and freely mingle with the clientele. I stayed in this betting shop (hereafter referred to as B.S.I) for an initial period of eight weeks. I then revisited it for a further four weeks after a four-months' lapse and finally returned to it again for a further three-week stint towards the end of my empirical research, almost a full year after the original series of visits.

Largely in an endeavour to seek to counterbalance the impact this 'respectable' and integrated part of East London had made on me, as well as to observe gambling in an environment in which personal and social restraints were likely to be less pervasive and evident, I decided to subject the material gathered to test in another betting shop in a sector of East London, as contrasting and divergent as it was possible to find. Having surveyed various alternatives, my choice fell on the larger and busier of the two betting shops in Cable Street, Stepney (hereafter referred to as B.S.II). In all probability this street is still the leading contender for the unenviable title of principal metropolitan crime and vice strip. Cable Street, though by now having passed through the era when, in the words of one local sage, 'It had become so dense that those who weren't coppers were welfare workers stumbling over social researchers or their likes', still well deserved Downes's description of it as 'a compound of culture conflict, transience, demographic upheaval, poverty and insecurity, overcrowding and of total human depression and affliction found only in the crevices of our society'.[2]

Experience had by that time taught me to desist from describing myself as being engaged in a survey or on a research project. Nothing else seemed to serve as a more effective antidote to relaxed interaction, to easy discourse, or behaviour uneffacted by the consciousness of being in the presence of an observer, a judge. Instead I had acquired the habit of introducing myself as an author looking for material for a book on leisure pursuits with particular emphasis on betting. I had equally, at an early stage, learned to discard the use of the emotive word 'gambling' wherever possible, particularly in reference to any activity in which the subject being questioned was himself engaged. Only the very exceptional individual was prepared to see any terms other than 'betting' applied to his activity in connection with the subject being discussed. In this role of 'author' I found myself amongst a clientele largely composed of down-and-outs, vagrants, derelicts, methers,* prostitutes, petty criminals, and drunks. After the initial period in which I appeared to have attracted an undue number of confidences and confessions, I was accepted as an insider without inhibitions or restraints. I was even permitted the privilege of asking direct questions and of taking notes, while at the same time being exempt from the peremptory, aggressive demands for so-called loans to which members regularly subjected each other. In fact, even the more notorious scroungers proudly declined my offers of 'subs' at times when their luck was in particularly short supply, limiting the amount of non-reciprocal help they were willing to accept to a glass of beer or a cup of tea and a bun.

I had during that time made the acquaintance of two young men who had, in the years following the passing of the Betting

---

* Methers: Methylated-spirit drinkers whose main habitat is 'Itchy-Park', adjoining Spitalfields Church.

and Gaming Act, built up a successful chain of twenty-odd betting shops, entirely in East London. Of the many valuable pieces of information imparted by them, none aroused my curiosity more strongly than their descriptions of, and speculations on, their most lucrative single set of premises, a betting shop in Mile End. This betting shop (hereafter referred to as B.S.III), poky and meagre even by local standards, had, being directly adjacent to a gaming club, for some time become the regular haunt of a set of men who, according to my informants, spent each and every afternoon circulating from betting shop to gaming club and back again, and betting in each constantly in considerable sums, apparently not minding how often or how much they lost. These people allegedly did not follow any recognized gainful occupation—how could they, when all of their afternoons were passed away in gambling?—the origin of their resources seemed obscure, while their funds appeared inexhaustible. In the opinion of my informants and that of their staff witnessing their daily pursuits, their clients were an assortment of crooks, ranging from petty criminals such as housebreakers, dippers, screwmen,* and thieves to hold-up men, gang-leaders and underworld racketeers. Having had my curiosity excited, I decided to try and take a closer look at this phenomenon. In view of the speculations as to the likely means of livelihood of the clientele, I considered it unavoidable, in this instance, to depart from my otherwise firm resolve of not sailing under false colours. Adopting for the purposes of 'infiltration' the fictitious guise of a temporarily out-of-harness businessman who, having recently sold out a small enterprise in a seaside town, was, while awaiting the proceeds of the sale, devoting himself to his leisure hobby of gambling, while carrying on negotiations in respect of a future field of action. This disguise, though making it obligatory to perform as player and bettor, spared me the necessity of betting in other than the most modest stakes.

Although effective in achieving acceptance and integration for me, I am anything other than proud of this deception which, as is so often the case, proved to be unnecessary. Instead of the anticipated bunch of assorted gangsters, I found these men, though by no means averse to the occasional sally into illegality,

---

* Dippers: pickpockets; Screwmen: skilled burglars, safecrackers, etc.

to be, other than the untypical few, members of respectable, hardworking professions. The majority were independent taxi-drivers working the most remunerative metropolitan routes,* some were market porters of a supervisory grade† and a few were stallholders and marketmen, whose pitches were of a sufficient degree of profitability to permit their owners to restrict their working week to Saturday, possibly Sunday (in Petticoat Lane) plus a further two half-days. Their ages ranged from the early twenties to the late seventies, all were products and residents of the local neighbourhood and virtually all were distinctively Jewish. I dubbed these men, in whose close company I spent several weeks, in spite of their philosophy of 'when work interferes with play, stop work' (as expressed by the manager of the gaming club) the 'Frustrated Entrepreneurs'.[3]

The chapter following is an attempt to describe as well as to analyse some of the sociological ramifications of the Gambling Situation. Before turning to the material itself, I feel it incumbent upon myself to repeat that the observations are confined to one single type of gambling activity within one particular subsection of London and that they need neither be relevant to other types of gambling activities, nor need they necessarily find themselves substantiated by future research undertaken in other parts. Despite these reservations, particularly in view of the reinforcing material adduced in previous chapters, I feel justified in submitting that the types of action and interaction I have sought to outline will serve to indicate not only the integral part gambling plays within the working-class urban culture, but that it will also throw light on some of the social functions gambling performs as well as the contribution it makes to the maintenance of structural order and equilibrium.

The following initial hypotheses suggest themselves for consideration in the text to follow:

(1) If empirical observations of gambling in action reveal that, in this activity, the economic motivations are either total or that they predominate to any significant extent, such evidence would

* Largely the evening and night hours at the larger West End hotels, Heathrow Airport and the Air Terminal.

† These, again, working unconventional hours, generally from five o'clock in the morning until midday.

stand in confirmation of the assumption that gambling is a materialistically dominated activity. If, however, other non-economic elements were shown to be of equal, or even of greater impact and significance, then the activity of gambling would need to be defined in terms beyond being a pursuit of material gain.

(2) If these elements were to be of sufficient power qualitatively to transform an institution, we would be justified in assuming that they possess functions and implications beyond the manifest and that they are part and parcel within the larger framework of individual and communal existence.

(3) If, by means of participation in the activity of gambling, individuals can be considered to acquire:

(a) a superior perception of their environment,
(b) the means of expanding their personalities,
(c) the satisfaction of needs of which they would otherwise be deprived;

then we are justified in suggesting that, at least within the cultural environment of which such was held to be true, the activity acts as a positive agent in the direction of individual comprehension, development, and self-integration.

(4) If, by means of mutual interaction in the activity of gambling, social groups achieve:

(a) reinforcement of cohesion and integration,
(b) affirmation of their communal value systems;

if mutual interaction is effective in:

(i) the exercise of social control,
(ii) the socialization of recruits;

then we are justified in claiming that the activity of gambling, at least within these dimensions, whatever its possible consequences in other spheres, performs a positive function for the social order at large and that it helps to enhance social solidarity and continuity.

'Let us not take it for granted that life exists more fully in what is commonly thought big, rather than what is commonly thought small.' (Virginia Woolf, *The Common Reader*).

The East End of London has provided rich material to the social observer during the past hundred years. Nowhere else were the miseries and degenerating distortions of the unadulterated phase of *laissez-faire* industrialization more apparent in such abundant measure, nowhere else could the entire complex spectrum of human misery and degradation be found to be more completely assembled. From Mayhew to Dickens to Booth to Jack London and finally the Webbs,[4] social consciences were aroused by the chronicles of exploitation, brutality, vice, inhumanity and despairing hopelessness, possibly best summarized by Jack London in *The People of the Abyss*:

No more dreary spectacle can be found on this earth than the whole of the 'awful East' with its Whitechapel, Hoxton, Spitalfields, Bethnal Green and Wapping to the East India Docks. The colour of life is drab and grey. Everything is helpless, hopeless, unrelieved and dirty . . . Here lives a population as dull and unimaginative as its long grey miles of dingy brick. Religion has virtually passed it by and a gross and stupid materialism reigns, fatal alike to the things of the spirit and the finer instincts of life . . . A new race has sprung up, a street people . . . They have dens and lairs into which they crawl for sleeping purposes and that is all. (p. 13)

Throughout, the East-Enders were described as abandoned, rudderless wrecks with only the faintest vestiges of social comfort, social awareness and responsibility. Whether it is thanks to the benefits of social reforms, or to the transition into the more advanced stages of industrialization, or thanks to the more systematic and incisive analysis of more rigorously equipped social observers,[5] not to mention the vast demographic changes set in motion by the upheavals of the last war—mass bombing, evacuation, emigration—the image of the East End has undergone a radical transformation. The emphasis on misery and degeneration has given way to acknowledgement of the positive factors to be found in the environment. Cheerfulness, optimism, spontaneity, a capacity to adapt to changed circumstances without a loss of identity and above all vibrant, co-operative community life are given due credit and recognition. True poverty, unemployment, overcrowding, slum dwellings and thriftlessness do persist, but the victims find shelter and protection in the deep, dense network of family and community life. They are sustained by the corporate, co-operative consciousness, the individual's readiness to offer succour and self-sacrifice—be it thanks to primitive, traditional attachment to kinship roots, to comradeship or through practical awareness, that their own turn to ask for help may come next. In this environment human findings and frailties are taken for granted. Occasional and even recurrent bouts of voluntary idleness, drunkenness, brutality and infidelity are generously condoned; imperfections are regarded not as the shameful abnormalities of Puritanism, but as inevitable components of the personality structure. Power and Law—of which the visible representatives were the means-test man, the bailiff, the rentman, the 'gaffer', the 'beak' and the 'copper'—are held in scant respect. Infraction of the legal code is a daily spectacle, adroitness in evading detection a positive prestige symbol.

The recurring certainty of the daily struggle, the inescapable limitation imposed by the manual worker's wage, the humdrum monotony of the daily toil alone create a background against which gambling, free from the complexes of guilt which overhang it in other social environments, flourishes in all its forms. The daily flutter on the horses, the evening visit to the dogtrack, the weekly ritual of the football pool, afford not only amusement and necessary diversion, but hopeful, even if unreasonable, expectation of a windfall; the winning coup which, when it does materialize, will allow, while the money lasts, profligacy in the grandest manner, extravagance which even when it is enviously mocked, will be respected and admired. The gambler is the social norm, the non-gambler the deviant oddity.[6] Traces of the tradition termed by Hobsbawn 'social banditry'—taking from the rich to give to the poor, of not using violence other than in justified self-defence—still survive.[7] The ethos of being confronted by an antagonistic authority—all-embracing and all-powerful and yet, by virtue of its self-seeking greed, vulnerable and even pliable—is deeply embedded in the culture. If you cannot match 'Them' in confrontation, get even by trickery, subversion, barefaced deceit, submissive insubordination. In this *milieu* the street bookie, in the pre-1960 betting legislation days, was in his element. Although nominally outlawed he practised his trade with little effort at concealment. His pitch, his clerks and runners were universally known, his pledged word sufficient cover for any bet, his reach long enough to make default a hazardous extremity; his wealth and success regarded as objects of communal pride and his ability to triumphantly defy the Law served as comforting evidence of the asinine witlessness and egotistical corruption of the mighty and powerful.[8] Since liberalization of the betting laws, the legalization of ready-cash off-course betting in 1960, the disappearance of the street bookie is not the only change in the East End scene. Not only have the Greater London Council and the local authorities completed the work, initiated by Hitler's bombers, of the destruction of the worst areas of slum housing—the intricate, interwoven network of tunnelbacks, of clusters of decaying terraces—replacing them largely with tall, imposing, uniform and impersonal blocks of flats, but concurrently with this removal of one of the major bulwarks of indigenous community existence, other cornerstones have yielded to the processes of social change. The poky corner shop, the focus of parochial life, where regulated closing times, mechanical efficiency, space utilization, strict economic orienta-tion were in scant presence; where gossip, communication and, as was often dire necessity, credit were at all times available, has given way to the bright, brash, impersonal efficiency of the supermarket, the chainstore, the launderette. The working-man's pub—at once vilified and romanticized by his 'social betters'—the refuge in which arduous toil, enforced submissiveness, domestic disorder could, however briefly, be obliterated in the company of his chosen mates, where the humbled working man could reassert his individuality, his unique personality, has disappeared. Its place has been taken by the chain-operated, pseudo-elegant, contemporarily-decorated, hygienic public house, in which the landlord is a stranger, where spontaneous relaxation has been superseded by the juke-box and the omnipresent tele-vision set, where excesses are strictly barred and almost unthink-able. The introduction of the television set into every home, the increasing level of ownership of cars—the former tending towards social contraction and the latter expanding the universe of experience and contact—have further led in the direction of weakening the fabric of community life until, as some claim to detect, the same anomic mass existence, as had previously been diagnosed in other quarters of metropolitan life, appears to pervade.

However, wherever one goes, a new but quickly familiar

phenomenon has arisen—the betting shop. How do these fit into the social scene, do they conform with the recent trend towards facelessness or do they, as an accidental by-product of their creation, provide a recharge, a centre of resurgence of the other- wise waning channels of interaction and intercommunication?

Bethnal Green (B.S.I)

The betting shop which forms the subject of our discussion lies close to the centre of a long-established, well-known East End street market, a market in which the large number of stalls offer a rich variety of commodities, chiefly foodstuffs and apparel. The accent is on price, on 'unrepeatable' bargains, clearance lines, bankrupt or fire stocks, with occasional innuendoes to bargains owing their value to 'stuff being nicked'. The market is patronized largely by the local population, a heterogeneous mixture of White, and Black, Gentile, Jew and Moslem, of firmly rooted and transi- ent, locally born and bred and recently immigrated. The district is predominantly composed of manual workers, with a large element of dockers and watermen, and of workers employed in the small-scale family businesses concerned with the manufacture of furniture and of clothing—often evolved from the ill-famed sweat-shops—and a smaller component, socially almost indis- tinguishable, of traders, merchants, small shopkeepers, and stall- holders. The level of occupational training is meagre, the bulk of incomes within the lower regions of the semi-skilled ranges of the industrial workers' brackets. A large proportion of wives within the active age groups go out to work, at least part-time, finding their employment mainly as machinists in the vast number of clothing workshops, or as shop assistants, cleaners, with a few aspiring to clerical levels. Local industry is confined and meagre, located anywhere suitable premises can be found or has tradi- tionally come to be established, freely intermingled with resi- dential occupation. Several large-scale concerns—a flourmill, a cement works—have been founded and draw the major part of their labour force, male and female, from the area, but appear as yet unintegrated into the community.

Strikingly obvious is the coexistence rather than the conflict between the old and the new—the intermingling of sparkling launderettes and of male boutiques with the traditional East End 'Caff'—dark, dank, reeking of stale tea leaves and of slop; the super-modern chainstore and the chaotic secondhand dealer; the mini-skirted factory girl, still wearing her curlers barely concealed under her headscarf. Fashion shops, record shops and to no lesser extent betting shops abound. The diminishing majority of the last are still owned and managed by the independent entrepreneur—frequently the ex-street bookie or his clerk—but an increasing proportion are now chain operated, in the hands of a manager controlled by head-office. They all seem to be able to count on their stable, regular clientele, the reliable hard core of backers who remain loyal to the betting shop of their choice. Although punters, apart from other considerations affecting preference, will, after a prolonged unsuccessful run, be inclined to switch custom, will try their luck in a different environment— expressions such as 'Mark's shop is a bock* to me' are not infrequently heard—they will, unless their luck in the new betting shop changes phenomenally, unless within their new orbit they rapidly form new allegiances, tend to drift back, making little effort to conceal their peccadillo, submitting good-humouredly to the kindly banter on return—'so you found that their runners are the same as ours'. Naturally, some punters will change under impact of external forces—new job, new home, a new set of mates—and many others, the 'floaters', will lay their bets at whichever betting shop happens to be most convenient at the time. But each betting shop has its hard core of supporters, loyal, steadfast, ranging elsewhere briefly to break their luck, to avoid the embarrassment of a long streak of winning bets, or to gain new insights by exchange of opinion with a different set of students of form. Within their own betting shop they are known and addressed by their first names, or even more often their nicknames; their foibles, preferences, idiosyncracies are known and taken account of, their moments of glory, their splendid exploits are fully recalled in surroundings familiar; their near-misses given a sympathetic ear, their prestige firmly established and regularly reinforced by new deeds of valour—the successful bet, irrespective of volume of winnings, made in the face of overwhelming

* Bock: ill-omen.

odds, in defiance of expert opinion, the result of personal courage and firm resolve. Their honour, prestige and self-respect will be revalidated by withstanding, without flinching within the range of public scrutiny, the assault of a sustained losing run, by display of the appropriate mixture between elation and restraint at their moments of triumph. Each subtle nuance of action and reaction will undergo the litmus test of judgment by equals, will serve— not as on first impact one might assume, to divide the wheat from the chaff, to separate the leaders from the mass in competitive encounter, but rather—to sustain the common values, to confirm the image of what man ought to be like—resolute, independent yet co-operative, humorous, modest, indifferent in the face of danger and of adversity.

Zola suggests, on the basis of a participant study in the United States within a social environment not too dissimilar to the one studied by us, that the predominant motive of the punter is to do down the bookie.[9] He views the activity of gambling as being dominated by the ethos of the personal duel until death, the encounter between David—the punter, isolated, lonely and outgunned—and Goliath—the bookmaker, powerful, proud and representative of superior predatory power. Triumph of the weak by any means is justified; total, complete ruin of the bookie the ultimate goal of the encounter (however disadvantageous in objective terms such annihilation might be to the punter). Each series of bets is a personal contest, a competitive activity in which success will serve to establish excellence, superiority over the herd, or at least some modicum of personal worth—'What do they think I am, a Nobody?' Such observations may accurately reflect the American scene, they may well be true of a society in which competitive success—the stiffer the contest the better, the more devious the means the more glorious the triumph—may in itself be a culture goal. They may well be the reflections of a system in which the bookmaker, prescribed and outlawed, is a more convenient, comprehensive scapegoat.

They are certainly not true of the field of activity observed by us. Study of form, deliberation and selection may be isolated and even secretive. Winnings are personal, but each triumph belongs to the unit, the entire group of which, paradoxically, the book- maker—after all, the owner who is footing the bill—forms an integral part. Minor regular winnings occur constantly and these are collected without much comment on either side; but the coup —not assessed primarily in quantitative terms, but rather as a matter of quality, the outfacing of heavy odds, the courage to defy the majority successfully, to think and act independently—is, not only rewarded by due personal recognition of the winner, but by expressions of common jubilation and exhilaration, in which all the regulars, not least the owner, spontaneously take part, not as a tribute to one punter's excellence, but as common triumph over the massed forces of the outside, over the superior external powers, a victory of 'Us' over 'Them'. This struggle is free from signs of tension and strain; losses are borne with poker-faced composure, are nonchalantly shrugged off with a casual smile— 'always picking wrong 'uns', 'can't pick a winner for toffee', a self-mocking phrase, usually of stereotyped character 'wouldn't know a winner if I saw one', 'what's the odds, easy come, easy go'— after all, defeat in the face of the overwhelming odds facing 'Us' is anticipated and thus, in itself, not shameful. But lack of character, of moral fibre are. Fruits of one's knowledge are granted open-handedly, when asked for, and are given without imposition of inferiority. Yet it is but rarely solicited—is one not facing an incomprehensible foe, a superior combination of nebulous forces; not united in subtle alliance to do 'Us' down—that after all would be amenable to analysis, to comprehension and exploitation —but fighting their own battles, for their own benefit by their alien system of logic, taking 'Us' as expendable supply material for granted. But possibly for the very reason that intrusion into the thought processes of 'Them' is a virtual impossibility, triumph becomes all the more precious and sweet.

In this world strong, rigid sex-differentiation continues to exist, the male and female universe follow different paths, their separation almost retaining forms of ritual avoidance. The morning hours, from opening time at ten to midday belong to the women. Soon after the shop has opened, after the racing pages of the morning press and the early editions of the evening papers have been pinned to the walls, the females start trooping in. Their bets are already written out on slips of paper with total stakes neatly added up and usually they proffer the exact amount of cash. Stakes are modest, a daily maximum of 30p with a minimum

of as little as 5p. The majority of bets are of the various combination types—doubles, trebles, accumulators, yankees*—multiple
bets usually made up of the short priced selection of the racing
experts of the morning press, in most cases the *Daily Mirror*
whose 'nap' selection—the pick of the day—figures in some form
or another on almost every slip.[10] Comments connected with
betting are minimal, even when winnings on previous day's
racing are collected—these are pocketed without emotion or
comment, rather in the manner of drawing Family Allowance
from the Post Office. Conversation is nevertheless lively and
intense, concerned chiefly with matters of family life—enquiry
into health, husband's new job, daughter's council flat, with
particular concentration on topics relating to babies—perennially
a favourite working-class topic. Occasionally some banter of
ambiguous strictly circumscribed sexual overtones (such as the
admiring 'Had a rough night?'), always some comments on the
quality and content of last night's 'telly'. Not by any means are
these exchanges one-way traffic. To a no lesser degree than the
bettors', the history, background, family life of the two proprietors—H. and J., themselves products of the environment—and of
M. the female clerk, are known and stable subjects for discussion.
When winnings of moderate amounts are handed over, H. or J.
will usually pass some encouraging remark 'It's time your turn
came up', 'That'll be a little treat for the kids', 'Don't let the old
man get 'is 'ands on it' and when a really big win comes up—one
elderly regular, a woman in her late sixties, had won £67 on a
20p wager—'The first big draw in all my life', an event highly
improbable, but the designed outcome of this type of bet, the
multiple—the handover acquires almost ceremonious overtones.
The cash is slowly counted out with considerable emphasis, the
bundle of notes handed over and received with undisguised
jubilation—no trace of that haughty restraint the male takes it

---

* All these are multiple bets. Doubles rely for successful outcome on selection
of two winning runners; trebles on three winning runners and accumulators on
any nominated number of runners. In all these cases, any losing selection results
in loss of entire stake. In the case of yankees however where eleven bets are
placed on four runners, any two successful selections ensure some return.

The majority of bookmakers are prepared to accept multiple-type wagers on
placed runners, allowing the bettor, subject to double initial stake, to cover
against the eventuality of one or more selections being beaten into second place.

upon himself to display in similar situations—and without the least overt trace of rancour or recrimination; after all this win, representing a relationship between stake and winnings of something like 400:1, a series of results against which the management cannot budget, afflicts the bookmaker most cruelly. A few final remarks as to the most fruitful manner of disposal, free of condescension or dogmatism, are passed on, local legend such as the tale of the old regular who with her £120 win just before Christmas had fitted out her entire family, including all grandchildren and then had enough left over to stand her Darby and Joan Club a 'proper do', recounted in details often rehearsed and repeated.

It is possible to state with confidence that in this, as well as in other cases when money is paid out to regulars, the owners share in the local triumph. Identification with the group is sincere, heartfelt and genuine, despite the fact that such rejoicing is, being jubilant at an event damaging to one's interests, paradoxical. True enough behind the scenes, in the little back office invisible to the public, the owners will silently, in the course of the race commentary, cheer for the horses carrying little of their money. They will rejoice when betting slips heap into the losing pile at the end of a race, they will utter a mumbled curse when a big win (to them, loss) shows up and particularly when, as happened not infrequently, losses in course of the day exceed takings with accumulated longshot bets still running against them. But once the amount of the big win has been calculated and particularly when the number on the winning slip has been related to the face of one of the old-timers (no effort is made to conceal resentment when an outsider strikes a coup) the process of group identification takes over, 'I suppose the old dear can do with the few bob', 'It's time Ted's luck changed for him', and by the time pay-out comes, the transformation from the role of the bookie to member of the community has been completed, rationalized by 'If they backed nothing but losers, they would soon stop coming'.

Strangely M. the female clerk—forty-fiveish, bustling, articulate, humorous and humane, possessing strong reality awareness —is allowed to stand apart. Not by any means is she an outsider, in fact her personal knowledge of the lives of the clientele is the most highly developed, the most up-to-date. Yet her official role

—that of the paid functionary—allows her freedom of action, comment and above all detachment denied the other, though personally more directly involved members of the establishment, the two partners. The accepted differentiation between the private self—the indistinguishable member of the local community—and the public self—the functionary, the authority's representative—permit her both participation in private gossip, extending even to consultation on form and race performance, as well as an official role she is expected to assume immediately she acts in her appointed capacity, in particular the handling of her employers' money. To this latter role the right of caustic comment—'Why don't you give someone else a chance', 'You got the luck of the devil', 'What do you do with it all'—are granted. Detachment, 'Your second draw of the day', 'I saw you pounce and knew you had a good 'un' and public identification with the boss's cause 'If this goes on much longer we'll have to close down', 'They've got it made' are permitted without causing offence, without the least overspill of resentment into the private role. The public after all expects the paid functionary, the hireling of authority, to be 'Anti-Us' and they feel no surprise when such expectation is fulfilled. Whilst at the same time, the same process permits the owner's re-identification with the environment in which love of contest, valour, conformation of mutuality are common values, greater than those of mundane consideration of personal profit, of private gain.

The morning session, as said before, belongs to the females, supplemented however by a section of male old-age pensioners. This group of males in retirement occupies an indistinct twilight zone in the world of the betting shop. It seems that those who have accepted relegation into the limbo of dependence and of non-productivity, who have resigned themselves to their loss of function and of independent survival in the male world of swagger, assertiveness, dominance over the females, who have undergone the metamorphosis into meekness, dependence, acceptance of domestic democracy, have at the same time voluntarily, without any act of rejection by their former associates, transferred into the less demanding world of the female. Their betting times, types of bets, division of stakes, reaction to winnings and to losses begin to resemble the group into which they have moved. Whilst others of the same age, or even older, manage to retain a firm foothold in the male universe, exhibiting the same characteristics of virility, dominance, decisiveness, superiority over their domestic group as their younger, occupationally productive mates. Whether the dividing line hinges on greater or lesser disposal of independent funds, on sufficient means to face, on equal terms, the requirements of male hegemony; whether it is a matter of a greater or lesser degree of sturdy health; whether it depends on the retention of an independent household, or whether it is largely a matter of spirit, of power to adapt to changed conditions, of determination not to falter, is difficult to assess. Yet the contrast is striking. Whilst the majority almost appear to welcome refuge into the less strenuous regions when the fibre begins to weaken, others—such as Charlie, by all appearances in his late seventies, yet still hale, hearty and confident—retain a hold over their former domain, still manage to hold their own, often with something to spare, in the quest for recognition of those who count; still demand, perhaps now with a greater edge of aggressiveness, to have their voice heard in expert discussion of form, to have their opinions taken account of in achievement of consensus.

For the world from which they refuse to be parted is of tougher fibre than that into which the bulk of the contemporaries has withdrawn. One single lapse from common standards, from mandatory norms is enough to spell exclusion. And yet, strict as segregation may be, it is even then not total. For even in this exclusive male order there is a niche for the untypical, the exceptional female—the Amazon, who refuses to be daunted by the fact of her natural biological inferiority. The woman who is confident, brazen enough to stand up and be counted within the male universe. The good sort, the woman of spunk able to take her drink glass for glass without descent into maudling sentimentality, incoherent splutterings; capable of outfacing her man in direct confrontation, in violent dispute without refuge into the weapons of the weaker sex—tears, tantrums, nagging, recrimination, appeal for sympathy to the outside world; capable of independent survival in the world of the betting man, where knowledge of form, of performance, of interplay of odds, confidence in personal judgment, unswerving pursuit of the chosen course are essential prerequisites. Such women, the select few, are without reservation accepted into the male clan, are without differentiation accorded equal place in the afternoon session, the time when the serious business of real betting has begun to run its course.

By midday the *habitués* have taken their places against the two counters above which are pinned the pages of the daily press featuring the racing news and forecasts. They intently examine the records.[11] The majority are satisfied with intense scrutiny of their favourite source of information* but some punters will repeat the process in front of other clippings before finalizing their selection. Conversation, consultation, even between those who entered together, is minimal. Attention to fluctuations in ante-post odds, as reported by the 'blower', is by all appearances negligible; demeanour is grave, studious and reflective. Towards the approach of the starting signal for the first race the bets start trickling in, on the announcement 'They are under starter's orders' a sudden momentum builds up. Although superficially reminiscent of the effect of the words '*Faîtes vos jeux*' on the roulette table, it lacks the latter's atmosphere of compulsiveness, of feverish excitation, of suddenly becoming aware of new fancies not to be missed, the moment when eager hands compete in their efforts to pile new heaps of stakes on the table. Each punter makes his final choice, hands over his betting slip but once the bet has been completed, all interest in the race appears to depart. Attention is once more fixed upon the clippings in consideration of the next event and even during the climactic stages of the race in progress, the time when the announcer discards his customary neutral intonation, only a barely noticeable inclination of the head towards the loudspeaker, an imperceptible pause in the study of form, betray involvement and interest. Once the race is concluded, the results and final prices announced, laconic comment—'They must have been preparing him for a killing', 'I fancied his chances' (but backed another), 'Wouldn't touch him at these lousy odds'—addressed to the assembly in general is expressed strangely pronounced with equal authority by the majority of losers as the few winning punters, now collecting their winnings without permitting themselves, other than possibly

* The *Daily Mail* appeared to be a particular favourite of the initiates.

for a jauntier, more assertive angle at which they dangle their cigarettes, the least flicker of emotion. Indeed, time for ceremony, regurgitation is short. Races, even only with two meetings per day, follow each other at intervals of no more than fifteen minutes so that no sooner has the announcer given the final result at one course, than the transmitter will switch over to the other, with on-course betting, by that time, in full swing.

Bets follow a pattern different from that of the morning session. They are almost invariably single selections—one horse only—rather than the multiple preferred in the morning. Rarely does selection fall upon the short-price favourite, but most frequently on horses with odds in the intermediate zone. Bets are usually 'win only', so that the entire stake, usually no less than £1, is staked on one single outcome of a 6:1 to 10:1 chance. The proprietor's books find themselves thus, by a process almost resembling the operation of Adam Smith's 'intervention of the unseen hand', without purposive action on their part, almost in perfect balance. The morning bets incline towards the multiples in which favourites are a strong preference (often runners turn into favourites by the mere fact of being chosen by the mass dailies' experts) while the afternoon crowd will largely omit these from their selections. So that loss on the one will usually be compensated for by takings on all the others, with the likelihood of a large win if a rank outsider, completely unbacked, upsets form by coming in first and against this the certainty of a heavy loss in the event of a winning accumulator bet, as well as the romping home of one of the local favourites. (Some horses, by virtue of some terminological or emotional association, will attract the support of virtually the entire community, almost in the manner of the local football team.)

Occasionally, meetings will be organized so that the races at two courses are run simultaneously. This will allow punters to back 'across the card', to link two horses for the same race at each of the meetings, in a double. This is an arrangement which is highly popular in the neighbourhood, inducing punters to deviate from their normal pattern, the single-choice bet. At other times only one single horserace meeting will be held and on such occasions the 'blower' will transmit reports on one of the afternoon sessions at one of the dogtracks. On these occasions a marked change in atmosphere and betting habits will be manifest. Dograces are timed at intervals of only fifteen minutes against the thirty minutes break between horseraces. The commentary, devoid of all refinements, will confine itself to identifying runners by no more than numbers, omitting all mention of names. The entire activity will acquire an air of immediacy, urgency, affecting the public in the form of greater intensity, excitement. This is the one occasion when punters appear to allow themselves deviation from their usual detachment, their normal habit of resisting all allures of progressive betting*—a tendency previously identified as a feature of roulette but otherwise absent from the activity we are discussing. Whilst in the case of betting support for horseracing, prestige and location of the track appear to be irrelevant, the volume of betting on the afternoon sessions on dog-tracks will considerably depend on proximity and familiarity of the track. Distant tracks such as Oxford are regarded with indifference or even hostility (H.—'lovely city, but lousy track, I lost ninety quid in one day—making a book'). Others such as Hackney Wick, Clapton, Walthamstow, or the 'sister track' at Hendon will arouse interest, attract enthusiastic support. Names of runners are familiar, their past performance well remembered, the winning traps are singled out—there exists among dograce bettors a powerful legend alleging that at each track certain traps, irrespective of runners, will produce a much larger quota of winners than would statistically be probable (a hypothesis, it must be added, unsupported by empirical evidence)—and conditions favouring certain runners are recalled as the dogs are paraded. Whilst for horseracing, the punters will be satisfied with second-hand information, such being the best they can get, their betting support for dogtracks will vary in relation to the personal knowledge and experiences which, as regular attenders, they have been able to acquire.

As the afternoon drags on, no perceptible change in atmosphere occurs. Some regulars—mainly the retired, the shiftworkers and

---

* Progressive betting refers to the tendency of seeking to reverse past losses by progressive inflation of money staked. Thus, a bettor having lost £1 on the first race, would stake sufficient to cover his initial loss plus a further sum to equal initial intended winnings on the second race, a similarly inflated sum on the next and so on. Since introduction of the latest system of distribution of Family Allowance, this practice is in racing circles sarcastically referred to as 'clawback'.

the out-of-work will remain through the entire session, others will from time to time drift back from their nearby places of work in order to note results, collect winnings and to linger long enough to renew study of form before placing fresh bets. Others will, again as a regular habit, confine their visits to the daily midday break. An atmosphere of fatigue may slowly seep over the assembly, but self-discipline, universal display of fortitude, haughty yet modest indifference to the vagaries of fate remain unbroken. Each new manifestation serves to reaffirm common values, to reinforce solidarity, to revalidate the actor's self-image, to re-emphasize honour and reputation, as expressed in Calderon's phrase '*Soy quien soy*'—I am who I am.

From this universal male ethos some, however, stand exempt. One early afternoon two swarthy, sharp-featured men marched in, distinguished in this assembly by their immaculate appearance, their brazen self-assurance and their apparent indifference to the necessity of prior study of form. They stayed in self-imposed isolation long enough for each to back two fair-priced winners in the following two races, to collect their winnings, to award a defiant last glance of nonchalant disdain to the assembly and then to depart. What place these 'hawks' occupy in the structure of the betting shop world is obscure—whether they are themselves those independent professionsals who by stealth, manipulation or bribery succeed in obtaining advance knowledge of a coup; whether they are merely the big-timer's minions, spreading their master's bets when operating a coup;* or whether they are just smarter, more astute backers possessing sufficient self-restraint to bide their time until a 'hot one' comes up—and their expert judgment in placing their bets at the very moment when their selections were offering the best odds, suggests this alternative— their bearing clearly differentiates them from the group (According to H. 'These blokes come from out of town, I guessed there

---

* When operating a coup—most frequently derived by advance fixing of a race by means of illicit doping, drugging, overfeeding, overexercising etc of intended losers, or by concealment of true form of the intended winner by display of deliberately planned slow times from all but an inner circle—it is essential to exercise discretion by not being seen or known to have placed substantial bets. Avoidance of such contingency at the same time assures the initiate of more favourable odds, as sudden influx of 'big money' instantly depresses the odds. The practice is therefore to 'spread the bet'—to split the wager into a large number of small bets to be placed by different persons at different premises.

was something up.'). Although convention demands acceptance of their bets, the bettors as outsiders are exempt from the moral code of the group. They need not make any attempt to disguise jubilation and triumph, they are able to refuse the group affective participation in victory, they are isolated, despised and feared representatives of the self-centred, exploitative, merciless world of the outside.

Nor does the moral code impose rejection or sanction on the non-integrated. The neighbourhood has a long history of absorption of immigrant groups, a long tradition as 'melting-pot'— Irish, Jews, Lascars, Poles and in recent years an assortment of Coloureds. Each group in turn has faced intolerance, opposition, and even violent rejection; but each has in turn bowed to the storm, has ducked, dodged and trimmed until, though distinct and separate, acceptance and integration has been accorded; each making, in the course of integration, its own special contribution to the common culture. Colour alone has ceased to carry any stigma; without distinction or discrimination, White and Black make their claim to public recognition. Yet lacking the privilege of being British-born, of being locally reared, the immigrant is pardoned, while on probation, ignorance of the unwritten code of strict observance of emotional neutrality, of phlegmatic gravity, of subversive submissiveness to the decrees imposed by 'Them'. Joe, a virile, young and handsome West Indian, possibly the most ardent devotee of gambling of them all, has as yet failed to absorb the norms. Unashamedly, yet with naïve courtesy, will he approach fellow punters to solicit information; without invitation will he proffer advice to the expert engrossed in his private study of form; with the sublime unconcern of the ignorant will he infringe the local taboos—the unmentionable existence of the cash nexus 'I shouldn't be losing all this money'; the conflict of interests between the two sides of the counter—'More money in your pockets'—with undisguised, animistic show of emotion will he react to the blower's account of the race—'Honey, be good to me'; with open scorn and dismay will he receive the news of his losses and with uninhibited joy will he claim his occasional winnings (which his lack of self-control itself makes rare indeed). Yet his deviance is endured with tolerance and is even subtly controlled and gradually diminished by the vaguest hints and even the occasional distinction of special praise from the unofficial leadership of the group, until nothing but colour—an unimportant detail—will distinguish him from the other members of the fraternity.

Cable Street (B.S.II)

'You have not only given up your life, all your interests, private and public, the duties of a man and a citizen, your friends (and you really had friends)—you have not only given up your objects, such as they were, all but gambling—you have even given up your memories.' (Dostoyevsky, *The Gambler*.)

In respect of physical background and facilities this betting shop, housed in the extensive ground-floor quarters of a formerly substantial commercial property, would be considered superior not only to the one previously described, but further to the majority of other betting shops in the locality. Spacious, well-ventilated and lit it provides ample elbow room for the clientele, served—this being one unit in a prosperous chain—by a manager, four counter clerks, three general clerks, a boardman and two cashiers. Nor is the external appearance of the clientele, at a superficial level at any rate, much different from that found elsewhere in the district. Apparel is perhaps a little more seedy, complexion somewhat more pallid and wan, racial intermixture more wide-flung. But these factors alone would not account for the overpowering, immediate impact of dislocation and disarray. We have entered the arena in which the ragbag of social discards, the very bottom crust of the urban proletariat, leavened by a constant minor trickle of seamen on shoreleave, have come to do their daily betting.

Dedication to the cult of gambling is intense among this group of men of whom only the very few—the local barber, the café proprietor, the cutter from the adjoining clothing factory, the gasman—follow a paid regular occupation. The rest belong to the army of workshy, of unemployables, of regular patrons of 'The Assistance', 'The Labour' and 'The Gift Shop'.* While funds

* 'The Gift Shop': term by which one or the other of the local charitable institutions is generally referred to.

permit, their home will be the local 'kip'.* When these funds have come to be exhausted, in summer it is the park bench and the all-night 'caff' in wintertime. Most of them still carry a faded photo of a mother now old and neglected, of a wife and family once loved but now no longer seen, the address of a sister whose invitation to come and stay they have been on the verge of accepting for a number of years, while others declare that their footloose ways, their terror of routine and responsibility had always stood in the way of formation of stable ties. For all of them, home or family life, as is commonly understood, does not exist. Social existence is circumscribed within the narrow circle of the 'caff', the 'boozer', the betting shop and the 'Exchange'. Sexual activity is for even the most virile and young male limited to one or another of the local 'brasses', one of the set of good-natured, ageing, dimwitted 'pros' who will, even in the course of her afternoon's off-duty visit to the betting shop answer the casual 'How 'you doing, Lil, you're looking better today' with a coquettish 'What 'you after, you greedy bastard, a quickie?'

A few will from time to time accept a few hours casual work—sweeping a yard, washing a car or two, or moving some rubble—others will eagerly volunteer their services as looker-out, as decoy or tool-carrier, as bottom-grade recruits in one of the local gang operations. Almost to a man will they, on demand, flash the Seamen's Union card now long expired when claiming to be 'just having a breather between ships'. But most will, when pressed hard, accord with the view resignedly expressed by Mike, pointing to the betting shop: 'This is my life now.'

Study of form within the accepted meaning of the term does not exist. Only spasmodically will they sidle up to the racing pages pinned against the walls and even then, more often than not, do so in order to sound one of the occupants for information and advice. Habitually selection follows by means of a peculiar form of group consultation in which emotional, irrational factors, such as 'He sounds a good'n', 'With a name like that the fucker ought to piss home', a jockey's record as to past good or bad luck—'The cunt B. owes me a win, he's let me down time after time'—or reference to odds in terms of irrelevant abstraction—

---

* 'Kip' (or doss-house): would be one of the charitable institutions for the destitute, such as the Y.M.C.A. or the Salvation Army.

'8:1, just what I need to get out of stuch'*—will predominate over all others. The groups themselves are loose and open-ended, each containing no more than two or three core members with others giving merely fringe allegiance. Resolution is fickle and even the most casual attachment to a new group before the bet is placed is likely to shatter the brittle thread of confidence, arousing fresh waves of uncertainty and doubt.

In the course of the early stages of the daily programme, spirits are high, elation general and diffuse. Forgotten are yesterday's disasters and humiliations, a new day has dawned (for most of the *habitués* literally so, when only a few will be willing to confront daylight much before midday) when lessons hard-learned will now be fully applied, when ill-luck, for so long a constant companion, will once and for all be triumphantly overcome. At last the choice is made, the bet written out and handed over—the amount staked carefully concealed from even the closest associate—the race begun. Commitment is total, involvement absolute, the 'blower's' commentary almost drowned under the continuous barrage of cheers, encouragement and bitter invective. The final result is greeted with utter despondency by the many and with jubilant rejoicing by the fortunate few. The winning ticket is triumphantly paraded round the room, the alleged amount won inflating with each presentation.

The first couple of losses can generally be sustained with resignation. Did one not, after all, at one time have the winner, only to be talked out of it by that fat, useless bastard over there? But this, one will not allow to happen again, from now on one will stick to one's choice. Though, is it safe to ignore the advice so vehemently dished out by Joe, who after all backed the 10:1 winner in the last race? On the other hand, had not the same, self-appointed prophet only the day before been reduced to spongeing round the room for a few measly snouts?† Better follow one's own devices, or might it not be best to go and have a chat with that crowd by the door? Val, over there, is usually a good judge when it comes to Irish horses, or is it in the race after that the Irish horse is entered? Tension is beginning to have its effect. Concentration, not intensive at any time, flags even further. Adhesion to group becomes ever more fitful, uncertainty as to

* Stuch: trouble.　　　　　　　† Snout: cigarette.

whom to heed or to approach ever more perplexing, recall of recent near misses too painful to bear. Emotional strain of such magnitude cannot allow itself to be contained in the couple of paltry quid one has, in actuality, been able to afford to lose. With each moment of anguish and disappointment the losses recounted will expand until their imaginary volume will reflect the actual pain felt at the inescapable reality of near-empty pockets. Spatial stability becomes intolerable, the urge to be elsewhere, overwhelming. The ritual circuit from betting shop to public lavatory on the street island, thence to the 'caff' at the opposite street corner for a hastily swallowed cup of sweet tea and then back to the betting shop, of even briefer duration. Tempers, not over-courtly at any time, fray even further. Outbreaks of the most tempestuous, violent verbal aggression which, contrary to the bystander's firm expectation invariably stop short of the implied and anticipated physical manifestation, become more frequent and inflamed.

Finally, with two races still to be run, at the very moment when luck was beginning to turn, when a 'certainty' was just begging to be backed, pockets are empty, even of the reserve earmarked for the night's 'kip'. But whom to 'blab' for a sub? Is it to be Alf who's been coining it all afternoon, or Reg whom one rescued from a similar tragic predicament only a couple of days ago, or should it be Jock, still flush with the loot of last Tuesday's screw? Alf has by now surrounded himself with an admiring entourage of subsidized hangers-on. Reg's indifference to reciprocity is notorious, so the choice finally falls on Jock who, responding to the request, couched within the most ingratiating terms normatively permitted—'For God's sake, lend us a couple of quid, man'—with the anticipated barrage of bragging invective—'You lousy sod, you think I stick my neck out to keep you? I keep telling you there's money to be made, but you prefer to spend your last few coppers standing in the boozer with your fucking arse hanging half-way out of your pants'—will at least fork out the half-quid for the next race. Alas, the 'certainty' will, once more, turn out to be another disappointed hope.

Is the bitter taste of defeat the one and only sensation experienced in this world? Today Alf's luck has been in. By the time of the last race he has backed four winners out of eight, managing to

amass the sum of twenty-four pounds. Proudly, having bellowed a
final vituperative 'That'll set you fucking bastards back a bit' at
the cashier, does he proclaim to his entourage 'Fifty quid I've
taken off these bastards today, shows you it's bloody guts that
counts in this game.' With princely grandeur does he hand a
pound note to each of his principal lieutenants before marching
at the head of his troop proudly into the boozer, there to command drinks all round, as befits the 'King for the Day'. Yesterday's disappointments and defeats have passed into oblivion,
tomorrow's loneliness and frustration now seem a long way off. A
few rounds of drinks and the entire group has, however tran-
siently, achieved the transformation, passing from the camp of
the despised and the vanquished into the world of the victorious
masters.

Is there no way out from this universe of disinheritance?
Familiar faces would suddenly disappear without trace, inquiries
eliciting no more than a vague 'Might 'ave taken unwell or
something—I'd better look 'im up tonight' (an undertaking not
meant for implementation), to be followed on re-inquiry by an
even vaguer 'He's got folks up north, reckon that's where he's
gone'. By that time the few personal traces would be wiped out,
direct inquiries at different quarters would end up in a blank.
Some, true to Jock's philosophy, 'I need something done to me
inside, been suffering with me stomach for years, got a doctor's
letter an' all. But I'm buggered if I go in till winter come, let the
bastards feed me when it's cold outside' might have retired into
hospital, others into the 'nick',* yet others might just quietly have
faded away. Mike was the exception. Still in his early thirties,
powerfully built, dynamic and virile, of resonant voice, his
demeanour was more suggestive of the Killarney plains that of
the backwaters of Cable Street. Yet the pitiful state of his clothes,
the glaring early symptoms of malnutrition, and above all the
obsessional vagaries of his betting behaviour marked him out as
inevitable candidate for the vortex of disintegration. It was he
who had described the betting shop as 'this is my world now'.
One day, suddenly, he had disappeared, none knew his where-
abouts. A few days later, by chance, I ran into him a few turnings
away, carrying a dozen or so shirt-boxes tied together. He had

* Nick: prison.

visibly smartened up, his suit was clean, his shoes polished. 'A friend of mine has lent me a hundred quid to get back on my feet. I'm starting up in business, wish me luck', was all he had time to say. Cynically I expected him back in the cauldron within a few days. Yet until the end of my stay he had not reappeared. Shortly before I left, one of the few remaining old-timers remarked 'Saw that chum of yours, Mike, the other day, making good, looking busy and rushed. Had not time to talk to him!' This information, however, aroused no interest in the assembly. Another Mike had, after all, for some time now been filling the vacant place.

Mile End (B.S.III)

THE FRUSTRATED ENTREPRENEURS

Both as a matter of principle and institutionally, modern society tends to enlarge the domain of regulated competition, or merit, at the expense of birth and inheritance, or chance, an evolution which is reasonable, just and favourable to the most capable . . . From this arises the nostalgia for crossroads, for immediate solutions offering the possibility of unexpected success, even if only relative. Chance is courted because hard work and personal qualifications are powerless to bring such success about.

In addition many people do not count on receiving anything much on personal merit alone. They are well aware that others are abler, more skilful, stronger, more intelligent, more hardworking, more ambitious, healthier, have a better memory, and are more pleasing and persuasive than they are. Also being conscious of their inferiority, they do not trust in exact, impartial, and rational comparisons. They therefore turn to chance, seeking a discriminatory principle that might be kinder to them. Since they despair of winning in the contests of *agon*, they resort to lotteries or only games of chance, where even the least endowed, stupidest and, most handicapped, the unskilled and the idolent may be equal to the most resourceful and perspicacious as a result of the miraculous blindness of a new kind of justice.[12]

Gambling as work is not by any means an easy occupation.[13] In betting on horseracing an intricate network of complicated variables has to be taken into account: the animal's performance during the present as well as in past seasons; the cycle of fluctuations of form over time, over a range of distances and at a variety of courses; the weight carried, the ground and weather conditions, favourability of starting orders; the jockey's performances at various times, in various races as well as for a variety of stables; the trainer's record and his incentive to do well in a particular race. The relative merit of each of these factors has to be assessed, and their combined value, as reflected in the particular odds, evaluated against those of the other runners.

To these tasks our present subjects, whatever their degree of eventual success, are no strangers. Their discussion is knowledgeable, expert and informed, ranging from the commonplace —'Never seen 'im do well when the going is soft'; 'Too short a distance for a strong finisher like him'—to the more complex— 'D. hasn't ridden three winners on the trot for more than two seasons'; 'Give 'im a few pounds, and he never fails to fade a couple of furlongs from home'—extending even to speculative inference as to manipulation—'Stands to reason they're holding him back for a coup, he's in there just for an outing'—and at times not even excluding the animal's sexual peculiarities—'Last three times they made 'im hot favourite, he didn't come nowhere. They just could not make it out. At last they found the dirty bastard used to rub 'imself off on the box. Mind you with a tool like he's got, you can hardly blame him. Saw 'im on the Telly running at Sandown a week last Saturday. Blimey, I said to Morry, we can't bloody lose, we've got five legs running for us.'

Such reflections however, casually delivered to the assembly at large, supply no more than the small change of daily intercourse. Internal competition for recognition as fearless speculator, as ruthless major operator, as resourceful pseudo-entrepreneur provide the major substance. Blatant self-confidence to rise to the top in merciless confrontation, to beat the market by manipulative skills, to weather unflinchingly temporary reverses, neither to grant nor expect quarter, to transact at all times on the most propitious terms, to outflank and outwit one's competitive rivals form the major currency of exchange. In this setting, selection is firm and abrupt, once made is assumed to be obvious and incontestable. 'Kirkdale's the fucking winner in the next race, there isn't another horse to touch 'im,' Sid announces authoritatively, affirming his choice by demonstratively backing it with a fiver. His challenge is at once taken up and answered in kind. 'You must be nuts putting your money on this load of crap,' Joe counters, 'you wouldn't catch me backing that cripple against my bloody canary; Dagenham Piper will leave 'im at the post.' Ken follows with his public declaration: 'The two of you don't know the first thing about racing; give me Persian Warrior any day. They must be off their rockers offering 'im at sevens.'* In this manner it goes on around the room, each major contestant making his public affirmation and substantiating his choice with the appropriate capital investment while denigrating his rivals' wares in the process. Even coincidence of choice does no more than mute conflict of interests—'You made the right choice for the wrong reason; lucky you find yourself in good company'—though competition is confined to status equals and no attempt is made to vanquish one's status inferiors.

Discernment of the most favourable moment for placing one's bet is almost uncannily precise and uniformly taken for granted. Failure to seize the best possible terms is subject to instant reprisal—'If I ever open a book,† you come and bet with me all day long. To punters like you they ought to give a gold watch every six months'—though denial of guilt will, with no lesser vehemence, be pleaded in mitigation—'They're betting like maniacs in this race, half of them don't know what they're doing. In a race like that, believe me, you're better off knowing fuck-all about the game.' Convention dictates strictest affective neutrality in commercial transaction. Relations with the staff are strictly instrumental, limited to the business at hand, devoid of personal context, though true to the motto 'Never trust Nobody', each betting slip will be minutely scrutinized for possible defalcation. Whereas within the group, conflict is universal, total and brutally severe, in contact with other groups, particularly social inferiors, relaxation and even a mild degree of fraternization—'After all, if I can't do you a good turn once in a while, I might as well be dead' after a successful tip—is permitted.

The blower's race commentary evokes neither the stoic calm found in Bethnal Green (B.S.I), nor the frantic emotional turmoil noted in Cable Street (B.S.II), but typically produces a series of comments suggestive of physical presence at the race:

* Refers to odds of seven to one.
† Become a bookmaker.

'That's the boy, let the others set the pace'; 'Don't let these bastards pin you on the rails, use your bloody whip, boy'. Successful progress of one's mount elicits triumphant acclaim— 'What did I tell you, there isn't another to touch 'im in this race', while anguish at failure even to hear one's choice mentioned allows itself to be dissipated by 'This stupid bastard don't know the first thing about announcing; my little boy could do a bloody sight better'. Nor need even final defeat necessarily deflate complacent self-confidence—'I'd like to know what they've been feeding the poor fucker all the week, more likely than not they've been feeding 'im on treacle tart'—and even a prolonged series of setbacks can be absorbed—'These crooked bastards, if they don't stop soon the whole bloody game will be ruined. Even the starter must be getting his whack.'

It is not indeed the degree of financial success, but masterful display of requisite commercial skills which establish status and prestige. Volume of stakes—though within the 'top league' the fiver is the near-universal norm—are at all times variable and even occasional total abstention—'Never touch a Selling Plate; they're no more than a bookie's bloody benefit'—conventionally sanctioned. Only collapse of morale will spell defeat and expulsion. From the early manifestations—expressed by 'I don't mind taking a knock, but this is positively diabolical'—to the final surrender couched in terms such as 'If I don't stop soon, I'll go mechula'.* Of the two available means of capitulation, total withdrawal—'I go and see what's going on next door;† the air in here stinks'—is the less reputable (provoking a jeering 'What's the matter, Sid, you pooped your pants, you're in such a hurry to get out'); while the alternative of 'agonized reappraisal'—self-relegation into the lower spheres—is more highly respected, occasionally even arousing a rare, untypical flash of compassion— 'You'll be better off, Jack, betting so you don't get skinned; you're a bloody fool staking it big, when you know fuck-all about the game.' Reception into the lower regions after an introductory hostile phase—'Just because you can flash a few fivers you think you're a Ganzer Macher'‡—to be accorded with the appropriate

---

* Mechula: Bankrupt.
† 'Next door' refers to the adjoining gaming club.
‡ Ganzer Macher: Big Shot, Big Operator.

admixture of rancour and bitterness—'Once a Nebbich, always a Nebbich.'*

Though by no means explicit or formalized, the system of status-division is firmly entrenched and might be classified in the following manner (in descending order of ranking):

(1) The tycoons: the major, independent entrepreneurs, haughty, fearless and tough; outranking those below not merely in terms of capital invested, but also in assertiveness, voluntary risk exposure and intensity of internecine rivalry; exclusive, indifferent to public opinion.

(2) The minor entrepreneurs: emulative of and deferential to tycoons; status conscious, contemptuous of masses—'This place is getting so packed, you can't hear yourself think.'

(3) The artisans: modest, moderate and adaptable, yet inclined to sudden excesses and extravagances; resentful of patronage— 'You go and bet with your own mob, we aren't looking for none of your etzes';† internally co-operative through willingness to exchange knowledge and information, but strictly observant of the subcultural taboo concerning financial autonomy 'Never borrow, never lend'.

(4) The Schnorrers:‡ the pauperized mob, able to bet only meagrely and intermittently, soliciting largesse, avidly seeking patrons whom they will loyally and submissively serve—'Go get me twenty Seniors, Nifty'; 'Put me a fiver to win Bright Boy and mind you bring back the news of the last race'. Service to patrons is prompt and exclusive, even to the extent of being prepared to out-face the patron's status equals (On return Nifty disclaimed knowledge of the fate of runners other than his patron's and declared to Len, who was insistent, that he had not seen the Board. 'What's the matter,' Len challenged, 'you wearing dark fucking glasses?' 'Send your own man, if you want them that badly,' Nifty replied, 'you don't give me no orders').

(5) The Non-Competers:
(a) The Occasionals
(b) The Young on Probation
(c) The Veterans: exempt from active competitive participation and ranked according to criteria of sagacity and of being reposi-

---

* Once a Nebbich, always a Nebbich: Once a Nobody, always a Nobody.
† Etzes: Advice.   ‡ Schnorrers: Beggars, Indigents.

tories of lore—'He started as hurdler back in '61, then had a couple of seasons over in France; then they brought him back and sold 'im for fifteen hundred guineas up in Doncaster. You ask me, he's never been no good to nobody!'

Mobility, frequent and continuous in both directions was, as a rule, unistageal though untypical cases of ballistic advance were not unknown.* In the event of promotion, integration depended largely on betting in acceptable denominations, but to a no lesser extent on polished display of the appropriate 'class' characteristics. Age discrimination did not exist, subject only to norm-conformity the young were accorded complete equality, though deviation was instantly reprimanded—'Don't get in the way of people who come here to bet. If you want to play games, go back to the fucking playground' to a small bunch of youngsters (20–24 years) who were noisily mimicking jockeys' actions in course of the race commentary. The betting shop, recognized as the major field of action, accordingly achieved status precedence over the 'Spieler'.† Ranking earned in the betting shop automatically transferred into the 'Spieler', the small minority refusing to take part in activity inside the betting shop only able to acquire rank when combining extraordinary skill at the card table, with complete denial of the validity of the alternative—'I suppose if you ain't got the sense to play a decent game, you got no choice but to do your money on the gee-gees.' The fiercest antagonisms, the crassest status inequalities, however, ceased to count once the boundaries of the betting world had been left behind. Immediately they entered the outside world, affectionate amity and undifferentiated mutuality is re-established between old friends, the status values of the external world re-acquire total recognition.

A FRIENDLY GAME OF HEARTS

As usual, the air was thick with noise, smoke and perspiration; as usual all the five tables in the 'Spieler' had become occupied by

---

* Len, a relative newcomer, no more than twenty-two, achieved meteoric integration into the élite by matching them not only in willingness to hazard, but by outflanking them even in assertiveness: 'You old fogeys get in a fucking rut spending your life in this stuffy hole; it's not what you know, it's who you know what counts in this world' he insisted only a few days after admission.

† Spieler: Gaming Club; usually providing card games.

two-thirty in the afternoon; as usual crowds of kibitzers* were surrounding the tables, their voices drowning each other's in the post-mortems following the play of each hand. But contrary to custom the two high-stake tables directly to the left of the entrance were almost totally bereft of spectators. All action seemed concentrated on Table Four where, moreover, the despised and derided game of 'Hearts' was being played ('I'd rather go in the khazi and wank myself off' Paul had contemptuously replied to an invitation to make up a four in that game only a few days earlier) —and even then for no more than paltry ten pence stakes. The game of Hearts, though simple and mechanical, only slightly upgraded from the identically named nursery game, consists in broad outline in throwing one's opponents unfavourably designated cards—all cards in the heart suit scoring minus one and any one of the four queens scoring minus six for the final holder—while trying, in the course of following suit, to achieve a minimum final holding of unfavourable cards. The winner of each hand is the player with the lowest ultimate minus score. In spite of its simplicity however this game allows considerable scope for the exercise of flair and ingenuity, while, at the same time, providing an ideal vehicle for the enactment of personal feuds.

At first sight the composition of the quartet seemed anything but remarkable. None of the players could, by even the remotest stretch of imagination, be classed within the top levels of the club hierarchy. Both Bernard and Sid were as relatively infrequent attenders only marginally integrated, being by virtue of their

---

* Kibitz: Spectator. This term, in common with the other Yiddish terms quoted in the course of this Section, does not lend itself to literal translation into English, a language which lacks the character of duality, the simultaneous sweet-sour connotations embodied into the Yiddish. Thus the word 'Kibitz', though implying spectator, carries in its original meaning the concept of right of admission, of comment and involvement, possibly even extending to the possession of technical skill superior to that of the participants. 'Schnorrer' (Beggar) suggests a legitimate claim to sustenance and support as well as the poor man as caricature of the wealthy. 'Mechula' (Bankrupt) denotes not only the loss of resources, but suggests also the shedding of the yoke of duty and of responsibility, while 'Etzes' (Advice) carries with it the implication of advice unwanted and unwelcome, as expressed in the saying 'Mit deine Etzes bin ich versorgt' (With advice like yours I have more than my fill). Little wonder that the Yiddish language has not only survived, but has achieved deep penetration into the lingo of the world of the fringe.

lighthearted attitude to the activities at hand, anyhow marked as potential deviants. Cecil—immaculately dressed, articulate, informed, prosperous and successful—one of the very few members whose internal aspirations matched his external existence as wholesale merchant, and yet one of those incongruous individuals who despite their public worth, by virtue of some minor character irregularity (in Cecil's case a powerful inclination toward self-pity and a tendency to crack under verbal assault) find themselves singled out as scapegoats and butts. Finally there was Joe—pugnacious, ebullient, irrepressible, quick-witted, and sharp-tongued; the perennial Kibitz, forever disrespecting the spectator's first commandment, 'Kibitz keep stumm';* not only constantly interrupting play, but proffering unsolicited advice having seen more than one player's cards; though admired for his tenacity and feared for his refusal to acknowledge the superior power of overwhelming odds, universally despised and detested, the constant target of vilification and abuse—which however seemed only to reinforce his determination to challenge all-comers all of the time.

It was however the status and character of the audience, rather than that of the players which unmistakably stamped this as a special occasion. Joe, having for once discarded the kibitzer's role and exposed himself as performer, found himself flanked by Ken and Sam, the Club's principal 'scribes'—members who though desisting from competition for the supreme seats of power nevertheless, as immaculate performers and infallible interpreters of the code, were uniformly awarded top-hierarchy recognition. Bernard had the young, utterly fearless and dedicated Phil at his side, who at an early stage of the proceedings had insured against status loss by making it smilingly clear that 'me and Bernard are partners in the penny-farthing game'. Sid, who had initially attracted only meagre attention was soon, by virtue of adroit play, by liberal dispensation of cigarettes ('As long as I'm winning, you fellows help yourself to my snouts; as soon as I lose, they go back in my pocket') finding himself ringed with a fair-sized crowd of supporters, being, in the process even granted Hymie's, the old-guard's approval—'You played this hand like a master, Sid, even

---

* 'Kibitz keep stumm': Spectator keep your mouth shut (Do not divulge privileged information).

I couldn't have done no better.' Cecil was, as usual, surrounded by an unruly, gleeful mass of observers, responding to his efforts at self-justification ('What a fucking hand I had dealt me, it needed a miracle not to end up with the whole lot'), his appeals for affirmation of particular ill-luck ('There isn't another fellow in the whole wide world who gets the shocking cards I do') with malicious derision, not even bothering, while hands were in actual play, to tone down their debate as to relative merits of the runners in the race to come; even occupants of other tables permitting themselves in Cecil's case to disregard the established right of turbulence at the conclusion of each hand, spitefully throwing across a 'Why don't you stop moaning, Baldie, you give me a fucking pain in the neck'. Not that Cecil—it was after all he who had enriched the language with the original 'I piss on you all the way to the bank', explosively released on a defeated opponent in one of his rare moments of triumph—was a sluggard in the art of verbal counterattack. With phrases such as 'If you rotten shysters held my hands, we would have had three heart attacks round the table by now' and 'Cut the inquest, let's get on with the game; the way you fellows hold an investigation, anyone would think this is the Board of Trade', he did his share to enliven the fray.

It was Joe, however, who acted the central figure in the drama being performed. His guardians' earlier remarks (Sam: 'You shoot your mouth off all day long, but to watch you play gives me a pain in the arse' to which Ken mock-placatingly added: 'Leave 'im alone, Sam, he don't know no better') he had been able to parry without bother ('Who's forcing you to watch; if you don't like my play, why don't you go back to the shop and do the rest of your money?'). By now the undisguised malice of his style—'There's a little beauty for you, pity I don't have a dozen more to bung on you'—the open scorn towards his opposition—'It's a fucking shame to take your money, fellows'—had virtually united the other three in common cause. But what was even harder to bear was the mounting evidence of disparity between words and deed, his frequent need to supplement original sources by drawing upon reserves (Calling forth a 'That's the boy, Joe, circulate them before they go bloody mouldy'). With reluctance he had already seen himself compelled to abandon his natural flamboyant, freebooting manner in favour of greater caution and discretion. With an exasperated 'If I have to watch your game much longer, I'll have a nervous breakdown', Ken had by now ostentatiously taken up a position behind Cecil's chair, whose game he was in a short while masterminding. Joe's plaintive lament, 'Three against one, you call this fair play', had instantaneously found itself squashed by Sam's adjudication: 'Look who's calling for fair play. Anyway everyone's playing for themselves as they ought to be doing. The way you played that last hand, you turned the 60:40 chance you had into a 40:60.' Emboldened by the enrolment of the élite to his cause, Cecil suggested sarcastically 'If you apply to my secretary, I'd give you lessons on how to play the game at two guineas an hour; if I could trust a twister like you to pay'; and Sid observed, 'Pity we couldn't get a decent fourth, we might have had a proper game.'

Hymie's propitiating 'I thought this was going to be a friendly game of hearts; the way it's turned out it's getting worse than an Irish wedding' had already a while ago fallen on deaf ears. By now the attention paid to the game, the heat and controversy it was arousing was beginning to resemble the pitch, as a rule, reserved for only the 'Cup-Finals'.* Playing under maximum pressure and against natural inclinations a game cautious and constrained, Joe's game was beginning to show cracks. Hesitation, doubt and even regard for public opinion were becoming apparent. At last the fatal slip occurred; Joe covered a card led towards him with

* Among the card-playing hierarchy, an unrecorded, yet semi-official ranking-order existed. This was of sufficient elasticity to cope with minor fluctuations such as normal single-rung ascent as a result of a series of victories. At times however, after a period of relative prolonged stability, dissent would arise, usually provoked by nothing more than a status dispute between two medium-ranked members. Confrontation could not be avoided and resolution became possible only by 'Duel'—victory to be conceded to the winner of three or more out of five two-handed games. Yet in spite of the fact that protocol for the resolution of such conflict did exist, one single act of challenge and confrontation would, more often than not, spark off a chain reaction, finally engulfing even the top levels of the hierarchy. A series of play-offs would result (though challenge was by convention restricted to players directly above oneself in the ranking-order) and the final play-off was termed 'Cup-Final'. By that time allegiances had hardened and were expected to be backed with appropriate stakes. Harry who acted as bookmaker on these occasions would set the odds (margins needed to be most carefully assessed and were subject to constant fluctuations as the games progressed) and he would directly challenge supporters ('I thought you were a pal of Dave's, where's your stake') to translate allegiance into action.

an honour-card when the correct percentage play would have been to duck. Immediate uproar ensued the moment the transgression was discovered. With a final agonized 'That's the worst fucking hand I have ever seen played in my life. Do me a favour, Joe, keep away from the tables', Sam abandoned the scene, adding 'If it's a choice between the two, I'd rather have you kibitz me than have to watch you murder the cards'. Almost at once Bernard suggested 'Don't you think it's time we packed it in, the game is beginning to get on my fucking tits'. Directly following, the game folded up; the crowds dispersed, Cecil and Ken leaving the table with arms on each other's shoulders ('Just shows you, if I get my share of cards, I can teach the whole gang a trick or two'). Shortly after, Joe's raucous voice could once more be heard leading the kibitzers' chorus. Not without trace of kindness Phil, who had meanwhile resumed his more normal role as player, leant across his shoulder: 'Do us a favour, Joe, give us a bit of a break; we've heard nothing but your lousy voice all afternoon as it is.'

Summary

The principal findings contained in the foregoing sections may best be tabulated in the following manner:

STRUCTURE

	Roman Road (B.S.I)	Cable Street (B.S.II)	Mile End (B.S.III)
(i) *Selection Preference*			
(1) Method of choice	Deliberate, informed, personal but co-operative; irrelevance of favourite/non-favourite	Chaotic, confused, emotional; antipathy towards favourite	Expert, authoritative, resolute, investment-minded, pro-favourite

	Roman Road (B.S.I)	Cable Street (B.S.II)	Mile End (B.S.III)
(2) Emotional attitude to event	Indifferent, detached, absence of overt signs of involvement	Total; progressing from gay to desperate; compulsive	Minimal; Participants firmly convinced of supremacy of personal critical judgement
(3) Level of expertise	Reasonable, rational prepared to learn from experience and from each other	Minimal, irrational, responsive to rumour and hearsay	Maximal, absolute, individualistic, averse to counsel by others
(ii) *Betting Performance*			
(1) Response to win	Controlled; communal participation in triumph	Orgiastic, prestige conferring, boastful exaggeration of sum; share of cash proceeds but not of prestige	Anticipated outcome of event; conducive to upward mobility
(2) Response to loss	Anticipated, humorous; disinclination to progressive betting	Rebellious though regarded as inevitable; tension creating and leading to escalation of stakes if funds permit	Protestation of fraudulent conspiracy; affirmation of quality of choice; status destructive if compelling withdrawal or reduction of stakes
(iii) *Social Arrangements*			
(1) Rank order	Egalitarian, non-differentiated *Gemeinschaft*;[14] emphasis on character and steadfastness in adversity	Anarchistic disorder; short lived supremacy of successful	Hierarchical, mobile; irrelevance of *Gesellschaft*;[14] irrelevance of external status

	Roman Road (B.S.I)	Cable Street (B.S.II)	Mile End (B.S.III)
(2) Personal Relation-ships	Mutually protective; universalistic[15]	Tense, imper-sonal; verbally aggressive; financial mutuality only	Competitive, merciless; antagonistic; particularistic[15]
(3) Clients v. Manage-ment	Mutually reinforcing; fraternal; diffuse[16]	Hostile; conceived in terms of direct confrontation	Impersonal; service oriented
(4) Male-Female	Sex-differentiation and avoidance; male hegemony	Female confined to sex role	Undifferentiated; ranked according to betting performance and achievement
(5) Elderly	Availability of self-selection of operation in male or female sphere	Regarded as inferior, typically exhibiting visible signs of dis-integration	Award of honor-ary elite rank to patriarch steeped in knowledge and folklore
(6) Young	Tolerant, preparedness to instruct and initiate	Preponderance of young as norm-setters	Equality if mature i.e. achievement oriented; contemptuous of playful
(7) Outsiders	Tolerant receptive; readiness to socialize and to integrate	Unpredictable; wavering from acceptance to relegation as scapegoats	Integration subject to norm-conformity and to hierarchy subordination
(iv) *Value System*			
(1) Ideology	Communality, mutuality, co-operation; respect for self-discipline, fearlessness, order and tradition;	Nihilistic, severed from social main-stream; self-deprecating, passive, failure-conditioned;	Materialistic individualistic, utilitarian; 'jungle philo-sophy' of ruthlessness, survival of the fittest,

	Roman Road (B.S.I)	Cable Street (B.S.II)	Mile End (B.S.III)
	denial of competitiveness, self advancement and personal pride	deriving from renewed failure experience confirmation of personal inferiority and consequent unwisdom of social participation	mercilessness towards defeated opponent; hierarchical, prestige conscious, mobility oriented
(2) Social control	Isolation by withdrawal of integration	Absent	Communal sanction by imposition of failure situation
(3) Ideal image	Autonomous, co-operative 'working man'; free spender	Amoral success, big time sponger non-violent crook able to subvert social order	Successful entrepreneur in external world, selfmade businessman
(4) Negative image	Bad loser; compulsive gambler	Wage-slave; conformist	'Softie', individual lacking assertiveness and push

FUNCTIONS

(i) *Personal* (All: B.S.I, B.S.II, B.S.III)

Facilities for exercise of decision taking, judgement and choice. Socially valued subject matter of shared knowledge and expertise. Acquisition of familiarity with management of complex set of variables; system building as regular habit available for transference into other life situations.

Availability of choice from large range of standardized, institutionally sanctioned roles (e.g. Sage, Jester, Barrackroom Lawyer, Philosopher, Neophyte, Rebel, Greek Chorus), providing outlet for fantasy roles, vicarious experience and affording opportunities for cultivation of talent and development of virtuosity.

(ii) *Social*

(*a*) *Roman Road* (B.S.I) Affirmation of fraternal co-operative community; socialization and integration of newcomer; arena in which working-class subcultural values of mutuality and universality supersede external values of competition and achievement. Self-contained universe of order and stability, acting as insulator against rapid, externally imposed and incomprehensible change in outside world.

(*b*) *Cable Street* (B.S.II) Self-created retreat in which the disinherited, the social misfit can vent revenge upon his oppressors by denial of validity of external value systems, by desecration of the principal symbolic 'deity'—money. Sublimated experience of participation and thrill by group withdrawn from social system.

(*c*) *Mile End* (B.S.III) Creation of fantasy world of capitalist system *en miniature*. Exercise of manipulative and entrepreneurial skills by individuals deprived of facilities for expression of those, due to life situation or to personal flaws, yet dominated by ideology of virtue of competitive struggle and achievement. Denial of personal insignificance and failure subject to competence within substitute systems.

The following conclusions may be drawn about the hypotheses posed within the initial section:

(1) No less than the public at large, the actors themselves (i.e. those who take part in gambling) define the activity in economic terms. It would be impossible to determine whether the actors' self-definition is the result of the concepts *a priori* imposed upon the activity by the external culture, or whether the public's definition derives from the interpretation put upon the activity by the actors themselves (which is the cause and which the effect?). It does, however, seem clear that although the economic factor is, in actuality, only one among a number of others, it is the one factor which all gambling situations have in common and it is accordingly, being representative of every situation, the one which is nominated as being dominant or even exclusive, whereas in actuality it may be no more than secondary or even subsidiary.

The actors are by no means ignorant of, or indifferent to, the fact of the balance of financial odds being in favour of the management and the commercial organizers of the activity. They are fully aware that, over a sufficient period and in respect of a sufficient number of transactions, their losses *in toto* will exceed their winnings. Deriving, however, from this activity a variety of non-pecuniary satisfactions, otherwise totally unattainable or available elsewhere only at a higher cost, they enter the gambling situation willingly, paying an economic price for non-pecuniary satisfactions. In these terms, participation in the activity of gambling is neither an irrational appeal to blind chance, nor individually or socially damaging and disruptive.

(2) The empirical material overwhelmingly suggests that the institution of the betting shop has undergone a qualitative transformation. Having been originally created as a purely 'Operative Institution'—one whose duties and functions are clearly enunciated and unique, confined in this instance to the single economic performance contained in the activity concerned with the placing and taking of bets—it has come to be transformed into a 'Regulative Institution'—one fulfilling a manifold variety of functions and providing for a multitude of needs.[17] Although it would be naïve to expect a permanent and on-going institution in which people over a considerable period of time regularly interact to confine itself rigidly to the exact terms of its charter and not, after a while, to acquire such secondary features as channels of interaction amongst the personnel and the public, as well as the establishment of specific sets of norms, customs and etiquette, it would, on the basis of the adduced evidence, seem safe to conclude that:

(*a*) Gambling as the action pattern it is today did, by and large, exist prior to the institution of the betting shop;

(*b*) the action pattern acted upon the institution and not the other way round; in other words, it was gambling which transformed the institution of the betting shop and not the institution of the betting shop which changed the nature, and in all probability the extent, of gambling;

(*c*) the containment of the action pattern, previously disparate and diffuse, as well as the effect of the institution *per se* upon the action pattern, is likely to have led to a considerable degree of regularization and routinization of gambling, consequences which are considered invariably to produce control and restraint to a greater and an increasing extent.

(3) Considerable sections of the total community are, by virtue of the prevailing social arrangements or in view of their personal shortcomings, denied attainment of the ends proclaimed as most valuable and desirable by those in moral authority. Having, however, as a result of the socialization process, internalized affective orientation towards the normatively prescribed means as well as ends, they are reluctant to resort to non-legitimated means in the interest of the attainment of socially elevated ends.[18] For these individuals the gambling situation provides the perfect shadow system, within which retreat from the external failure situation is achieved and where, in a circumscribed and regulated setting, a 'miniature version' of the external value system can effectively, by reciprocal subscription to the common code, be acted out and can be made, by the process of acting out, to serve as a sublimation of the 'real thing'. Such acting out in a self-created fantasy setting will not only provide communal solidarity, but will for the participants provide scope for the development of personality and for more effective modes of transaction with the external environment.

(4) In the course of participant observation inside three different institutions within a limited locality and a relatively homogeneous social environment, widely divergent sets of attitudes and behaviour in relation to the activity of gambling were found to prevail. This would suggest that gambling means many things to many people and that sociological concepts of type-situations postulating situational affinity, in which different sets of situational needs and values prevail, rather than in terms of massive, undifferentiated subcultural groups, may more effectively reflect social reality.[19]

However, in all cases it was found that regular interaction within the group does reinforce group cohesion as well as affirm the individual's personal system of values. The betting shop was found to be a vehicle for social control imposed by a variety of means; furthermore, in each of the places observed, regularized and institutionalized means of socialization of recruits were found to exist.

Notes

1. See for instance Booth, C. (1902); Bott, E. (1959); Harris, C. (1927); London, J. (1903); Mayhew, H. (1851); Robb, J. H. (1954); Young, M. and Willmott, P. (1957).
2. See Downes, D. M., *Delinquent Subcultures in East London*, unpublished Ph.D. Thesis, London, 1964, pp. 224–5.

   See further the *Observer*, 21 August 1960: 'The western edge of the Borough of Stepney, immediately east of the City of London and the Tower, has got itself a bad reputation. The Cable Street and Spitalfields areas were badly bombed, and much of the housing there is still ruinous and unsanitary. In this vacuum, from which much of the pre-war population has moved away, people from all parts of the Commonwealth—West African, Pakistani, Maltese, especially congregate . . . There are drinking-clubs, all-night cafes, which are the headquarters of prostitution, thefts, fighting, the drug trade and organised gambling.'
3. The relationship between Jewish religious dogma, Jewish national character, Jewish entrepreneurship and Modern Capitalism has been analysed and described in Werner Sombart, *The Jews and Modern Capitalism*, T. Fisher Unwin (London 1913).
4. See note 1 above.
5. See particularly Burn, W. L. (1964) *The Age of Equipose*, London; Bott, E. (1955) 'Urban Families: Conjugal Roles and Networks', *Human Relations*, VIII (4); Self, P. J. O. (1960) 'Voluntary Organisations in Bethnal Green', in Bourdillon, A. F. G. (ed.) *Voluntary Social Services*.
6. See Mayhew, H. (1851) p. 46: 'It would be difficult to find in the whole of this numerous class a youngster who is not—what may be safely called—a desperate gambler. At the age of fourteen this love of play first comes upon the lad, and from that time until he is thirty or so, not a Sunday passes but he is at his stand on the gambling ground.' Although this refers to a specific group of the urban proletariat—the costermongers—there is no reason to believe that their habits were, within their environment, unusual. See also Chaloner and Henderson (1956) p. 855.
7. See Bendix, R. (1964) *Nation-Building and Citizenship*, New York: John Wiley, p. 44.

   '. . . such non-cooperation merges on a second type of social unrest, which Professor E. J. Hobsbawm has characterised as Social Banditry. In contrast to millenial radicalism . . . this is a fundamentally secular and conservative response to physically superior powers, which are conceived as alien interference with an established way of life.' From E. J. Hobsbawm, *Social Bandits and Primitive Rebels*, The Free Press, Glencoe, pp. 57–92.

8. In an unpublished manuscript entitled *The Neighbourhood Bookmaker Entrepreneur and Mobility Model* the author, Robert D. Perruci, describes how, in an ethnically underprivileged slum neighbourhood, the bookmaker as person provides a success model as well as means of social mobility to those who will attach themselves to him. His domination of the local agents of law-enforcement, universally presumed to be on his payroll, lends particular glamour to his operations.

9. See Zola, I. K. (1963).

10. It must be added that no direct information as to the proportion of these bets in which wives act merely as their husbands' messengers is to hand. Such practice, if widely prevailing would serve to undermine some of the conclusions of male–female differentiation. However, personal observation, examination of handwriting on the betting slips, and particularly the virtual uniformity in type of bet in the course of the morning session inclines one to the belief that the greater majority of these bets originate from the person placing it, the woman.

11. The majority of dailies and particularly the mid-morning editions of the evening papers, report in intricate detail, by use of a sophisticated set of symbols, totally meaningless to the non-initiated, particulars of past performances, weight carried, jockey, trap order, starting odds, ground conditions, class of opposition, performance against present competitors, placing in recent outings, weight carried in present race, anticipated starting odds, jockey's record and finally in many cases a probability rating for the present race, an amalgam of all the various factors weighted according to a particular expert's evaluation.

12. See Caillois, R. (1962) p. 114. Caillois classifies games which, according to his definition, have functions and significance well beyond the immediate, under the following categories: (*a*) *Agon*—Competition, (*b*) *Alea*—Chance, (*c*) *Mimicry* and (*d*) *Ilinx*—Emulation and disorder.

13. Work, in this context, is not intended to imply income-producing pursuits within the orthodox definition, or even the supplementation of income by a part-time occupation, but the application to an economically non-productive activity of factors conventionally associated with the work situation, i.e. systematic effort, endurance of routine, application to detail, as well as in the present instance, exercise of mental skill, of memory and of rational choice. A similar definition has been argued by Robert D. Herman (see 'Bibliography') (pp. 87–104).

14. Distinction proposed by F. Tonnies (*Community and Association* 1887; English translation, The Michigan State University Press, Michigan 1957) in which *Gemeinschaft* (Community) is defined as 'intimate, private and exclusive living together' and *Gesellschaft* (Society) as 'public life'—associations united by rational agreement of interests, entered upon consciously and deliberately.

15. Universalistic and Particularistic: The choice between treating individuals as individuals in a multiplicity of roles (universalism) and

regarding them in only the role they play as members of classificatory groups (particularism).

This distinction, as well as the definition in note 16 below, is contained in the Pattern Variables as defined by Talcott Parsons in *The Social System* (1952) pp. 58–9.

16. Diffuse: Regarding the actor as the provider of many services.

17. The definitions of 'Operative Institution' and 'Regulative Institution' derive from the description and analysis presented by S. F. Nadel in his book *The Foundations of Social Anthropology* Cohen and West (London 1958).

18. The adaptive processes available to socially underprivileged individuals and groups in order to resolve anomic situations originating in defective mechanisms without the special system derive from Merton's now classic, definition. Merton, R. K. (1967) ch. IV: Social Structure and Anomie; pp. 121–60.

19. 'It is probably more fruitful to think of lower-class families reacting in various ways to the facts of their position and to relative isolation rather than to the imperatives of a lower-class culture.' Hylan Lewis, *Culture, Class and Behaviour of Low Income Families*, Paper presented to the Conference of Views on Lower-Class Culture (New York City, June 1963), p. 43.

The concept of type-situations as a sociological method of analysis is persuasively argued by E. Liewbow in *Tally's Corner* (1967).

CHAPTER VI

Gambling Profiles

In addition to the activities outlined in the foregoing chapter, I spent in the course of something like twenty months a great deal of time in various local cafés and pubs, at dogtracks, gaming clubs and other betting shops. In each of these places I declared my research intent, made myself known, struck up conversation at every opportunity, sounded views and opinions, tested reactions and took notes. At an estimate, I would say that I spoke to no fewer than five hundred people, in one way or another, directly on the subject of my research.

Yet I felt that there was still an important component missing from my inquiry, the unknown group of people who were non-visitors to betting shops, cafés, pubs etc., the non-gamblers and non-attenders. I accordingly decided to supplement my research by a series of door-to-door interviews. I had, at an early stage of the empirical activity, been struck by the wide divergence in residential accommodation. On the one end of the scale the modern, well-appointed, post-war Council flats—abundant in natural daylight, open spaces and up-to-date domestic equipment —and on the opposite end the decaying, dilapidated Victorian terraced houses, of which a large proportion had come to be designated sub-standard slums, together with a distinctive middle group consisting of more substantial properties which, though privately rented and relatively old, had been externally renovated and internally updated. I hypothesized that, as between these divergent qualities of accommodation, divergent sets of habits and attitudes towards gambling would exist. That those least stimulated by their physical environment, those whose life chances were the most depressed, would be more prone to fall victim to the temptations, distractions and fantasies associated wit h

gambling, while those at the opposite end of this particular scale
—those best housed—would, being the most thriving, most
aspiring also be those most resistant to gambling lures. A hypothesis, incidentally, which soon proved to be entirely unsub-
stantiated. By means of the Electoral Register I selected from
each of these three groups on a random basis a total of 18 households, intending to interview the principal Householder in each.[1]

In only one instance was the interview refused, in all the other
53 cases, though frequently in accordance with the dictum 'I
invest, you bet, he gambles' having to overcome such initial objections as 'I doubt if I can help you mate. You see, I don't gamble',
the interview was successfully completed.* In most cases in
which the above objection was voiced I found, in the course of
subsequent conversation, that not only the householder but
frequently all other adult members of the household were
regular bettors on horseracing, football pools, bingo and sometimes also on dogs. By deliberate preference, reinforced by the
results of a small-scale pilot set of interviews, I carried out these
interviews, lasting anything from twenty minutes to as much as
four hours—some in the presence of other members of the household, others with the householder alone—in as informal a
manner as possible. Though asking each of the subjects, in the
interest of structure and consistency, a few basic questions as to
the types, volume and frequency of betting, I avoided imposing
any rigid pattern on the interview, aiming instead at maximal
empathy and mutual understanding.

I do not consider myself to be endowed with any talents above
the ordinary for eliciting response and interaction and yet I feel
that in each and every area of study I speedily and fairly effortlessly
established contact and active participation. I consider two
fortuitous factors—in the first place my evident chronological
maturity† and in the second place the obvious traces of my foreign
origin—to which Ferdynand Zweig also paid tribute in connection
with his empirical research[2]—greatly assisted me in my task. But
to an even greater extent, I feel I owe whatever limited success I
might have had in achievement of co-operation to my firm

---

* Refusal rate 1.85 per cent.

† I was born in Vienna in July 1922, was, therefore, 44 years when I came to the
project.

resolve to impose upon myself as firm a check as possible on all impulses towards manipulation, exploitation, moral judgement, and over-hasty conclusions. I stand, as yet, too close to the experience to be able to evaluate my mistakes critically. From past experience, the awareness of these tends gradually to mature and then to haunt one for a long time to come. I have already started to rue occasional premature tendencies towards pigeon-holing and also incidents when I discovered myself holding forth, when availing myself of the opportunity of learning by listening to others would have been the better course to follow.

The influence the observer exerts upon his environment is always difficult to assess, particularly by the observer himself. As mentioned before, I considered it in one instance[3] unavoidable to conceal the nature of my enquiry, a move I began to regret the moment I had become committed to it. Apart from the fact that it inhibited probing and questioning, the unreality of my position and the constant awareness of the deceit I was practising on my unsuspecting subjects preoccupied me to the possible detriment of the task I was engaged in. In other instances, where I found myself cast in the role of 'The Author', I feel that after an initial, brief period of mutual self-awareness, my label soon ceased to matter. What William Foote Whyte postulated of the environment in which he conducted his research, namely that acceptance of himself depended on the personal relationships he was able to establish and on the opinions people formed of him as an individual, held true for me as well.[4]

The major part of the present chapter is taken up by ten 'Gambling Profiles', a brief account of some of the more outstanding characters encountered by me in my various activities. I do not claim for these, lacking control material and continuity, the status of case studies, nor would I seek to maintain that they are either exhaustive or universal. Rather, taking the view that the employment of the method of 'type situation' might afford the most effective means of insight into some of the sociologically relevant implications of gambling, I have chosen to depict in this context the extreme rather than the average individual in the particular working-class area. I trust that by outlining a number of type situations, I have succeeded in illustrating not only the particular set of orientations a specific number of individuals bring to the gambling situation, but that I have also managed to suggest the part gambling plays in the total fabric of social existence. By learning to understand how conduct, seemingly irrational, would appear rational and overwhelmingly consistent from within a different social perspective, we may learn something not only of others, but also of ourselves.

Section II is an attempt at a brief differentiation between gamblers and non-gamblers within closely similar social background and environment. As I have tried to indicate earlier, we must not only seek to analyse the covert satisfaction contained within the gambling situation, but must further attempt to establish by what means other individuals who do not gamble manage to achieve a corresponding set of satisfactions, or the types of accommodations they manage to make with their environment when being deprived of these satisfactions altogether. I freely recognize the shortcomings of my own material for these purposes and the limitations these impose upon any conclusions I might be tempted to draw. But I consider that deeper and more systematic efforts in this direction will eventually allow a degree of differentiation, sufficient to possess a considerable amount of predictive validity.

The Sportsman

Jack J., a fifty-three year-old bachelor, lives by himself in the ground-floor flat of a decaying row of houses, having to share front entrance, bathroom and lavatory with the two upstairs tenants; one a bright, cheerful, butcher's apprentice and the other, 'a real cuss, a proper subject for a psychiatrist such as you', a minor customs official, the same age as Jack, who had recently taken as his third 'wife' an eighteen year-old runaway, younger than his own daughter. The gloomy interior, the fraying sparse furniture, the half-made bed in the corner hardly served to suggest being in the presence of a member of that rare community—a Master in the Art of Life.

For most of his life, until a few years ago, Jack had been a State-Registered Nurse on outside duty with the local Council. For the past six years he had been working on a three-shift rota in the local Old Peoples' Home, previously the local Workhouse, where he had first been employed many years ago when newly qualified. Certainly things had changed in the meantime. Whereas previously 1,000 old people had been herded together, there were now no more than 120. No longer was it necessary to produce a pass to leave the grounds, the huge iron-gates now stood open throughout the day and the inmates could, subject only to curfew, come and go as they pleased. Nor were the old people required to do chores for their food; now they could, if they chose, do little jobs for fag-money to supplement their weekly 75p pocket-money—another innovation. What with carpets on the floor, television, hot water and outings—in fact, the very next day the old people were due to travel to the Brighton races in three coachloads, with crates of beer loaded in the back and a bit of cash for a 'flutter' as a present from the Governor—an outsider might not know the place was even the same. But to the 'poor old bastards' inside, it was still the old Workhouse, the place where you came to die. As soon as the heavy iron gates closed behind them, as soon as they looked at the high grey walls, they knew it was the end. For a while their folks continued to come and see them—you'd be surprised, no sooner do old people get sick or infirm, than their relatives suddenly find that they have not the room to provide for them, or that they have to go out to work and cannot look after them, in other words, they become a 'bloody nuisance'—but after a few visits they drop off. 'One of the old boys might say to me: "My son, you met him last time he came, will be here this afternoon, he promised to come." I know quite well how he grumbled about the fare money, I know the old boy won't see him again. I just say "You go and have your afternoon nap, mate, I'll call you if he comes and if not, I might take you for a little walk round the park." After a few months they just cease to care, they become apathetic like the others, just sit and sleep with their eyes open. If you pass by them when they sit to watch the television, they don't even know you're blotting out their light. Part of the trouble is they mix them all together*—the imbeciles, the infirm and the good ones—and another is they give them nothing to do, not even a few games to keep them

---

* According to Jack, the official admission age was 65 years, but due to lack of staff and accommodation, in practice, inmates' ages ranged from 74 to 98 years.

occupied. You wouldn't believe it, we've got a beautiful billiard-room with two full-sized tables, it has been locked for the past two years, because a couple of the old boys started a fight over a game. A few, when they can, do a bit of gardening, they come and ask me and I tell them "you go ahead, mate, if the Warden sees you, don't say I told you."

'It's all centralization now, rules made in some far away office and uniforms. Me, I never wear one, when they see you in it they don't recognize you. They say "You're from the Council, aren't you?" and walk away. And then, the young warders don't want to get their hands dirty, to them it's all money for old rope. The first time you ask them to help you shift a corpse, they're off. I say you have come here to help the old people and that's your job. They no more want to mess their beds, or have to be washed or buried than you want to do it, mate; if you can't stand it, get out and work in a factory.'

Did it not upset him emotionally to continuously see people he had cared for die, did he not get attached to them?

'You can only cope if you treat them all alike, individually I don't know them. It you get to feel sorry for any one of them, you might as well pack up. While you made a fuss over one, you are neglecting another half-dozen. The way I look at it, they've come here to die, so I am here to make it as easy for them as I can. It's funny the way it happens, the light just goes out. One moment they lie there and ask me, "Hold my hand, Jack" and I say to them "Take it easy, old cock", and a minute later they're gone. I wash them down, carry them to the mortuary and tomorrow another one is lying in their bed. Mind you, this job plays havoc with your social life, my mates knock on my door and call out, "Come and have a drink, Jack" and I call back, "I'm just off to work." "Blimey", they say, "Why don't you pack it in?" I wouldn't dream of it as long as they don't make me wear uniform. I'm as free as a bird, got all I want and can, at least, believe I am doing my little bit to help my fellow creatures instead of sweating my guts out in a factory to buy the missus another frock she doesn't need.'

While on the subject of leisure, what did he do with it, did he go in for gambling at all?

'Oh yes, I like a flutter as much as the next man, wouldn't be normal if I didn't.' It transpired that Jack placed bets on horse-racing with fair regularity. A two-pound 'up-and-down double'* in the betting shop every Saturday and most weekdays the odd few shillings, usually adding his stake to others' bets. He did not profess to any special knowledge or deep interest in form, in fact he was happy to defer to the selection made by others wherever these had proved successful in the past. There was, for instance, an old fellow, name of Meyers in the Home, must be about 85, who had quite a knack of picking the winners. He could not afford to bet much himself, but you'd be surprised at some of the winners he picked. At times his choice was so odd that the others just laughed at him—they all liked a bit of a flutter, always had their noses stuck in the papers, gave them something to do—but in the end, more often than not, it was old Meyers who had the last laugh. He was quite a scholar, old Meyers, used to be chief-clerk or something in a shipping-office, knew the life story of all the horses, jockeys and even the trainers, could talk about it for hours, though Jack guessed he just had a lucky touch, or maybe just a lucky run. Jack had recently made a point of following the old boy's advice, treating him to a packet of fags when his tip came up and had only last Saturday won £18 on a double.

Was his interest in betting related to active interest in racing as sport, I asked, did he go to any meetings and if not what was the attraction?

No, racing had never appealed to him, he could not bear to stand still for any time, not even in a pub, nor did he like to be surrounded by crowds without being able to move away. Betting was a separate activity which had its independent charms. Firstly, as his old Dad used to say, 'You have to speculate in order to accumulate',[5] but quite apart from that, what other harmless pleasures were there for the working man, what else could he natter about for hours at a time? And what a grand sport horse-racing was, or come to that even the dogs, where you were only watching it on the telly. Thoroughbred animals, the finest in the land, pictures of health and beauty, in peak condition, ridden by the topmost professionals, each trying his honest best to beat the others in a fair battle, surrounded by crowds, everyone deter-mined to have a good time. Added to that the thrill of knowing

* Refers to selection of several runners, each linked in double harness.

that one of them carries your money, your hopes of striking it lucky; maybe just a few bob, but still enough to make your heart miss a beat or two. And if you lost, so what, it was only money you would have wasted on something else.

Did he then, as he seemed to imply, accumulate his winnings? Save, to see it fought over when they took him to the old-people's home? Lord no. The last few quid he had won, he had bought a new outfit for one of his nieces, a few records for another, given his brother's wife a couple of quid for herself—though he knew full well it would go straight to that 'silly bastard', his brother, who had not done a day's work in years; spent all his time and money in the betting shop, not even knowing how to bet like a man, just went on any silly hearsay; and then came home and kicked up murder if his dinner was not on the table, and that stupid woman ran round him like a puppy-dog, no use telling her, bending down to take his boots off. With the rest of the money he had treated himself to an outing in Southend. He loved fun-fairs, could spend hours in one of them. Then he finished off with a few beers and a song-and-dance. Could anything be more fun?

Did he not mind living alone?

He was never alone for long, only when he wanted to be. Always had one mate or another calling in, or one of his nieces— pointing them out by name on the coloured photographs proudly displayed on the mantlepiece—would come in with a friend to play his records until he sent them packing with a couple of bob in their purses. 'But' he added 'I've never seen a happy married couple. I won't even mention the poor devils in the broken homes I used to visit in my work. Just look at all my pals. They might tell me they are happily married, but if you suggest they bring the missus on one of our little outings, they scream "What and spoil my fun", they can't wait to get out of their houses to get together with the boys and, once we are out they get stuck into bird-hunting even worse than I do. They say to me "Who will look after you when you are old?" and I answer them "Look at them poor bastards in the Home I work at, they've all got wives and family, but when they get old, nobody wants them. I can't be worse off than they are." The only certainty in life is, that at some time you'll be carried out feet first. As for the rest, it's just a treble chance. Now let me make you another cup of tea, guv, and let me hear what you think about it all.'

The Rational Gambler and the Handicapper

Though in all probability not often encountered in real flesh and blood, the 'Rational Gambler'—in common with his counterpart the 'Rational Man'—is capable of fairly simple definition: A man who, having taken account of all relevant factors and having assigned to them appropriate values and priorities, will endeavour to reach his decision under the set of circumstances most favourable to himself, being aware at all times of the interests of others as well as of his own limitations and fallibility. The Handicapper is a figure probably more familiar on the other side of the Atlantic —a follower who not only busies himself in the study of racing information itself, but who also attempts to read between the lines. The 'wise guy' who, trying to keep one step ahead of the bookie would, could he do so, get his information straight from the horse's mouth; who, when losing, is likely to ascribe his failure to conspiracy and deceit rather than to personal imperfection or even ill-luck.

Both Thomas (the rational gambler) and Maurice (the handicapper) happened to be coloured immigrants, both were in their early thirties and both had lived in this country for over ten years. Thomas, a modest, slightly reticent well-spoken Trinidadian— dapper, slight, yet athletic, installed in a neatly furnished modern council flat—had for the past five years worked in the stores of the regional telephone exchange, proudly proclaiming himself a telephone engineer. Maurice, from Guyana, a skilled plumber in the East India Docks—tousle-haired, fiery, loquacious and self-assured—was living in the downstairs portion of a terraced house, recently condemned under Slum Clearance, his own flat in a state of seedy neglect. When I met him for the first time at three one Monday afternoon he had 'fancied a day off to do some decorating', yet the tools and implements were still stacked untouched in a corner of the room. Both men were fathers of young families, Thomas had three delightful, self-disciplined and yet uninhibited boys between the ages of two to six and Maurice had five children, including one set of twins, all under the age of seven. ('We don't want no more, didn't want the ones we've got until they come along; but once they come, you wouldn't want to be without them. This is no country for large families; at home folks have twelve children and don't seem to worry. I don't believe in family planning, anyway you can't trust these things; but, I guess, this time we'll have to stop.') Both men worked long hours, taking overtime and weekend work wherever they could— Thomas had worked for the past four Saturdays in a row and Maurice reported himself as working seven days a week (a statement which subsequent events established as highly unlikely), both wives were doing part-time evening packing jobs. The two men were strangers to each other.

Both men were keen bettors, both eager and regular students of form and performance, both occasional direct attenders at meetings. Thomas, at one time, had plans of becoming a professional jockey, even undergoing the pre-apprenticeship training, but had found himself in adolescence to be growing too tall. He still retained a vivid interest in pedigree, tactics and technique, though he doubted whether this afforded him any differential advantage. 'You can't look inside the animal's heart, just look how often form gets upset in something like athletics. You can train until you are pure muscle all over and then you get up in the morning and have a bust-up with your wife, you might as well not get under starter's orders.' Yet in spite of his long familiarity with the racing scene, he still retained his sense of wonderment and fascination. 'When I went to the dogtrack for the first time, soon after I came to this country, I could not believe my eyes, I thought I was in fairyland.' This sensation soon waned with familiarity, but at a later stage of the interview: 'This year I managed to get to the Derby for the first time in my life. I had dreamt about it since I was a little boy and it's even grander and more colourful than I had seen it in my dreams. I brought the programme home to keep as a souvenir for my kids when they grow up.'

Maurice's attitude was more utilitarian: 'I have no use for horseracing, too much of a fashion parade and a get-together for a booze-up to interest me. Besides, by the time you reckon up your fare money, your entrance, drinks and food, you need a couple of winners just to pay for that, let alone make a profit on the day.'

He regularly went to dog meetings, 'You've got to see what's going on to give yourself a chance, what you read in the papers is all balls. If these tipsters knew the winners they'd be bloody fools to blab them all over the front pages. I'm a good enough judge to form my own opinions.'

What factors did he take into account and what weight did he attach to each? 'You can even make a science out of this game, man. Sure, form and class count for something, but if they were everything there would be no point in having a race. There are things you don't see in the papers, nor even printed on the card.'* Such as what? I enquired. First of all the condition of the animal directly before the race. This, he said, a good judge could learn a lot about by close scrutiny while the dogs were being paraded. Then the owners' and trainers' intention, the way the 'big money' was behaving—all this again was ascertained by shrewd attention to the trend of betting as shown on the bookmakers' books as well as the totalisator scoreboards.[6] Besides, there were always the 'insiders', those who got the tip-off at first or second-hand of what was going on behind the scenes. If you got in with them, they were always good for a winner or two. Only last week he got a 'Tip'—a dog prepared as a 'trainers' benefit'—alas it lost; at 6 : 1 this was a 'cert', but unfortunately it got badly bumped on the second bend, 'you can't grumble at that!'

The methods employed by Thomas on dograce betting were less complex. He just concerned himself with the form in the previous two races—after all a dog, like a human, could change so much in condition in a couple of months that it was virtually no longer the same animal. He always gave consideration to trap position—some dogs were wide runners, so these would do well in outside lanes, others were railers who did much better from the inside. Oh yes, they nearly always tended to race in the same style, just as humans would do, that's why you had so much bumping. You might get a wide runner in trap two and a railer in trap six,[7] the whole bunch would turn into a mess at the first bend and only the trap one runner—whom he would then be likely to have picked—might escape the *mêlée*. He also took weight into account, each animal had a best weight, if he lost or gained a

* The racing programme giving intricate details of runners, trainers, times, order of finishing etc.

couple of pounds, you could virtually write him off. One time, a few years ago, he had struck the Jackpot, had won £94, he could still recite the winners.[8] He had noticed before the last race—by which time he had accumulated £35—that all the previous winners on the Jackpot had been visiting dogs from a sister track, so he plumped for the Walthamstow runner on the last ticket and when he won, he had been 'so bloody excited' he had run out for a taxi. There were still two races to go, he could not find a taxi, so he sat in the coach and waited for the crowds to come out. When he had come home, he had told his wife that he had lost all his money and even had had to borrow his fare home. Before she had time to get angry, he had thrown the bundle of money on the table and they had both cried with happiness. He had made sure the money would not go back to the bookies, they had gone out the next day—he had always made good use of his winnings— and bought a new three-piece suite for cash. But over the past two years he had given up dogracing, there was too much risk of losing more than one could afford and besides, he had developed new interests, such as records and recently photography. He still betted on horseracing, inclining to pick horses of good breeding early in the season and following these through. If you knew when to stay off them—for instance when the odds were too low, or when late finishers lacked a pacemaker—you could come out winning at the end. But he was getting disillusioned with what he termed 'petty gambling', you tended to fritter away your small winnings and when you had a long losing run, you were hard hit. His wife, who did not know the first thing about horses and did not even have the skill to construct her bet sensibly, was hardly less successful than he himself. Maurice had no such reservations, convinced as he was that he was 'on top in betting' and that 'if you are smart, you don't lose, unless your luck is out'.

I asked both men to keep a detailed log of their betting for one full week. At the end, Thomas had placed ten separate bets, all on horses; none on Tuesday or Wednesday, two each on Monday, Thursday and Friday and four on Saturday. Total outlay for the week had been £2.05, the biggest single outlay a 50p bet on Saturday. He had three winning bets: one of 40p on Friday, a 30p winner on Saturday, plus a £1.50 win at odds of 3:1 in his largest bet. His total winnings therefore amounted to £2.20, a net profit of 15p for the week. He informed me that the process of being observed had altered his behaviour in the direction of more intense concentration, as well as greater resistance towards temptations of fancy.

Maurice's log did not extend beyond Tuesday. It disclosed only 3 entries, all losers, losses amounting to £1.37½. 'You mustn't challenge your luck, the moment I gave up keeping record, I had a 7:1 winner come up; I promise though to send you a wire the moment I've made my first million.' I told this story to Thomas—'We all go through that stage' he reflected 'when we think we are Lady Luck's special favourites. When we get wiser, it's really a mug's game. But as long as I can watch the race on the telly and say to myself how clever I've been when I have won, as long as our wives and families don't suffer, where is the harm?'

The Professional

One is unlikely to remain in the company of regular gamblers for any length of time without the subject of discussion turning upon that mythical character—the professional gambler. The character, real or, as more often turns out, imaginary, who makes his living out of the activity of gambling. Questions soon reveal that this group of people is not merely of nebulous composition, but also of very wide definition—extending from the professional book-maker on the one end to the casual, short-time winner on the other. No doubt, a great many people earn their living from the gambling trade, but the majority who do so—bookmakers, casino operators, pools' promoters—are entrepreneurs, businessmen, operatives rather than gamblers, deriving their profits from the gambling of other people. It may indeed be the case, as one prominent bookmaker remarked to me that: 'If you were to take the ratio of gamblers—those who place bets—and non-gamblers throughout all the occupational groups in the country, you would find the lowest proportion of gamblers amongst bookmakers with probably mathematicians just below. Both of them know that the odds against them are stacked.' Nor do jockeys and trainers, bookmakers' clerks and croupiers rightfully belong to this category—the former group are professional sportsmen, while the latter are just paid employees. Whether to classify owners amongst the professionals or not is more difficult to decide. In the case of racehorse owners it is still probably true that the majority (in spite of the fact that 'The Sport of Kings' is said to have turned into 'The Sport of the Financiers'), though rarely disinclined to the occasional flutter, derive satisfactions other than financial from the activity. Owners of greyhounds are socially more heterogeneous, as well as being more divergent in their motivations. It is more than likely that the overwhelming majority find themselves out of pocket at the end of the year, while a few, either by collusion with their trainers and kennelmen, or thanks to particularly skilful personal manipulation of their stable, will show profits running well into five figures year after year.

In fact, though less frequent now than before the last war, ownership of racing greyhounds is still a not uncommon practice among the East Enders and still provides a positive prestige symbol. The decline in the popularity of the 'Flapping Tracks'— the unregistered dogtracks where all kinds of contrivance and villainy were commonplace, where it was possible (though not popular) to run dogs under different names at different meetings and where even the changing of the markings by application of paint was not unknown—has cut out a number of previous owners. Others, no longer prepared to spend long hours exercising their animals, or with the growth of Council Housing, no longer able to keep them kenneled in their back gardens, have not been willing or able to face the costs involved in keeping an animal stabled and racing-fit. Nevertheless, a number have remained as owners. The majority, no doubt, clinging to the status ownership confers, as well as hoping that sooner or later their trainers' tips will prove to be less consistently unreliable. Only a small minority could, with any validity, claim inclusion among the ranks of professionals. These would be the owners who, generally owning no more than a few dogs at a time, have learnt to discriminate between information 'good, so-so and diabolical' and who have acquired sufficient mastery over themselves to bide their time until a 'hot inside tip' comes along, often standing at the track throughout a whole meeting without placing a bet, yet keeping a close eye on each runner. The tout and tipster

—both salesmen of information of varying degrees of quality and reliability—the linkman and the snooper*—each benefiting by the inside knowledge and machination of others—would also be classed within the same group, though their numbers and identities might be more obscure, their tenure more uncertain, short-lived and precarious.

The only other group qualifying for inclusion among the professionals would be the 'professional backers'—individuals, or in some cases the group of persons, the syndicate—who facing the odds against them in whatever activity they select as their field of operation without the aid of contrivance or of inside information, are prepared to rely solely on their skills, their expertise and their superior judgement and not only succeed in winning the occasional few pounds, but are able to adopt gambling as a regular income-producing way of life.

Norman was a worthy member of that exclusive circle. I ran into him when, finding myself in one of the smarter areas of West London—St James's to be precise—I decided to pay one of the local betting shops a few visits. The contrast between this betting shop and my usual areas of participant observation was, not unexpectedly, startling. The bulk of the clientele was, once more, proletarian—local building site workers, waiters, municipal manual workers, domestics, and porters—but in addition there was also untypically a fair sprinkling of white-collar attenders—clerks, shopkeepers, housewives, as well as a regular trickle of proxies—messengers carrying the bets of their bosses or of members of their clubs. Yet even in this assembly Norman stood out—tall, well-groomed, expensively if a little flashily dressed, composedly prepared to pass the time of day with all-comers, yet languidly withdrawn. His study of form seemed casual yet deep, his winnings and losses regularly recorded in a little black book at the conclusion of each race. Contrary to common practice, he gave the form of the runners only the scantiest attention, scanning the race programme in his own copy of the 'Sporting Life' only in the most cursory fashion. But he keenly followed the fluctuations of the odds in course of the pre-racing transactions, staking his money almost unfailingly at the very moment when the odds were most favourable to him.

* Intermediaries passing 'inspired information' from the stables to confidants.

It did not take me long to get into conversation with him. In some of the races he seemed to show no interest whatever, half-reclining in his chair with eyes closed. It was at one of these moments that I approached him, declaring my purpose, as well as my admiration for his apparent financial success. 'Well, it is hardly surprising, you see I am a professional gambler, so I have to do well at it. Maybe not a very admirable profession', he continued, 'but as you can see it affords me a fairly good crust.' It transpired that Norman had been following this way of life for a number of years now, though he supplemented his income by freelancing as an insurance agent, an occupation that at the same time provided him with an identity comprehensible to the Tax Inspector. He was in his early thirties, married with one small child, commuting from his own suburban house in a slightly outdated model of an executive-type car. Funds, throughout the period of our association, seemed ample and lavishly disbursed, personal turnout, even at the end of a series of all-night card sessions, immaculate, unruffled and relaxed. What, I asked in the first place, were his sources of gambling income?

Racing first and foremost—the horses and the dogs, though the latter had only recently again staged a revival after the anti-greyhound tax legislation had been removed. Cards, with Poker at Gaming Clubs as the most lucrative single source of income. Baccarat only when others failed and roulette and other table-games never, as these allowed no edge whatever to skill and consistent self-control.

Well, how did he manage to overcome the inevitable unfavourable odds built into Racing, did he have any particular system or was he one of that small band of elect who 'got the whisper'?*

Inside tips, God forbid, in these Norman had no faith whatever. Why, after all, should those who risked their livelihoods and their personal freedom in doping or fixing in advance stick their necks out even further by passing the word to outsiders who would, no doubt, in their own turn, pass the whisper even further? Once you gave your ear to that kind of wishful thinking, you would soon lose all ability to discriminate truth from falsehood, good risks from bad ones, you might as well give up. He

* Inside, confidential information of rigged races.

had no doubt that racing was basically crooked, that horses were trained to win only certain races, that only a small proportion of entrants were really trying and that a large number of races were fixed in advance. The core of his system was to try to puzzle-out the methods by which the operators were trying to hoodwink the authorities as well as the public. Supposing that he, as an intelligent person, were the owner or trainer shaping-up for a coup, how, he asked himself, would he go about it? It would, first of all, be necessary to build up a series of defeats in order to be matched against lower quality opposition, to get favourable weight allowance and particularly to lengthen the odds, in other words to create a public illusion of being a failure, a loser. It would help to engage a non-fashionable jockey, as the popular jockeys, irrespective of mounts, always attracted a certain amount of money; preferably a striving apprentice, little known but on his way up, who given the chance would ride like the devil, who had not yet built up a circle of people who depended on him for 'news' and who would, moreover, be given a favourable weight allowance. To an owner operating a coup, prize money itself would be a negligible factor, so the coup would be more likely to be staged in a race in which the horse was running for a low purse and therefore in relatively inferior company. So there you were. Study the race card and all the form particulars first thing in the morning, mark the runners who had in previous outings raced in higher class, had been ridden by top level jockeys for high purses and who were even then rated of sufficient quality to be well-backed. Estimate what their 'true odds' ought to be in the inferior company in which they are now running and then check these against the odds anticipated by the forecasters. Confirm that the horse is rated as relative outsider—in other words that the anticipated odds are long. Strike out those races in which these factors did not operate, or in which too many contradictory explanations were possible. After that, attendance at the betting shop was essential. Watch the odds as soon as these appear on the board, confirm their coincidence with the early-morning quotes. Then look out for the moment, if the analysis proves correct, at which the operator at the track will be waiting to pounce with his money. As soon as his money starts going on, odds will start reacting. That is the time to turn yourself into the operator, discard all caution, pounce before odds become too short to be worth the risk. Then, lean back, light up and hope you have not made a bloomer. But do not allow yourself to become conspicuous, change your field of operation from time to time. Always choose premises owned by multiples, where the staff do not care whether you win or lose, and where they are anyhow too busy on their own little schemes to pay attention to you. Chat amiably to all as though your outlook were the same as that of the other punters, never get into arguments, treat everyone's point of view with respect. Never allow yourself to be tempted to bet outside the system, beware against too serious study of form—once you consider yourself a form expert your judgment gets blurred. Determine in advance how much each race is worth, don't chase your losses, though once you are playing with the bookie's money, you can allow yourself a little flutter. When your luck is in in a big way, hit hard, hit mercilessly, reach for the moon. Only two weeks ago he had backed four long-shot winners in a row.

Did it pay off? How did he cope with losing runs?

Naturally, at times, things did not work out. Then there was always the chance that the cards would be kind, or there was as final recourse his insurance agency. Unfortunately, the bottom was just beginning to fall out of cards, not even poker—a game in which traditionally the cool-headed, investment-minded professional had had a clear edge over the punter, the excitable, erratic amateur—could now be counted as a stable source of income. Where previously most clubs—and he was not referring to the West-End leading establishments, but rather to the third-rank gaming clubs able to count on no more than a limited clientele—had been glad to have a poker-game going to liven things up, they were now no longer eager to see their customers deflected from the games the management counted on for their own profits, nor did they relish watching their clientele being fleeced by a handful of professionals having, as a final irony, at the same time often to provide the victims with cash against the most dubious collateral. So the game was now being forced into the less salubrious establishments, less scrupulous about observing the law as to percentage deductions, not very fussy about the occasional resort to 'strong-arm' in order to recover debts. Such surroundings were not very congenial to the 'gentleman professional' whose success so largely depended on panache and atmosphere. But why spend sleepless nights (days might have been more apt in the present context), when in gambling it was always true that as one door closed, another was just opening and true enough, the 'gee-gees' were at the moment behaving just as the doctor ordered.

Would he continue to gamble if the percentage he was able to juggle into his favour were to disappear?

Did he understand my question right, did I mean to ask him whether he would gamble just for the kick of it? Not on your sweet nelly, just look at all these poor nuts doing their pieces. You would not see his arse in a place like that for dust were it not for the real hope of making money. He had no doubt that gambling was a curse and the institution of the betting shop an act of utter folly. Why else would anyone want to hang around these grubby surroundings, or stay up half the night in a poky, smoke-filled rat-hole, were it not for the love of money, the hope of winning some cash? If he were Home Secretary he would clamp down on all forms of gambling with an iron fist—though then it would probably go underground—certainly while there were villains like himself around. But now, he must ask to be excused, after all these were his office-hours—and by the way also his business premises—and duty before pleasure. The odds for the next race were just coming up, he must alas now return to work.

The Conman

The three o'clock race had reached its closing stages. I had moved away from the form-clippings along the walls in order to eavesdrop on some of the reactions to the commentary being voiced by a polyglot group of bettors half-way towards the counter. A hand touched my shoulder and before I had time to look round an unfamiliar voice was asking 'Fancy running into you here, I didn't know this was one of your haunts.' Acting, for reasons outlined above, in the assumed role of genuine punter in this particular betting shop,* exposure seemed immi-

---

* B.S.III, Mile End, where I had concluded it to be essential to disguise my true identity.

nent. But, in spite of my unfortunate inability to rapidly fit faces into unfamiliar surroundings, I need not have worried. When I turned, I was looking at a face I had definitely never encountered before. Having been reassured with: 'Sorry, old friend, I thought you were an old army chum of mine', I made to turn back to the group I had been detached from. But the newcomer clearly had not yet finished with me. His clammy hand seized mine. 'We were fellow officers in the 8th, shared some pretty rough times in the desert,' he continued.

I made a quick mental check: Age seemed to fit—probably 45–50—height and physique rather dubious, slight, seedy and soft; apparel and general appearance not unlikely—natty, tidy and smart, though slightly threadbare, but at the same time flashy and flamboyant, the cut of the blue serge suit slightly suggestive of the 'spiv' of the immediate post-war; accent and manner more than doubtful—though in speech less demotic than the usual, nevertheless a strong undertone of Cockney twang, the demeanour unmistakably the familiar mixture of the ingratiating humility and razor-sharp cockiness of the underdog on the make. All might be fair (and classless) in love and war, but my new friend's officer status, if authentic, would have been the scrapings of a rather deep barrel.

The situation however did not allow much time for reflection. 'Still,' he continued, 'now we have met, you seem a pretty good sort. Tell me, can you keep your mouth shut?' Peremptorily he waved aside my timidly cautious 'Depends on what the secret is.' 'Never mind that, you promise not to breathe a word and I'll show you how to make a packet.' Gravely I assented to keep my mouth shut for, 'If you blow your top, it's more than my life is worth' I was told. 'I only come in here to place one quick bet and then I'm off to the next shop to get my money on. You ask them, I drew a hundred pounds in here yesterday. If you don't spread your money around, they won't take it and in any case the price would go down. How much have you got on you?' Curious as I was to see the situation through to the end, I was beginning to rue some of the pitfalls of my false role. Revealing myself now as an observer would not only abruptly bring to an end the present scene, but would explode my standing as punter in the betting shop in which I had decided operation would, on other terms, not be possible. Yet the full implications of playing my unintended part to the end were unforseeable.* Clearly my new friend considered himself entitled to expect a meaningful stake now he had singled me out and yet at the same time gullibility, vulnerability to confident assertion were part of the role I had assigned to myself.

I decided to prevaricate. 'Where do you get your tips from, and anyhow why should you give them to me when we have never met before?' I wanted to know. 'Alright, so I do you a favour, who knows I might want a favour from you another time. Why should you look a gifthorse in the mouth? I'm sticking my neck out a mile roping you in, but in my line of business you've got to be a judge of character and I've decided you are a man of honour. Anyway, when the money starts rolling in, I don't expect you to be a miser. My office is just round the corner, I get the tip once a day directly from the stables—if you knew who's behind it, you'd have a fit. Nine out of ten piss home and today's is a bloody cert. It's just money for old rope. How much you got on you, fifty? Don't let the mob see you slip it to me, just pass it along quietly and don't waste any more time, I've got another two shops to get to before the race.'

Events were warming up, I had to withdraw either now or never. What probably swayed the balance in favour of further involvement, was less my commitment to the cause of social research, than my growing avaricious hope of being in on a good thing. Yet, all the money I had on me, apart from silver, were two single pound notes and one secreted fiver, none of which I was as yet willing to commit to the venture without further reassurance. Pointing to the race programme in the newspaper in my hand I demanded: 'Show me which one it is, you can't expect me to buy a pig in a poke.' My friend's finer feelings were outraged: 'What

---

* I had hitherto, while being able to mingle with the punters on equal terms, been able to restrict my stakes and bets to a minimum by use of a variety of stratagems—such as boldly walking up to the counter with a completed betting slip and a pound note in my hand and sliding back unobserved at the last moment, or betting 20p on the last race and making sure of being heard to say to the cashier, 'That's what I've come down to, I did my pieces on the favourite in the 3.30'. At the same time I was able to retain relative obscurity by attaching myself to the fringe rather than the centre of activity, by assuming the role of listener, of non-expert. The present involvement was threatening my existence along all the fronts.

do you take me for, a bloody shyster? I collected a hundred quid in here this morning, so do you think I need your measly few quid? If you don't want to trust me, you better forget it (nothing would have suited me better at that moment)—pretend we haven't met, I don't do business with dummies!'

Sensing my growing desire to take him at his word, he quickly added, 'You're throwing away your chance to get rich, once you get started you need never look back. I made over five thousand in less than six months, I tell you what I do for you, show me your money and I let you into the tip; it's in the 4.30 at Plumpton.' I had become aware that the initiative had passed to me, or at least that he was too deeply committed to write me off totally at this stage. 'I've had a pretty rough couple of days,' I said, 'all I've got on me is a fiver. But if you can convince me that I'm on a good thing, I can get hold of another twenty before the race.' 'Alright then, give me your fiver for now and get going for the rest.'

The tug-of-war carried on a while longer, I continued to insist on information before pay-off, while he, now negotiating from weakness, tried to hold out for cash in advance of revelation, dropping his final demand to payment of no more than one pound, a sum I was prepared to commit to the cause of research. 'Woodman in the 4.30 and don't tell a soul', he whispered conspiratorily when I passed him the money.* We parted as though both in a hurry to transact the business to follow. He, doubtlessly, had no more intention of implementing his supposed programme of visiting further betting shops to distribute his stake, than I had of trying to call on further resources, or even to bet any money on the 'tip'. Gordon—that was the name he had allowed himself to divulge to me in a whisper in the course of our negotiations which, I now noticed to my surprise, had lasted for over half-an-hour—moved towards the grille self-importantly while I went out for a cup of tea, ensuring absence until some time after the result of the 4.30 had been posted.

Woodman, though starting as 7 : 4 favourite, had not even made the first three, nor was Gordon anywhere to be seen. My afternoon encounter had, however, not gone unnoticed. No sooner had I posted myself at the result-board than I found Jack, who at

* Woodman was a much fancied runner, a short-priced favourite, a nap-selection in several of the racing papers, an unlikely subject of a hush-hush coup.

the time of my re-entry had been occupied in his daily final stage of the betting routine, the post-mortem disputation of the inner circle, by my side. Jack had since my first days in the betting shop been acting in a self-appointed role of part-mentor, part-tormentor, taking it upon himself to initiate me into the intricacies of the finer arts of betting, while at the same time critically demanding performance to expected standards on my part, as benefited a maestro's pupil. 'You must be a proper cunt to let that con-merchant make a sucker of you, a kid of five could smell him a mile off. Guys like him travel the betting shops kidding mugs like you they know something hot. The nearest they've ever been to the stables, is to kip in the hay when they're even more skinned than usual, a jockey wouldn't even spit at them. They con mugs like you for a few quid and run straight back to the boozer, don't even know the front-end of a horse from his arse. It's blokes like you that can't look after yourselves that bring that vermin into the shops.'

Before he had time to move back to the group with that well-timed reprimand I managed to ask: 'If you knew what he was, why didn't you warn me?' 'If you don't want to look after your money, that's your business, those who aren't born with enough sense got to learn the hard way. If I was to waste my time protecting every mug from his own foolishness, I'd need looking after myself.' Clearly my desire for exploring new areas had injured my status in the betting shop. I was standing in danger of dissipating the contacts I had established. For the few days following, my existence tended to be precarious. Though not actually barred from admittance to the fringe elements surrounding the inner caucus, I was denied confidences from that elect body. It seemed understood that my elevation from the ranks of the outsider had been rescinded.

Exactly one week after the original meeting I saw Gordon in the same betting shop. Driven by the twin desires to re-establish my standing in the group as well as to find out more about his trade, I decided to challenge him. This time it was my turn to tap him on the shoulder. 'I'd like to have a word with you about that matter we discussed last week', I said with all the volume and authority I was able to muster, conscious of the fact that open deliberate exposure in direct terms would constitute an unforgivable breach of communal etiquette. To his credit, Gordon appeared neither nonplussed nor unduly disconcerted: 'I just have a little unfinished private business with our mutual friend here to wind up, I'll be over to see you presently.'

Taking care to take up position close to Jack's group, I watched Gordon and his new associate out of the corner of my eye, ostensibly occupying myself in the mandatory study of form. This time he seemed to have been more fortunate in the choice of his 'client'. After no more than one instance of mock-outrage, after which 'our mutual friend' anxiously seized Gordon's sleeve as he was threatening to walk away—'If you're too dumb to appreciate someone who's trying to do a brave seaman a little turn'—a fiver passed into Gordon's hands, who not even having needed to disclose the identity of the 'hot one', added the note to his own 'wad', bulging from his breast-pocket.

Gordon's tactics, as I learned over a period, were really very simple. His trading capital was his 'spiel'—the glib, quick-witted, infinitely flexible mixture of enticing and cajoling, pleading and hectoring, revelation and mystery to which he subjected his prey. His intuition for the exact threshold of gullibility and cupidity of each particular 'client' was uncanny. Having persuaded his 'client' to part with cash without having had to disclose the identity of the 'winner', he would simply stake the money as though it were his own on the first or second favourite in the next race. If that proved to be a winner, the grateful client would not only be receptive to further information, but would happily part with a portion of his winnings. After all, as Gordon whispered, 'It costs me a small fortune to keep the boys on the track sweet.' When negotiations had been swift, Gordon was able to extend his operations to two further betting shops close by for the same race, backing a different runner in each, thus ensuring one grateful, magnanimous client. The pretence of having to rush to spread his money served as convenient cause of immediate withdrawal and made it unnecessary for him to face his disappointed clients again until time had healed the wounds. In addition to his instinctive awareness of each 'client's' optimum level of vulnerability, Gordon also possessed a first-class memory, enabling him to judge the lapse of time needed to assuage shattered expectations to perfection. Seven days' lapse was generally long enough to allow him to reassure disappointed clients—there was never more than one 'live mug' per betting shop at any one time—that 'all I know is my partner retired to the South of France last year and I shall join him fairly soon. But, as you ought to know, racing is a sport and therefore accidents are bound to happen once in a while. If you learn to stick with me, you'll be on the right side as from today. Today's tip is a real little beauty.'

His attack was almost exclusively confined to the unattached— those whose attendance was spasmodic, whose knowledge and intensity of interest were meagre, whose reason for attendance was largely to pass away the time. All of these attributes applied to the merchant seamen ('God bless the Navy' as Gordon allowed himself to let slip one day, when in his cups) who, pockets bulging, eager for a thrill, time to kill, formed a constant body of visitors to the betting shops in the area. Their suggestibility and vulnerability to temptation, their transient presence as well as their total absence of rancour, presented a wide-open target to the large variety of local sharpshooters. Gordon would play on their credulity with the virtuosity born of many years of subtle probing into the deeper recesses of his fellow beings' weaknesses and vanities. Even his well-hackneyed ploy of 'patting his wad'—the regular tapping of his bulging breast-pocket, alleged to contain the bankroll he was intending to stake himself on the 'tip', but in reality made-up of a few carefully folded pages of newspaper— found an unfailing response from his prey.

In spite of the constancy of response, his degree of material success seemed to fluctuate enormously. Some days his net takings must have fallen close to zero, while on other days an 'easy touch' would, virtually on the point of asking, part with a couple of fivers, almost apologizing for the paucity of his response to Gordon's challenging 'How much have you got on you, fifty?' However, though his trade and his methods were a familiar talking-point among the regulars, the community's philosophy of 'Every man for himself' and 'The sucker is fair game' protected Gordon from inhibitory action on the part of the élite,* as long as

* The warning given to me by Jack was the only occasion on which I noted interference with Gordon's activities and this, again, was only administered retrospectively. It was only given due, as I discovered later, to my occupancy of a unique role within the group, belonging to that ambiguous twilight zone between 'mug' and 'regular'.

he stayed clear of normative transgressions such as overtures to established members or straightforward fraud—taking of money without placing of bets.

All of this, however, I was to learn over a considerable period of time and very little of it from Gordon himself. When, in the first instance, Gordon had finished with 'our mutual friend' he came over to me. My position within the orbit of the main group was sufficient to alert him to the wisdom of discretion, when confronted by me with only having tolerated his 'spiel for a giggle'; while at the same time firmness in dealing with him helped to restore some of my damaged status with the group. Though steadfastly he continued to cling to his assertion of having special information to impart, of only having tested me to elicit my deeper worthiness for his information, he was willing to concede that he had 'spun me a bit of a yarn', offering propitiation by buying me a drink.

This invitation proved to be the forerunner of a series of further meetings in the course of which I got to know Gordon fairly well, though never being able to penetrate beyond his 'betting entrepreneur' façade. He was willing to go as far as to admit that times were not very good, that information was at this particular time a little disorganized, that the stables were under special surveillance and that tips were at the time lacking their usual reliability. 'That's why for the time being I am keeping my own money in my wallet,* I'm doing these blokes a favour giving them inside dope, it is only proper they should show their appreciation. [Only after a few doubles would his tongue loosen sufficiently for even this admission.] We are just organizing things right down the line at the tracks, once we get going, it won't be long before I buzz my old buddy to start looking for a villa for me at Monte. One more good season and I'll be warming my arse in the sun twelve months a year.' Custom forbade interrogation as to further particulars or reference to incompatibilities. 'I'd give an honest partner with substantial capital a half-way share, all legal and signed-up, but you lot of deadbeats would rather be mugs all your life, making the bookies rich, and anyhow the few lousy pieces you could lay your hands on wouldn't

* I never did see Gordon stake a penny of his own money, though when it came to buying rounds of drinks, he was able to flash the odd fiver.

interest me.' A final tilt of the whisky glass, a triumphant stare at the audience and back to action, morale reinforced.

The Essentialist

As a child may look upon his father, seeing in him an ideal, a unique model, a god-like personification of his own aspirations; the embodiment of perfection, of wisdom, of stability, glory, and virtue; the power which created him before his world began; which now preserves and sustains him; and in virtue of which he exists; so Plato looks upon the Forms and Ideas. The Platonic Idea is the original and the origin of the thing; it is the rationale of the thing, the reason of its existence—the stable, sustaining principle in 'virtue' of which it exists. It is the virtue of the thing, its ideal, its perfection.*

Bill was a dustman with the Local Council. I met him at a very early stage in my research, in the course of my surveying one of the local pubs as a possible operational headquarters.† I was sitting on my own in a corner when Bill approached me. He had picked up a pair of binoculars that day, I looked an educated gent, could I enlighten him as to their true value, or better still would I by any chance be interested in purchasing. The binoculars looked in excellent shape, I told him, unfortunately I could offer neither evaluation nor trade, I had come to the neighbourhood in course of my research on the subject of gambling.

That was a happy coincidence, he continued, for should I be interested, he had for the past months been struggling towards the perfection of a system, an ideal pattern of betting. Its essence was the construction of a set of combinations of trebles with two master-accumulators which, once achieved, would be used as a permanent model, it then merely being necessary to select the appropriate runners for each insertion week by week. He had been a keen student of psychology for a long time and had for some years subscribed to a monthly psychological magazine

---

* K. R. Popper, *The Open Society and Its Enemies*, Routledge & Kegan Paul, (London 1945), ch. 3, p. 26.

† Bill was throughout my stay to remain a faithful companion, a constant source of information and of interpretation, a contact willing to introduce me and to vouch for me, a friend in need and in adversity.

which he had seen advertised in his Sunday paper—if he could only think of the name, he was sure I would have heard of it or possibly even took it myself. One series of articles, some time back, by an American professor had made a particular impression on him. It seemed, according to the professor, that everything in this world had its own pattern. One only had to look at the regularities in nature, the immutable succession of seasons—of birth, development, decay, death and rebirth—to become convinced that a pattern underlay every part of our existence. The problem was to find this pattern, to study each phenomenon in its basic structure, to search for the key. He had all his life been a keen musician, with a natural aptitude for all kinds of instruments and had, without ever having been taught, always been able to play any tune anyone asked for on the piano. But he had never got beyond that, he had lacked the pattern. He had, in fact, been thinking for some time now of asking the music teacher at the local Institute where, once upon a time he had been attending for a few lessons, to give him the pattern of the more difficult pieces; one of these days he would get round to it, for sure.

The betting system, when revealed on the occasion of our next meeting, consisted of nothing other than a skeleton made-up of six separate components—a model in which six races, three each at two different meetings, were to be selected and these selections to be combined in eight trebles, plus one grand accumulator.* Bill maintained that the pattern was of primary importance, the choice of runners merely a by-product. So far the system had had a few trial runs, but success had been limited to no more than one winning treble, which indicated to him that there were still some deficiencies to be ironed out. Maybe, he reflected, it might be necessary to displace one of the existing props by another, say to remove E and F and to replace it with G and H. Surely, with my experience of the subject I could advise him in his dilemma. I suggested that it might be advisable to place the bets each-way as, in spite of the fact of such change implying greater outlay, it would provide a useful insurance. This he rejected—'Oh no, that would take the dare out of it, after all it is only a sport. There

* Say at meeting I: Choices A, C and E and at meeting II: B, D and F, with the following 8 trebles: ACE, ACF, ADE, ADF, BDF, BCE, BCF, BDE and the six-race accumulator: ABCDEF.

would be no fun left in backing a dead certainty.' The fascination consisted in the achievement of a perfect instrument, an operation in which the winning itself would only be affirmation of having achieved perfect solution, a reward for the labour entailed. To find the perfect pattern involved a lot of work, depended on skilful manoeuvre, on the employment of faultless strategy, but the solution lay just around the corner. What had been impeding attainment of his goal had been the usual distractions a working man was subject to such as the insensitivity of his workmates. ('They are a lot of puppets, they don't even know someone else is pulling their strings. They think there is no more to betting than just studying form, that's why they will lose all their lives, while those who know will always win.') Then there were the barrenness and indifference of his home environment— 'This system I am working on needs a lot of concentration, a focus where you can sit back and think, but do you think I can get it in my home? Not so likely. Not that my missus really is a bad lot, she never interferes where I go, not like the others. I can go where I please, but when it comes to Wifehood* she's a washout, all disorder and no system, even the dinner she puts on the table just anyhow. I have been meaning to make myself a proper desk —you know what I mean, with gate-legs and nice looking bookshelves—wouldn't mind going into production once I made the pattern, they should sell like hot cakes for caravans and such like. I've been talking about it to my son for some time now—mind you he follows his mother—it would be up to me to be the brains of the outfit, but then with all the brainwork and concentrating I have been doing, that should be just a piece of cake.'

A few nights later, coming into the pub at the end of some interviews, I found Bill, pencil poised, poring over a notebook. 'I think I've got it at last' he exclaimed as soon as he set eyes on me. 'I had a two-pound win only last Saturday, it's just a matter of analysis, no looking back from now.' He passed me his notebook. A few pages of cyphers denoting the structure of his betting system and some more pages filled with a series of single words, such as unique, practice, violence, formation, horror, etc, 'When

---

* Bill's conversation abounded with use of abstract nouns such as 'Wifehood', 'Dustmanship', 'Musicianship', 'Horsemanship', such terms implying absolutes, finalities.

I've got nothing else to do, I make it my business to experiment with the system in every possible form to get the perfect answer and at the same time I practise writing down the words I do not know to keep my brain active! Now I have got so far in my system, it's just a matter of time before I start winning in a big way.' I asked him whether he had ever heard of the familiar gamblers' saying: 'System going well, send more money.' 'That's different,' he replied, 'those systems they speak of are superstitions, make-believe. What I am after is scientific analysis, a strategy, a master-plan. No need to go through life with your eyes shut, not even when you are born no more than a common working man, I say.'

The Reluctant Gambler

It was not long after I had started visiting the small, old-fashioned pub on the corner opposite to the new council flats, that I became friendly with the crowd of 'Jolly Postmen'. An informal group, totalling perhaps a dozen, of whom no fewer than any six regularly spent their lunchbreak hours—between midday and more often than not, three in the afternoon—in the public bar. They spent their time playing cribbage, darts, shove-halfpenny, or just sitting drinking at their corner tables. All were employed at the local postal depot on the usual four-week rota of driving, delivering, collecting and sorting. Their relations with the other midday regulars—Arthur, the ex-barber prematurely retired due to a debilitating heart condition, Flo and Sid the old rag-and-bone couple and in particular with Jack ('Tarzan'), the scrap dealer whose yard on the opposite side of the road had been fitted with a klaxon to warn him of impending trade while he was engaged in the primary task of 'lubricating the works', the 'Greek Chorus' of elderly widows in the Ladies' Bar and the various other regulars and casuals—were amiable and friendly, but always short of mutual hospitality. Other than for special occasions, such as birthdays, weddings, anniversaries, wage increases or unantici-pated pay bonuses when shorts were introduced, beer was the order of the day, the average individual daily consumption rate ranging between five to nine pints for the session.[9]

I had, in the course of my second visit, opportunity to buy a pint of bitter for Alec who had temporarily detached himself from the group in order to inspect an old watch Arthur was offering for sale and had been asked back to the postmen's table, where, having disclosed the purpose of my stay in the neighbourhood, I soon found myself in animated discussion. Vic ('Hooker')—squat, powerfully built ('this stomach 'as cost me a fortune! I can't afford to lose weight')—acted, as was his custom on all public occasions, as spokesman, only from time to time turning to his comrades for confirmation.

He knew all there was to know about gambling, he declared, having himself in the past been a victim to the mania. Not to the extent of being, as you might say, an out-and-out compulsive as these poor wretches you could see down the 'Lane',[10] but bad enough to get himself severely into debt. He asserted that licensing the betting shops was the worst day's work the Government had ever done. True enough, there had been illegal betting with street-bookies before licensing, but then it had not been possible to place more than one single bet per day. You wrote out your bet in the morning, handed it to the bookie's runner before racing got under way and then you had to wait for the following day before you could bet again. Now things were different, punters were drawn into the betting shops to loiter there all day. If you waited for the pubs to close, you would not be able to get into the shops for the crowds inside. That was the trouble, the working man got a few drinks inside him, especially when he had been on spirits and he got the feeling that he could not lose, that this was his lucky day. They started off with 20p on the first race and when they lost, they doubled-up over and over again, confident that it was only a matter of time before their luck started to run for them. Before they looked round their wages were all gone and they were having to 'sub' from their mates. That was exactly how it had got him in the past; a few drinks too many—mind you, he had every reason to get himself tight once in a while, a man was only as good as his wife and he had got the worst wife in the whole wide world, she was not worth a 'fucking wank' (at this point the narrative was interrupted for several minutes during which time his mates assured Hooker that he was making it up, that it was his old woman who had had the ill-fortune to get 'the biggest, ugliest bastard in the whole world' etc.)—and you felt that this was the day when you were going to hit the bookie hard.[11] Of course things had never worked out this way, he had several times got himself deeply into debt to the tune of as much as twenty pounds at a time and had only been able to extricate himself by hard saving and copious overtime. But now he had learned his lesson, he had got wise to the fact that the bookies had got things in their favour in all possible ways—just look at the Dagenham coup a few years back, the bookies had stood to lose a lot of money, so they just refused to pay out.[12] Though the motto 'Live for the day' was still the only valid philosophy for the working man, it was equally true that you should 'never borrow, never steal', 'us postmen' had no need to go chasing around for kicks. He had got all the friends and company he wanted all around him, he had finished with gambling once and for all. On behalf of the rest of the group, Len seconded that 'us postmen' though always poor had no cause to be unhappy. Work was not hard, supervision easy, overtime freely available when needed. You had your pride, were respected and above all you could have all the fun you wanted without getting yourself into debt. For example, they got a bloody sight more fun from playing their 'crib'* without any stakes whatever than those nobs in their clubs who put thousands on the turn of one card.

Two or three weeks later—by which time my daily lunchtime visits had earned me 'honorary membership' in the group—while spending an afternoon in one of the betting shops I was frequenting, I suddenly caught sight of Hooker. He had just passed directly by the spot where I had been standing in conversation with one of the punters without giving any signs of recognition. Assuming that he had just dropped in to place a casual bet, I thought it best to carry on and to wait for him to approach me when he felt inclined to do so. It was just time for the 3 o'clock race. Hooker placed his 50p bet and then stood back anxiously, avoiding my eye, while the race commentary was being relayed. By his expression I judged that he had lost. He lost a further 50p on the 3.15, £1 on the 3.30 and by the time I left the betting shop at half-past four his usual cheery countenance had

* Cribbage, a near-mechanical card game, popular in pubs for insignificant stakes.

become clouded over, his customary smile had been replaced by an anxious, gloomy frown. His total losses at that time, according to my observations, had risen to over five pounds.

The following midday I found the 'Jolly Postmen', as usual, assembled in the 'Royal Arms'. Hooker was missing. Having sat down, I alluded to his absence in the most casual terms. 'He ain't come in today,' Jock observed, 'got himself a proper skinful yesterday lunch, went on shorts. When he goes that way there's nothing anyone can do, no telling what he will get up to. I reckon he hung around some betting shop all afternoon till the pubs opened and then got himself pissed like a parson till they'd chuck him out closing time.' At this juncture I considered it appropriate to mention having seen him the day before, hanging round the betting shop for most of the afternoon. 'I'm not surprised,' Jock answered, 'when he gets that way there's no holding him. He'll lie, borrow and blackguard to get his hands on enough to gamble and booze. The time before last they fished him out of the canal half-drowned. The Ambulance brought him home stark naked under the blanket. The wife called out "Where the bleeding hell have you been, you rotten bastard" and he answered her, "Been to the fucking strip club, can't you see?" I tell you, though, his old woman is a proper rotten bitch—we wouldn't say so when he is around—but she gives the poor sod a hell of a time, won't let him near her for weeks at a time and at the same time swears black's blue he's having it off with his sister-in-law. If I had her to live with, I'd do myself in, if I didn't do her in first. Every once in a while he just does his nut and then he's all right again.' I enquired as to the reason for his absence. 'Regularly after one of these bouts, he takes a couple of days off—there's so many of us postmen we just do a little more each. The Governor doesn't mind, it isn't his money after all, though I feel it's a shame on the poor bloody taxpayer. At first when he wakes up, he feels as rotten as hell, he tells us, and his missus feels so sorry for him, she takes a day off work to bring him his breakfast in bed and cook him his favourite dinner. For a couple of days they're so thick they just can't bear to leave each other and when he gets back to work, it is still all lovey-dovey, like a pair of newly-weds. Then, all of a sudden, she'll turn as nasty as a she-cat again.'

When I came in a couple of days later, Hooker had returned to the crowd. 'Fine old china* you are,' he remonstrated in my direction, 'pretending not to know me when you're with your mates.' 'Sorry Hooker,' I answered, 'you know what it's like when you are working, I just couldn't break away at once. When I looked for you directly after, I couldn't see you any more.' Magnanimously he waved aside further apologies: 'No offence, mate, I'd only dropped in to place a couple of bob on a horse the missus fancied. Just as well you couldn't get away, you might have done your money along with hers.'

The Reformed Gambler

Nothing about Bob C. suggested that the interview would produce any surprises. I found him seated in his shirt-sleeves, revealing a series of arm tatoos, in front of his television, evening paper on his lap. His wife, who had opened the door, resumed her seat on the settee immediately our conversation had got under way intensely studying a women's magazine, not saying a word for the first half-hour. At first Bob seemed hostile and suspicious, brusquely asserting that for all he knew I might be one of those encyclopaedia salesmen who, masquerading as researchers, were forcing their entry into houses and often succeeded in swaying the unsuspecting into signing contracts for goods they had no intention of buying nor any possible use for when bought.[13] On being reassured, his manner quickly changed and to an increasing extent he proved co-operative and informative, prepared to answer any question put to him.

The home was in close conformity with the usual standards found in these new, centrally-heated Local Authority flats. Fitted carpets, modern highly-coloured fittings and furnishings, plus the usual accoutrements of contemporary metropolitan working-class way of life—the 20″ television set (which though muted, as in so many other cases, remained switched on throughout the interview), the cocktail cabinet in polished walnut, the automatic record player, automated kitchen and so forth. A vast improvement on the previous low-standard house in Lea, though

* Cockney slang: 'China (Plate)': Mate.

involving much higher outgoings and depriving Bob of his little garden and his household pets. In fact, Bob asserted, the working man was now worse off than thirty years ago. His own trade—he was, now in the mid-forties, an electrician with the local borough —had in that period, in terms of income differentials, declined from first to forty-first place and even though his wife was, with both daughters grown-up and married, working full-time as a tailoress, there were so many things now to provide for that a working man had less money in his pocket for his own pleasures and interests than ever before.

Certainly, in his own case, the good old days of the last couple of years of the war and the early post-war had never returned. As a merchant seaman, able to lay his hands on quite a bit of 'stuff' then in short supply, he had got in with a crowd who knew how to make money; among them the racing manager at one of the local dog tracks, a trainer, a couple of owners and book-makers and even the racing correspondent of one of the dailies. His own background—'all the Irish are dog crazy, most of them keep a couple of greyhounds in the back garden. My father and two of my uncles used to train dogs for racing every morning on the heath, I had a go at it myself when I came over here and though I did not make any money at it, I soon got wise as to what was going on'—helped his entry and affirmed his position once acquired. The game was then wide open, lots of 'black money'[14] around, plenty of Americans with their pockets stuffed with cash and what with war work and later on gratuities, you could get away with murder. The crowd were so green, they'd stand for the three-card trick, they did not even trouble when one of the trap doors went up a full second before the others and one of the dogs shot out before the others had even looked at the hare. His own gang were so well in, that nine out of ten of the dogs they had 'prepared' would come in as winners. With the set-up they had, stretching right from the kennel to the book with everyone in between properly straightened out, they could hardly go wrong. At first, they had the sense to operate circumspectly, no more than one coup per meeting for three or four weeks, then give it a break for a couple of weeks to let the dust settle then, bingo, back to action. But human nature being what it is, they were not for long satisfied with what they had. Expenses were mounting with more and more people having to be sweetened, but even then there would have been no need to get greedy, to stretch it until eventually they had two crooked runners per meeting. Suddenly, the whole thing blew apart, one of the trainers was putting on the screws a bit too hard, a couple of the boys got into a bit of a fight; the Association got to hear of it and the whole 'bloody shoot'—trainer, training manager, bookie, reporter an' all—got warned off the track; that was the end.

But while it lasted it must have been very lucrative, I suggested, surely with certainties of that order and with accumulated winnings, he must have been able to put by quite a bit?

'I tell you, I used to win as much as five hundred quid on one single race, I sometimes had so much money in my pocket I didn't know what to do with it', Bob answered. It was at this stage that Mrs C. intervened for the first time: 'You might as well admit, it was easy come, easy go. You only said a couple of weeks ago you'd lost the price of four or five houses.' Bob did not seem to be shaken by this intervention of realism: 'Sure, I might have made myself a little nest-egg, but somehow you seem to get caught-up. You have to hang around with the boys to stay in the swim. What with drinks all round the house, taxis and tips, your hand is never long out of your pocket. After the race it's back to the pub for drinks, then on to the clubs. I used to roll home half-way through the night, not knowing where I'd been, who I'd been with or how much money I was supposed to have on me. You had to do it to stay in the crowd'—a stern admonitory look from his wife—'Alright, and that's not the whole story, you think yourself a bit of a big-shot walking round with all that money in your pockets and everyone kow-towing to you. You hang around the track, nothing to do but to wait until your runner comes up. Naturally you start getting interested in the card, you walk back and forth to the bar, you meet all kinds of low-lives, everybody gives you a different whisper, after a while you think the whole thing is easy. You back a couple of winners on your own and you begin to fancy yourself a good judge, and bang, by the time the next tip comes along, you are down to your last ten quid, or more often than not you've got to tap your pals for the stake money. I would have been a rich man now, if I'd stuck to my money and only backed the tips I got. There was an Italian in our mob, only just released from the Isle of Man, used to own a small tobacco-nist and was able to get hold of all the smokes and sweets the boys wanted.[15] Me and him sort of palled up, he used to say to me: "Bob, have a bit of sense, buy yourself a bit of property, you'll have something to show for it when it blows up." I wish I had taken his advice, he now owns a couple of blocks over at Stamford Hill, he gave each of his kids a house of their own when they got married. Another one of my pals turned himself into a professional, has never done a day's work since then, he now has twenty dogs of his own, employs his own observers at the meetings. He made himself five thousand quid last year and never paid a penny tax, never bets a penny unless it is a certainty. Mind you, he tells me his business is harder than working and I quite believe it, you can't even trust your best friend an inch. I just didn't have the sense to think of the future, or maybe the temperament was wrong, I never knew how to control it. Even after it all blew up, I wouldn't leave it alone until I'd lost the few quid I had left.'

Did he still gamble? I asked him.

Before he could answer his wife interposed: 'I make damn sure he doesn't, it was bad enough while it lasted, I managed to break him of it once, he knows I wouldn't go through it again, not for anything in the world. He only mentions the couple of pals who had the sense to hang on to their money, most of the rest finished in the gutter and that's where he would have been if I had not stood behind him.' Bob assented to these remarks, made in a matter-of-fact voice without bitterness or rancour, quite readily. It was not as bad as all that, there had been more good times than bad. He still kept in touch with some of the boys over at the X—mentioning the name of the pub in which the racing fraternity congregated on Saturday mornings—there was still information floating around. Some of the boys kept urging him to come along to the meetings, but he knew his own weakness; once he got started he could not see the end of it and besides, what with all the new commitments, he just had not the money to spare. Mind you, these had been the best days of his life, there was nothing like a racing crowd for generosity, good humour and cheer. No-one ever asked for help and went away empty-handed. What they had, they shared and even when they were all skinned they still had a laugh, they knew how to get the most out of life.

Did he then mean to say that some races were still being fixed? I continued.

The son of the trainer, as well as of the racing-manager he had been in cohort with were both now working on the tracks—'You can't make a corkscrew go straight all of a sudden'. Assuredly supervision was now much more strict, medical tests were regularly carried out on runners and furthermore the public had become much more knowledgeable and critical. But if you know the wrinkles—and after all some of the new generation of 'boys' had had the best education—and kept tight control, you could still help yourself from time to time. As long as racing and betting went together—no-one could control the amount of exercise or food a dog was getting, or even always see the little bit of extra that was slipped into their dishes—there would always be someone on the inside making himself a little pile; and good luck to them, was it not after all the same way fortunes were being made on the Stock Exchange and did not all Governments make use of the meanest and most immoral methods to get hold of the secrets of another? First make your perfect man, then you can have a system that is just and perfect. Until then, 'Where there's man, there is money; where there is money, there is dirt.'

The Compulsive Gambler

Mike and I were standing outside the betting shop in Cable Street. I had been trying to question him as to the system employed by him in making his choice, would he demonstrate his thought processes to me? 'You have to study form, otherwise you don't stand a chance,' Mike informed me, 'look for instance at the next race. I fancy Tamarisk, he weighs five stone eight-three ounces', quickly correcting himself when noticing my obvious recoil, 'what I mean, he is a five-year-old carrying eight stone and three ounces, that makes him bottom weight. His jockey is Busby who's always dangerous and last two times out he was second and third.'

'But look,' I interjected, 'the papers make him 7:4 favourite, does not this make him less attractive to you?' 'No they're wrong,' Mike averred. 'Sunshine will start favourite, Tamarisk will pay out at least 9:2.* But then, all these horses (pointing to three runners listed next to Tamarisk) are dangerous, any one of them might win, I wouldn't like to be off any of them. If I wasn't skinned, if I had any money, I'd back Tamarisk or Rapier, but who's to know, the whole bloody game is crooked.'[16]

Who did he think made the game crooked? I asked. Was it the jockeys, the stableboys, the trainers, owners, or bookies or perhaps all of them acting in combination. How would they, in his opinion, go about it? 'Look here,' Mike answered heatedly, 'you've got a horse running at odds of, say, 1:9 on. Some blokes will bet £900 to win a hundred, the bookies stand to lose millions, if it wins.'

The exact logic of this statement escaped me. 'Surely,' I tried, 'when the bookie takes £900 for each £100 he has to pay out, he stands to win millions rather than lose them. Anyhow the other horses will be backed and you will agree that a horse will have turned into an odds-on favourite just because the big backers . . .' 'You can take it from me,' Mike cut me short, 'when a 1:10 on chance races and gets beat, the bookies have nobbled the jockey. They've just gone to him and said: "Look here, mate, if you hold back or act exhausted, here's five hundred quid for you." 'But what will the owner say to this,' I wanted to know, 'wouldn't you say a horse is likely to turn into an odds-on favourite just because the big backers—the ones who could nobble the jockey—have got their own money on him.' By this time Mike was too testy for abstractions. 'This may all be very well,' he answered as parting shot before resuming his search for the Golden Grail, 'you don't know the ins and outs, I've been in the game long enough to tell you that the whole fucking set-up is bent. A 1:9 favourite, what's his name, anyhow it doesn't matter, got beat yesterday by a 40:1 shot. Now you can't tell me that's not crooked. Mind you, I'd rather back the 40:1, but that's beside the point.'

Tommy, who had for some time been hovering on the brink of our discussion, came over to join me the moment Mike left. He

---

* In fact Sunshine, who in the morning editions had been forecast to starting odds of 7:1, never fell below that figure in course of the ante-post betting, while Tamarisk, as predicted, started as 2:1 favourite and won by two lengths.

obviously considered me a 'Schmock punter' whom Mike had been trying to 'set up'.[17] 'You don't want to listen to that crazy cunt, he doesn't know the first fucking thing about racing or about anything fucking else!' he advised me. 'Who's ever heard of a racehorse weighing five stone eight, I ask you, that's the weight of a dog. Fancy a man fool enough to tell you a horse weighed five stone eight.* I know he corrected himself as soon as he saw you look surprised, but to talk such shit in the first place shows you mustn't listen to these cunts. Mind you, if I were you, I wouldn't let on you don't believe them, they are quite liable to throttle the life out of you.' My protestations implying that I considered such action rather harsh response to mere disbelief he waved imperiously aside. 'You see that khazi over there,' pointing to the public convenience opposite, one of the regular 'caravan stops', 'a man was found dead in there last night.' 'Murdered?' I asked. 'In this neighbourhood you don't ask no questions,' Tommy replied, 'or you soon find yourself in there with him. Look mate, all this violence this bunch bottles up inside them has to come out.'

All this was said in a strong Scottish accent with strange detachment, quietly and composedly. Tommy, even apart from this untypical apparent inner composure, stood out in this fidgety, pale-faced assembly by his fresh complexion, his clean, neatly-brushed hair and his reflective observant smile. By now he had gathered that I was unlikely to be the 'Schmock punter', the ignorant greenhorn hopeful of fastening onto the 'inside dopester' in the hope of inspired confidence but inevitably as befits his true deserts, duped, diddled and fleeced. 'Most of the time they only boast and shout, but once in a while they blow up.'

I asked him whether he was a local man and to what extent he was a member of 'the bunch'. He had been living in the neighbourhood for over ten years, was 39 years old, single and one of the very few who did not look at least ten years older than their chronological age. 'I live among them alright, but I try to keep myself apart. I don't smoke or drink and don't borrow, don't get involved with the villains and dodge when I see trouble coming along.' What did he do for a living? I asked. 'Nothing' came the

---

* The weight regularly quoted in the racing particulars is that of the jockey and not of the horse or the dog.

instantaneous reply, 'I've never worked in my life, I cannot live without my freedom. I wish I could settle down to a job, I've tried a few times, but never stick it longer than a week. I know I cannot work indoors, I feel stifled and imprisoned, but even when I've tried to work out-of-doors—I worked on a site* only this summer for four days—as soon as the foreman says to me "Where have you been all day" I tell him to stuff his job up his arse and I'm off again. I get about ten quid a week, and when I'm really desperate I can wheedle a bit more to get a new pair of shoes or a shirt, but you've only got to look at me to see it doesn't do me much good.[18] That's where it all goes'—angrily jerking his thumb over his shoulder at the betting shop—'there and the fucking dogs when I've got a few bob to spare. It's like a disease, you can't get away from it. I kid myself I'm different to that scruffy mob, but it's got me just like it's got them, except maybe I stop when I'm skinned. These cunts don't care what they do to get their few bob to gamble with. Me, I've had plenty of offers to come on a job, but I keep well away, I don't want to get involved with the law, I value my freedom too much.[19] Not that I do anything with it, I just hang around till the Shop opens. I might sit in the park if the weather is good or even spend a couple of hours in the library, but as soon as racing begins I'm on parade, doing my pieces like the rest of them. I don't spend anything, or practically nothing, on my bed—perhaps 30p a night in one of the dosshouses, that's all you can call them; a cup of tea in the morning and a plate of eggs and chips later on. The other ten quid goes on racing,[20] and then I'm usually skinned by Friday, so I can't even bet when I fancy a horse.' Pay-day, in respect of the various sources available to Tommy, appeared to be Monday. Monday and Tuesday, Tommy would back in denominations of one pound; with average luck there would be enough left to back in units of 25p on Wednesdays and Thursdays. By Friday these would have shrunk to 12½p and Saturday could only be sustained as betting-day either in the event of an untypical run of good fortune in the latter part of the week—success in periods of maximum resources would induce runaway betting and invariably to total bankruptcy at an early stage of the betting week—or the generosity of other members of the fraternity within different

* Site, in this context, means building-site.

stages of the weekly cycle, or experiencing a series of successful wagers.

Saturday was the nadir of Tommy's existence, the day on which betting funds were totally lacking, when nevertheless force of habit compelled full-time attendance at the betting shop. By mysterious, perverse, satanic intervention, the very day on which all his 'fancies'—unbacked—came home: 'I've stood out here with tears in my eyes when I've seen the results come up on the board, when one after the other of my horses has come in first and me without a penny in my pocket. Can you wonder that all this violence our mob bottle up inside us comes out once in a while. Something snaps and you just blow up without being able to help it.'

Haphazard aggression, vindictive yet pointless destructiveness were indeed in strong daily evidence. I was denied—or possibly spared—the witnessing of any acts of severe personal violence, but soon came to be aware of a stream of other acts originating from the same sources. Not unexpectedly, public property was regarded as fair game for pilfering or defacement, but a whole cluster of other acts of explosive frustration-discharge soon came to be familiar experience. For no apparent reason one person would pounce on a newspaper being studied by another and tear it to shreds, feet would be trodden on with vicious deliberation, a group member who only a few minutes ago had sought one out with the intention of patiently offering enlightenment on some matter one had previously shown interest in, would turn on one with 'Why the fucking hell don't you fuck off, we don't want any spies around here.' I soon learned to take it for granted that such outbursts would provoke neither resentment nor retaliation but that being passively left to peter out, they would quickly subside and, more often than not, finally even help to reinforce mutuality. By all accounts, physical assaults, though resisted and not always ending harmlessly, followed a similar pattern—haphazard, almost detached, aimless and inconclusive.

'Of course I do not always lose, I've had some decent wins from time to time, only two weeks ago I drew thirty quid on two winners, but I always end up the same way. Sometimes I think I am worse off when I do win, the whole bloody lot expect you to treat them and to bung them a couple of quid when they run out.

I never do anything with the money, I may have a blow-out and a few doubles instead of pints, but before I get round to buying myself a decent pair of shoes the money has run out again. You've only got to look at me to see that I am a bloody sponge, just like the rest of them, I can't even fool myself that I am any better. I tell you I love my freedom, but what do I do with it, the truth is I just can't settle to regular work. It's the system which is all wrong, they shouldn't give blokes like me money unless we work for it. There's plenty of work to be done on the roads, they should make us do a day's work before they give us a day's money and no more at a time. But then, you may as well be bloody dead if you don't have a thrill to look forward to. You ask me why I gamble and I tell you, it's the thrill. I know the game is crooked and that I haven't a chance, but when I've put my money on a horse and hear its name on the speaker, my heart stands still. I know I'm alive. You might have your last few bob riding on the horse, you know if it loses you've even lost your pastime, it's the excitement, the thrill that gets you every time. For us it's a pastime as well, I haven't a wife or a family, or even a room of my own, so what else have I got to look forward to, except to pass the time in study of form?

'Mind you, when I'm skinned, I'm skinned, I don't beg or borrow, I just do without, I can't go up to a bloke—not like Jim—and blab him for a few bob. Now Jim, he's got the cheek of the devil, when he's flat he'll squeeze a nicker* out of somebody and then he'll finish the day with a hundred quid in his pocket. No one can say no to Jim. I've seen him blab the last quid out of a stranger at the dogtrack and then laugh in the poor bastard's face. At least the villain has a skin as thick as the devil to enjoy what he is doing. Me, I just suffer, I'm just falling to pieces in front of my own eyes. If you offered me a million pounds now to lead a normal life, I could no longer do it. The only thing that could save me would be if they cut off my money altogether unless I did some work for it. But this they will never do as long as I can lie and connive my way round their silly little laws and regulations. So, what is there for me to hope for?'

* Nicker is Cockney slang for pound note.

The Non-Gambler and the Anti-Gambler

To all outward appearances there are few visible differences between the 'Non-Gambler', Alan G.—an employee of London Transport who had some six years previously, having been a bus driver, been transferred to less strenuous duties due to having a cardiac condition—and the 'Anti-Gambler', William W.—a printer with one of the national dailies, on permanent nightshift for over ten years.

Both men are in their early fifties, slightly built, soft-spoken, unassertive, slow to formulate thoughts and feelings. In both cases the wives, present throughout the interviews, seem to be the dominant partner; their presence more positive, their views more readily available, their powers of analysis and articulation more pronounced, both ready to answer on their husbands' behalf at the least encouragement. Both Alan's modern ground-floor council flat as well as William's privately-rented house in the same street where he had been living for some thirty years, bore clear, unmistakable signs of relative affluence, of systematic domestic care and application, of pride in one's home and possessions. Both reported minimal contact with neighbours— social life being confined to one's own immediate family—no more than the feeblest personal interests and hobbies, total absence of occupational ambition and only the slightest interest in outside affairs. Each family had one grown-up son. William's twenty-year-old an apprentice printer. Alan's son now twenty-two, a B.Sc. Physics graduate recently, after merely one year's training, qualified as B.O.A.C. pilot. Neither man, nor their wives, had any interest in gambling, none had, according to their reports, ever set foot inside a betting shop—nor were they ever intending to do so—nor had they over the past year or so, to their recollection, spent any money on gambling of any sort, other than the few pence on the occasional raffle-ticket, or possibly the office sweepstake. Gambling was no problem to any of them.

By the time that stage in the interview had been reached, a series of differentiating marks were beginning to come into focus. Where Alan's solid and sombre furniture was clearly the ac-cumulation of many years of careful budgeting and bore, though immaculately preserved, every sign of domestic use, William's home, equally spick and span, with its brightly polished cocktail cabinet and its plasticated hi-fi was of much more recent vintage. It was more modern and contemporary, but at the same time more flashy and flamboyant. Mrs G., a clerk with a city firm, though ready with her answers well in advance of her husband, was satisfied to guide his replies, to affirm his testimony, to applaud his character, to defer to him in the minute areas of divergence. Not so Mrs W.—exclusively a housewife, suspicious, assertive, and equally 'faster on the draw' than her spouse—in contrast to Mrs G., the one who directed fire, if not directly at her husband's personality, at least on any of his views the moment these threatened to diverge from orthodoxy; sniping with deadly precision at any targets looming-up from the enemy camp, as for instance her views on her neighbours.[21] While Mrs G. seemed to feel that hers were 'pretty nice people, as far as I know, we just don't seem to need them very much', Mrs W. had a different perspective: 'We don't have anything to do with our neighbours, we hardly know them to say good morning. This used to be a nice neighbourhood once upon a time, but it's got very rough. What with the blacks moving in all over the place, it's getting more like Mombasa than Bethnal Green. You should see all the white girls who shack up with these blacks, half of them not old enough to get married. It's the kids I feel sorry for, it can't come to any good with them spreading all around us. It's high time we kicked a few of them out, let alone allow more into our country.' Mr G. also expressed himself on the subject of coloured immigrants: 'The way I see it, we can't go on letting them in just as they like, the country just is not big enough and what with the housing shortage and now the unemployment, it's bound to lead to friction. We've got them all over the place, as you know, some good, some bad, some indifferent. Most of the time you hardly notice the colour now, but give me one of my own any old time, you know where you are with your own kind.'

On the subject of possessions and personal consumption— total household incomes were roughly similar—Mr G. modestly declared: 'We have never had more than enough, but have always been satisfied with what we can afford, what we can't pay for we do without.' The W.s were more aspiring, as their two pedigree miniature poodles—'They cost me thirty quid, but we have always been fond of dogs'—and their new Jaguar, parked outside the front door attested: 'I have got used to nightwork, have done it for most of my life. I have also got used to all the luxuries I can buy with the extra thirty per cent pay I earn working nights. We've had our holidays abroad for years now, last year it was Majorca, this year we are thinking of Greece. The wife told me the boy wanted a suit a few weeks back, I gave him forty quid to go and be measured for the best. I made him open a bank account with my own bank when he was twenty and now I make certain he puts by a couple of quid each week. He's just beginning to grow up to learn to appreciate the value of money. It's a good lesson when you realize that in life you can't get nothing when you have no money to pay for it. He's a good boy, works hard, has clean habits, keeps regular hours, it won't be long before he'll have a trade that will bring him good money all his life.'

When it came to discussing their son, the G.s were at their most voluble: 'Naturally we were a little disappointed when he told us he had decided to become a pilot, he had always been a brilliant scholar, he was the only boy from the whole area who got into University. His professor at Bristol pleaded with him to go on to his Ph.D., he said there was no limit to where he could go with his brains. But we have always respected his wishes and we felt that if that was what he wanted to do, it's all right with us. Now we are glad he has made up his mind, with his qualifications he's got his pilot's licence in a year and he is so enthusiastic, there is no limit to his prospects.' There could be no doubt that their son's career and accomplishments were their favourite topic, that the vicarious fulfilment they experienced in all his successes—his early grammar-school entry, his effortless integration into his new environment, his sixth-form prefecture, the ease with which he merged into the life at University, his popularity with his friends of both sexes, his manifold talents from the driving of cars to skill in debate—served as focal point to their own lives. Prodded by his wife Mr G. was willing to admit that he had done his best to 'encourage the boy, to smoothe the way for him', but other than for their lifelong preparedness to establish and maintain the correct backdrop for him, they disclaimed direct share in his triumph.

As regards gambling, Mr G. inclined to attribute his personal abstinence to early negative conditioning. His own father had been an inveterate gambler whose losses had constantly deprived the family of necessities, whose excesses had led to frequent family conflicts and whose self-indulgence and inability to resist temptation had finally led to his mother's early death. Personally, he had always been uninterested in gambling in all its forms, but was willing to concede that to most people it represented an interest, a pleasure they could indulge in without doing anyone any real harm. Only excess was harmful and deleterious, but then excess in any direction was. William W.'s sentiments, echoed by his wife, were less permissive: 'I'd put a complete stop to it, if I had my way', he declared with considerable vehemence. 'It's a bloody disgrace those fellows waste their time loafing in the shops when they should be getting on with their work.' The suggestion that, as would apply to him, some of these alleged daytime 'loafers' might be shiftworkers in their off-time period, he impatiently brushed aside. 'Be it as it may, there could only be a tiny minority of these and they should be doing something better with their time than squandering the money that should go into their home.[22] Chaps at my works, earning the same money I do, owe half their wages by the time they draw their pay. Their life is made up of gambling, particularly now they've got the betting shops. They go in there with ten quid in their pockets, by the time the second race is over that's gone, so they've got to borrow some more to get it back. When they win once in a while, say thirty quid, it's drinks all round and a fiver a race instead of two, in two days they're back where they started. For them money has no value, it's an illusion. A chap in my son's firm won three hundred quid a little while back, I worked it all out for him, told him to pay off the money he owed on his car. Do you think he did? Not so bloody likely, in a month it was all gone with nothing to show for it. There's only one winner and that's the bookie. You can see them riding around in their big, shining new cars. Where do you think that comes from? The bleeding poor punters who won't learn their lesson, no matter what you do.'

If this was the case, I enquired, would it not be futile to try to stop it, was it not a fact that gambling had been rife even before the changes in legislation?

It was nonsense, he declared vehemently, to assume that people knew best what was good for them, give people a pick between what was good and what was bad and they would always fall for the latter. Once you made things hard to come by, punished a few really hard, who just would not learn to obey the law, the others would soon realize that they had to fall into line, that those who ran the show really knew what was best. 'It's all this self-indulgence all around you, when you don't have respect for private property, proper discipline, your moral code soon starts to crack. Once that packs up, we'll all be back in the jungle, mark my words.'

The Bookmaker

Jim had been partner in the betting shop for the past three years, having originally had the cash required to purchase the half-share advanced by his father-in-law, himself a betting shop proprietor in another area. Bookmaking, in one form or another, had been his profession since he left school at the age of fifteen in the last year of the war. At first as casual runner for a street bookie then, some four years later as tic-tac man at racecourses, later again as clerk with a bookie alternating between legitimate bookmaking at racecourses and sub-rosa activity from a backroom and finally as right-hand man to his father-in-law until he, on retirement, had sold the betting shop owned by him. In the course of his advancement he had left the Bethnal Green area into which he had been born, and had, five years previously, taken the first steps along the traditional Jewish 'escape route', paying a deposit on a modest semi-detached at Stamford Hill.[23]

His spiritual roots had remained in the East End to which his work continued to bring him back six days a week. Nostalgically he recalled: 'Those days we were all of us poor, every household had known poverty and unemployment at some time or another. Quite a few of them were used to living with it most of their lives, but we were all of us poor together. There was nobody to envy or whose possessions you were craving for. When somebody needed a bowl of sugar, they'd give an empty cup to one of the kids and the first door he knocked at who had any for themselves, would fill it up for him and more often than not, give him half a loaf to go with it. The first thing you'd do when the pay packet came into your home, was to pay back your debts; if you had enough, with a little to spare. Mind you, the blocks were like little villages, in some streets there was nothing but one single family, no more than two or three names, what with uncles, brothers-in-law, second cousins and great-grandchildren. So in a way, you were really helping your own. When you got married, you just moved in upstairs and by the time you had a kid or two, one of your relatives had died or another had persuaded the rent-man to let you live in their upstairs.'

Had things changed so very radically, and what had been the cause of these changes? 'Once it gets started you don't know where it began. One neighbour puts by a few quid, gets himself a carpet in his parlour. At first everyone comes in wide-eyed to admire, before you look round, every woman is nagging her old man until he gets himself into debt and buys her one. No sooner have they made their first payment, than someone gets ahead and buys himself a hall carpet to go with it. As soon as you've got the first few pieces together, you notice what a hovel you are living in and suddenly the East End is no longer good enough for you. Once you get the feeling, you don't know where it comes from, nor have you any idea where it is leading you to. One part of you makes fun of your neighbours the way they've let themselves get caught in the net, another part is beginning to enjoy the new comforts you have managed to get hold of yourself. One thing is sure, the feeling of neighbourhood goes, now it's every man for himself.

'Of course, that's only one part of the story, a fat shilling coming into every home, the Welfare State, the skyscraper Council blocks on our doorsteps, foreign travel, the T.V., things were bound to change. The kids get educated and they pull us along, after all that's what we are all working for, a better life for the kids. Not that these things can't go too far, the kids get so much money, they think it just grows on trees.' Turning to Harry, his partner: 'Only last Saturday Pete [the owner of a nearby chemist shop] was telling me of a kid of fourteen comes in with his school cap and buys himself a dozen skins at a time.[24] My own kid tells me that in his school, half the kids refuse the free milk that's given to them and that the kitchen staff just fiddle it for themselves. I'm all for not letting anybody go short, but with all this welfare, half the stuff goes where it was never intended. Just take a look at the Family Allowance, they were meant to help the mothers feed and clothe their kids, but with some of them, the more Family Allowance you give them, the more they bang away; the more they yentz,* the more welfare they get till in the end they're better off not working. You see them hang around here all the afternoon.'

This comment provided a neat transition-point to the subject of Gambling. Had there been, I enquired, according to his experience, a marked increase in gambling due to the institution of betting shops?

'In this area you learn to gamble before you learn to read. I was playing pitch and toss for sweets before I was even old enough to go to school. The working man in this country has always liked his bet, it's his fun, his excitement or call it vice if you like, but it's his way of pitting his wits against somebody else's. And, he doesn't mind if he loses as long as he gets a fair run for his money, there's always another day. Of course there is more money spent on gambling now than there was, say, ten years ago—isn't it true of everything else?—but if you ask me if there would be less gambling without the betting shops, neither I nor anyone else can give you the answer. Around here you were never short of someone to take your money if you wanted to lay a bet, you could walk into any pub you wanted and you'd see a bloke in the corner sorting his slips.† The police knew full well what was going on, the copper on the beat used to have a pint and lay his bet at the same time. The only difference, the way I see it, is that they don't need to send their kids to the street-corners to get their bets on, they can walk in here whenever they please and be sure of getting paid out if they win. The few loafers and toe-rags you see hanging around, who make this their second home, who are stupid enough to leave behind the money they should be spending on their kids' shoes and who make a nuisance of

* Yentz: Yiddish word for sexual intercourse.
† Slips in this context is taken to refer to betting slips.

themselves when they go skinned, we'd much rather be without in the first place. Only you can't throw them out, the poor buggers wouldn't know what to do with their time.'

Did he have much trouble with misbehaviour, for instance fighting or loud obscenities? I asked. 'We haven't had a fight in here since we opened up, if you treat them decent they come to realize you are trying to make a living, same as they do, the few who enjoy trouble soon go elsewhere. You get the occasional punter who swears black's blue that you are trying to chisel him out of his winnings—more often than not it's the women who do it—no matter how often you calculate in front of them, they'll still go away calling you an effing twister. Or you get some fighting drunk who's out to pick a quarrel, I just tell him to piss off and next day he'll come in and offer you a fag.'

I remarked on the fact that, in this particular betting shop, I had noticed almost total absence of 'bad language', was this to be attributed to the presence of their female clerk? 'I always say a woman working in here is like working in a pub. You can't afford to be fussy, after all you're running a business. If you stopped them giving vent to their feelings or talking a bit of smut once in a while, you'd soon be punting to yourself. But, on the other hand, it isn't nice, they know we don't like it. When it gets out of hand, one of us just goes outside and tells them to pack it up. There's a great big Irish brute who comes in here a couple of times a week, had a few beers inside him, he started effing and bloodying a few weeks ago, threatened to break my neck when I told him to wrap it up. I didn't get into any argument, just said it would be childish to lose a licence just because a grown, intelligent man couldn't speak without dirt. Haven't had any trouble from him since.'

Did he himself gamble? I asked him. 'This is a funny business, when you are losing money you are working hard computing the winning bets. When you are standing still you are making money, it's then you might be tempted to try your own luck.' Harry, his partner, took up: 'George, my ex-partner wouldn't leave it alone, as quick as he took the money, he handed it back to the bookie. He just could not see a short-priced favourite get beat. The first day we opened he took three hundred pounds out of the till to back an odds-on to win a hundred, the bloody thing fell at the second fence. We used to row about it, it was the only thing we ever fought over, but it did no good, it ruined us in the end.' 'I wouldn't say I am different to the next man,' Jim resumed, 'we all like to have a flutter once in a while. There's nothing wrong in taking the wife to the dogs for a night out, as long as you make up your mind to lose a few quid and be done with it. But once you let it interfere with your business, you might as well put your lock on the door, you get as bad as the rest of the credit punters, you think the day of reckoning is never going to come. Before you look round your credit is ruined, you can't even find anyone to take your lay-offs,[25] when your licence comes up for renewal you find your name has begun to stink all round the neighbourhood. We've lived and worked around this neighbourhood from the day we were born, whatever happens, my good name is more important to me than the few quid I might make once in a while boxing clever.'

Notes

1. This survey has in previous parts of the text been referred to as Household Survey and some of the findings are incorporated in Chapter III.
2. 'The fact that I was a foreigner writing about the Englishman for the Englishman aroused curiosity and circumspection. Was that a handicap or a help in my enquiries? People often asked me. Some reviewers of my books believed that this fact helped me considerably, and so did the late Lord Beveridge who, in his preface to my first book, wrote: "It seems likely, indeed, that the fact of being a foreigner made him in some ways easier to talk to than if he had been one of ourselves against whom, for that very reason, we might need to put up defences and exercise reserves". On the whole I am inclined to agree with this.' Ferdynand Zweig (1967), p. 27.
3. This refers to B.S.III, Mile End.
4. 'I soon found that people were developing their own explanation about me: I was writing a book about Corneville. This might seem entirely too vague an explanation, and yet it sufficed. I found that my acceptance in the district depended upon the personal relationships I developed far more than upon any explanations I might give. Whether it was a good thing to write a book about Corneville depended entirely on people's opinion of me personally. If I was all right, then my project was all right; if I was no good, then no amount of explanation could convince them that the book was a good idea'. Whyte, William

F. (1943), *Street Corner Society*, University Press, Chicago, p. 300.

5. I constantly came across instances in which sayings, attributed to one or the other deceased parent, were quoted as justifications for deeds and attitudes. These sayings were usually couched in terms of the most simple homilies such as 'As my old dad used to say, you can't have the cake and eat it', or 'I've always remembered my mother telling me "all that glitters is not gold"' (A bird in the hand . . . run before you walk, bricks and straws . . ., etc, etc). These sayings, though overwhelmingly very general, did not always, though quoted, serve as prescriptions for conduct; in the present instance Jack's professed motives for betting and the actual manner in which he disposed of his winnings show wide divergence. The voice of the superego, once due verbal homage has been paid to it can, in per-formance, be safely superseded by the ego-demands?

6. Totalisator scoreboards are electrically controlled devices displayed at all tracks giving the public a complete, up-to-date record of the fluctuations of the tote-betting on the different runners, allowing minute-to-minute assessment of odds.

7. There are six dogs running in a dograce, each released from a trap, numbered from the inside to the outside numbers one to six.

8. The Jackpot consists of naming six winners in six nominated races by way of a system in which tickets are bought before the first race and selections are made race by race, with winning tickets being carried forward. The first loser disqualifies. A consolation prize is given for five winners.

9. To the enquiry as to the danger of prosecution, possible conviction and disqualification under the breathalyser tests, I was given the answer that the Police did their best to look the other way in the case of infringements, that they were loath to initiate proceedings, that it was an unwritten law that confrontation between 'Crown and Crown' was to be avoided in view of the likelihood of unpopular publicity as well as the futility of 'robbing Peter to pay Paul'. I was unable to check on the authenticity of these statements.

10. Brick Lane, Stepney, in common with Cable Street, the receptacle of a large variety of social misfits and outcasts.

11. A classic example of the process termed displacement, in which a substitute object on whom it is safe, or at least legitimate, to vent anger and frustration is chosen in place of the real cause of these emotions; the real cause on whom it would be unsafe or unacceptable to discharge these feelings, or whose sanctions in the event of such discharge would cause consequences even more painful than the original emotions. Instead of hitting his wife, Vic tried to hit the bookie.

12. In 1961 a gang of East-End 'Wide Boys' attempted a coup at Dagen-ham Dogtrack by 'fixing' the winner and runner-up in one of the races, backing the two dogs in combined forecast at tote-prices with a large number of bookmakers away from the track and 'blocking' the

windows at the racetrack just before the race, not permitting members of the public to bet on the tote at all. They then backed all the other dogs running in the race fairly heavily and bought one single 1op ticket on the 'fixed' forecast, thus inflating the return. The actual forecast, after the dogs had duly finished first and second, was over £500 for a 1op ticket and the gang stood to win several hundred thousand pounds on their bets placed with bookmakers. After many months of discussion and negotiation the Bookmakers' Association finally advised their members to refuse to pay out and to declare all bets on that race as null and void. This event has now passed into the East-End folklore. In countless conversations this matter finds itself referred to in a large variety of interpretations, undergoing a large variety of transformations in the process. In spite of the anti-social character of the coup—when after all ordinary visitors to the track were by strong-arm methods 'persuaded' to desist from attempting to place bets—this matter has already acquired a strong Robin Hood connotation 'To rob the rich to pay the poor'.

13. I was to encounter this charge on numerous occasions in the course of the interviews, though as I was to learn, none of my subjects had ever directly found themselves at the receiving end of such tactics. It did appear, however, that many of the wives had at some time fallen victim to the guiles of daytime 'tally salesmen' who had frequently managed to foist on them household commodities and gadgets of questionable quality and utility at highly inflated prices. I began to suspect that the husbands, enraged at their wives' gullibility, were feeling that they owed it to themselves to demonstrate to the household how to unmask and how to deal with one 'of them Johnnies'. The ease with which it was possible to propriate them, though certainly a tribute to their humanity, suggested that they would prove no less vulnerable than their wives to the assault of bogus researchers.

14. Black Money initially referred to money made in Black Market dealings or Black Market operations; activities which involved the buying and selling of goods outside the official legitimate ration-scheme. It later also came to extend to any money made in some illicit fashion, any money earned and not declared in any one of the manifold 'cash' dealings which had by then come to be not too uncommon practice. These nest-eggs, of course, could not be officially banked or declared and were often squandered at racetracks or in illegal gaming-clubs.

15. Under war-time emergency regulations aliens of enemy nationality had been interned in camps after the Fall of France in 1940, most of them being sent to camps on the Isle of Man. The majority—Jewish refugees from Germany and Austria—were released after a short while but some, largely long-term residents in Great Britain who had neglected to acquire British nationality and were unable to substantiate allegiance, remained in captivity for most of the duration of the war.

16. In common with my other informants Mike, who in normal discourse
made it a point of honour to use the words by polite society designated
as swearwords and obscenities be it as nouns, adverbs, adjectives, or
verbs never more than any six words apart, confined himself to
expletives no more powerful than 'bloody' when conversing with me
in my official role.

When addressing me as a member of the crowd inside the betting
shop, the pub or the cafe, no such inhibitions prevailed.

A fascinating study awaits the social researcher equipped with
perception sensitive enough to record and analyse the various norms
of the various rituals of 'swearing' in British working-class culture.
The range of words itself is limited, even impoverished, yet the
variability of form and nuance infinite. Instinctive observance of the
code persisted in all the various circles I managed to enter. As soon as
I revealed my identity, announced my purpose, it was taken for
granted that I was writing a book. As soon as I came to be classified
as 'author', I joined the species of 'poets', 'intellectuals', 'reformers',
possibly just one step short of the category of 'cranks', whose skin was
thin, whose sensitivity tender, whose fantasies too precarious to
withstand the full blast of manly discourse.

The professional tough would daintily apologise ('begging your
pardon') if inadvertently he had let slip one of the expletives in
conversation with me. However, occasions on which I was tactless
enough to breach the code by drawing attention to contradictions or
discrepancies evoked instant retaliation—reintroduction of the full
range of 'swearwords'—until I had paid due penance by condoning a
flagrant falsehood without comment. The worst *faux-pas* I could
commit would be to try to copy my companions' mode of speech.
Incomprehension rather than shock would be the reaction to such
indiscretion on my part, as though by stepping out of my alloted role I
had rocked a tender equilibrium.

This discussion might illustrate some of the pitfalls of social
research. Long-range survey, prepared questionnaires could never
hope to come even near to the threshold of free expression. Undisclosed participant observation lacks detachment and freedom to probe
beyond the most apparent levels, while even the most self-critical,
constantly self-adjusting, declared participant observer will react
upon his environment and will not be able to reproduce entirely
faithfully what he has set out to record.

17. Schmock-punter: Naïve, gullible, information-seeking bettor. In this
dockside area the well-stacked 'schmock-punter' is not the rarity the
environment might suggest. A constant stream of sailors, seamen and
assorted visitors, their pockets bulging with accumulated pay, dis-
gorged into the area—bewildered, pleasure-starved, hoping against all
past experience to the contrary for the thrill of a lifetime, the 'once
and for all'. Safe while protected by numbers, but helpless as the
proverbial Babes-in-Arms against the many sided, if disparate,

onslaught of the local pimps, tarts, conmen and grafters to whom they served as welcome sources of income and munificence.

18. Initially Tommy was very secretive as to the origin of his income, but soon disclosed that it was made up of money from the Labour Exchange, National Assistance plus two regular minor weekly grants from local Charity Institutions.

19. In this setting 'a job' means anything from a break-in, a little bit of drug-peddling, to 'doing over' a drink-sodden seaman. However, it is likely to stop short of organised, planned criminal activities in which teamwork, toughness and quick thinking in emergencies are essential.

20. The customary process of inflation in recall had by now raised the weekly income to £10 betting money plus perhaps another £4 for other items.

21. Although in all cases in which interviews were conducted, it was the male householder who was the subject of the interview, wives and from time to time other members of the household, were present throughout in a number of cases. A few were sufficiently deflected by the television programmes not to pay any attention to the interview, but the majority became involved to a no lesser extent than their husbands, eager to interject remarks from time to time.

22. William W. had told me at an earlier stage of the interview that he spent most of his own free time 'helping the wife around the house, doing a bit of shopping when she needs it, there's a lot of work for a woman running a home like this'. Towards the close of the interview, lasting altogether perhaps one-and-three-quarter hours, his wife twice reminded him that he had promised to dust one of the upstairs bedrooms before getting ready for work.

23. The process of Jewish residential emancipation is well-described and documented in Part III of Maurice Freeman's book *A Minority in Britain* (Vallentine, Mitchell & Co. Ltd, London 1955), the chapter titled 'The outlines of Jewish Society in London'. The author, Howard H. Brotz, relates how, in pursuit of social advancement, Jews attempt to move away from the original reception area—Whitechapel and environs—into more prosperous and ethnically more mixed parts with the North-West London Suburbs as the final goal. The majority follow (or used to do so) the traditional stepping-stones: Hackney, Dalston, Stamford Hill, Stoke Newington. A minority, more numerous since the Second World War, are able to achieve a direct leap into Hendon or Golders Green, their final sights now set upon the more prestigeful areas of Hampstead, Wembley and Stanmore, with Hampstead Garden Suburb ranking as ultimate peak. Amongst experts in residential leap-frogging the nature, velocity and content of the processes of advance alone are adequate symbols of solidity, substance on the one hand and of personal extraordinary quality of achievement and valour, or of unorthodoxy and ostentation on the other. Jim's performance of territorial change would to the 'expert' indicate modesty, conformity and reliability.

24. Skins: male contraceptives. The ritual of ownership and consumption of contraceptives has for a long period now been a status-symbol of the adolescent male in the 'respectable' sections of the East End (whose customs and folkways have in all probability never been more authentically and humorously depicted than in the stageplay 'Sparrows Can't Sing'). At a time of life when the middle-class boy is still seeking status recognition among his peers by display of the 'packet of fags' or accounts of early attempts at 'touch-ups', the adolescent working-class boy will proclaim his manhood in terms of 'real-life conquests', his self-confidence displayed (and possibly reinforced) by the packet of 'Briefs' or 'Skins' he allows to bulge from his breast-pocket ('Friday night is nuptial night'), the 'scalps' of his 'lays' commemorated in his rate of consumption. One is left to wonder how many unsmoked cigarettes on the one hand and unused contraceptives on the other, acquired with scarce resources in tense moments, find their way, sacrificed on the altar of conspicuous consumption, unused into the litter bins.

25. Lay-offs are clients' bets which the bookmaker for various reasons decides to pass on to other bookmakers on a small commission.

CHAPTER VII

Conclusions

Gamblers and Non-Gamblers

Gamblers

I would estimate that out of the 500 or so people, including the 53 subjects interviewed at some depth, I spoke to directly on the subject of my study, no fewer than 80 per cent of men and not very many fewer of the women, staked some money on at least one of the types of gambling activity with some degree of regularity, say no less frequently than once a fortnight. At least 75 per cent of the men, and something like 45–50 per cent of women, placed cash bets on horseracing throughout the year. The two major classic events—the Derby and the Grand National—were bet upon by all but the tiny minority implacably hostile to gambling.

Virtually all my informants staked money on football pools in the course of the English season. In the off-season, when promoters circulate football coupons relating to Australian fixtures, the proportion declined to something like 50 per cent for men and to 25 per cent for women.

Dograces were frequented by possibly 40 per cent of men and no more than half that proportion of women. I found, in contrast to the evidence submitted by those who studied this phenomenon in the early post-war period, that attendance at dog meetings was a yes-or-no affair, one either went no less often than once a month or not at all.[1] The occasional festive family outings, 'children and all', Zweig spoke of in the late 1940s have apparently, with the advent of television and the motor car, disappeared.

Bingo, despised and derided as mechanical and mindless by the men, had apparently turned into a waning fashion, now possibly

attracting no more than 50 per cent of the women, with particular incidence among either the very young, the newly-married or
the elderly. A number of men were, under closer questioning,
with an embarrassed smile prepared to admit that occasionally
'me and the missus go together, gives her a bit of company and
someone to buy her card'. I would, however, estimate these to be
fewer than 15 per cent. Casino games of any type were very
much a minority preference. I can call to mind no more than five
men (approximately 1 per cent of the total) who professed to membership of non-East London clubs in which table games such as
roulette, chemmy and craps were played. Possibly a total of 10
per cent of the men and certainly no more than 2 to 3 per
cent of the women, belonged to commercial neighbourhood clubs,
where card games for money—usually only whist, pontoon and
kalookie—were available. Participation in raffles, sweepstakes and
lotteries is now so near universal that it has ceased to be considerd
as gambling at all.

Irrefutably, in the community under study—and this is
probably true of most other similarly composed working-class
communities—the Gambler is the social norm, the Non-Gambler
the deviant oddity. To try therefore to enumerate the personality
characteristics of 'The Gambler', when this group forms
approximately 75 per cent of the population under review, would
not seem very illuminating.[2] I have, accordingly, decided to
designate as 'Gamblers' those individuals who confront the
questioner with a positive ideological attitude to gambling, who
will affirm that gambling is, even if not an absolute necessity, at
least a valued and significant feature in their lives, who will
declare that, were they to be deprived of gambling, an important
and treasured component in their daily life would thereby
disappear.

These individuals, perhaps as many as 20 per cent of all the
adult males—though no more than 5 per cent of the women—are
characterized by a general philosophy of tough-mindedness—an
emphasis on the superior virtues of self-interest, personal effort
and independence, a generalized suspiciousness of strangers and
outsiders, particularly of the motives of those in power and
control. They display a pronounced hostility towards the open-
handedness of the Welfare State, their antagonism usually being

focused on one particular sub-organ—'The way they make you hang around these hospitals is a bloody disgrace, someone ought to write about it'. 'To see the way the teachers dress nowadays, makes you sick; they look just like cowboys, no wonder the kids don't show them any respect!' Yet, this antagonism and distrust usually coexists with a considerable fund of tolerance for the foibles and weaknesses of others. Having probably seen their own resolutions frequently eroded by events, they might possibly have developed a sympathetic understanding for the inconsistency and variability of the human personality.

By and large, they show a greater awareness of public affairs than non-gamblers. Disinterest in the major national issues was, to my surprise, virtually total.[3] Public issues are taken note of, categorized as not belonging to 'Us' and then discarded as being sham and irrelevant. Yet, among the group of 'Gamblers' a noticeably greater inclination to identify slightly more deeply, to judge a little more critically and yet realistically seemed to exist. To the regular gambler, the racing pages of the daily morning and evening papers are the tools of his trade. However specific his interest, over a period of time some of this interest, and with it whatever emotional identification has taken place, is likely to seep into the non-racing spheres. A greater, even if still marginal, preparedness to involve and to participate than is characteristic of those whose reading of the national press may only be intermittent and irregular, is likely to prevail.

Throughout the community I found a total lack of concern with the prospects and potential rewards of upward social mobility. A possible change in the life situation was conceived only in terms of higher income, of having more money to spend on the same parcel of commodities and not ever in terms of possible occupational qualitative promotion, of attachment to superior-graded groups or of adoption of different sets of norms. Within this context, a noticeably more aspiring attitude seemed to prevail amongst 'The Gamblers', expressed in greater preoccupation with pay issues, with acquisition of consumer goods and furthermore a budget-awareness, a determination to make optimal use of one's financial resources.[4]

Non-Gamblers

I have decided to classify the 'Non-Gambler' into four different categories.

There are, first of all, those objecting to gambling on conscientious grounds—probably fewer than one per cent of the total—about equally divided between those who are, nevertheless, neutral towards the activity—'You see I am a Methodist, I wouldn't be allowed to gamble'—and those others whose opposition is active and vehement—'I'm strictly against it; it's what's bringing the country to its knees, no wonder they spit on our flag the world over'.

Secondly, those—perhaps two to three per cent of the total—possessing an absorbing personal hobby, such as fishing, rifle-shooting or even the pub—'There are only two things I live for, my pint of beer and my game of darts'. Such hobbies, if combined with a negative attitude towards gambling, will, as a rule, be of a social and associational character. A solitary hobby, such as tinkering with a car or with electrical equipment, is usually compatible with gambling.

Thirdly there are those, almost entirely veterans of the last war, within the age group of forty-five to sixty years—amounting possibly to almost five per cent of the total—almost uniformly self-defined as being 'in a rut'. Their reactions to challenge and opportunity seem docile and tame, their attitudes to their environment apathetic. According to them, there were lots of things they once enjoyed doing, many things they used to look forward to in the past, but this is now no longer so. Life has not turned out as they had intended, somewhere it seems to have gone tepid and stale, but even this does not seem to matter very much. Not that their life is in any way bad, the job alright, the family quite good, but nothing seemed to arouse them; in other words, they were in 'a rut'.

The fourth and last group, designated by me as 'detached young'—something like 5 per cent of the total, but as many as 25 per cent of the under-twenty-five male age group—is the sociologically most interesting and significant. These are almost entirely men married at an early age who by the time they reach their middle-twenties have a family of one or two young children.

Though resembling in some ways the 'privatized and instrumen-
tally oriented' young working men described by Chinoy and
Goldthorpe, they differ from these emancipated, technologically
trained groups in many respects, particularly as regards way of
life and life chances.[5] Our group of 'detached young' possess
only the most minimal education, have no occupational training,
their jobs are almost exclusively within the lower regions of the
occupational manual strata. In common with the other members
of our community they display sublime indifference to the prospects of social mobility. And yet, they are determined to break
out of the traditional working-class 'hand to mouth' way of life.
With tolerant contempt do they regard their forebears' humility
and submissiveness to their 'betters', no less than the older
generation's delusions of idealism and social reform. Like the
'automobile workers' they are home-centred, domestically
democratic, almost tender, prepared to take their share in the
household chores, ready to award their spouses domestic equality
and autonomy.

Towards the external environment they are, as they would
term it, 'Nobody's fool'. They seem keenly aware of all refinements of the ladder of success and despite their social disadvantages are intensely confident in confrontation with come who
may. What they are after is a bigger personal share of the 'loot'
and let everyone else outside their own immediate family look out
for their own. Their appetite for overtime is voracious, their
preparedness to uproot, to go where the money is best, absolute.
And even signs of deferred gratification—after all, the money you
put by will earn you money—are discernible in embryonic form.
Uniformly these men categorically say 'No' to gambling—'The
bookie won't keep my wife if she is short'—not for them the
slippery slope of alternating illusory hope and actual real-life
despair.

Maybe social convergence, if it does ever come to pass, will
arise from an unexpected unanticipated source?

Summary

The questions posed in the final section of the Introduction have, to a large extent, been covered by the material discussed in the relevant sections of the text.

It would appear that the legislative structure applicable to gambling in this country achieves widespread public recognition and support; that the laws governing the operations of gambling are in close conformity with the general moral and social values of the community; that the legal boundaries under which gambling functions are precisely and comprehensively defined and yet—as was demonstrated in respect of the recent changes in gaming legislation—of a sufficient degree of flexibility to provide for swift and smooth modification, wherever amendments come to be considered as essential or desirable. On the basis of available evidence, it would seem that the legal statutes are widely respected and observed and that infringements, wherever they do occur, are neither critical nor severe.

Although the amount of national outlay on gambling ostensibly appears to be substantial, it has been shown that a distinction needs, in this instance, to be drawn between outlay and expenditure and that expenditure represents no more than a portion of the total turnover. The total net sum expended on gambling seems, relative to outlay on other items of expenditure, neither excessive nor inordinate, nor would it appear to have expanded to a disproportionate degree in recent years. Gambling in contemporary Britain lays claim to no more than 0.25 per cent of the national employed labour force and to slightly more than 0.75 per cent of total national economic resources.

By all accounts, gambling constitutes, for the overwhelming majority of participants, a pastime rather than an addiction. Both frequency of participation, as well as volume of expenditure, appear to be moderate, and subject to personal self-direction and control. For no more than a small and numerically insignificant minority can gambling conceivably be regarded as unmanageable and obsessive.

Without doubt, both in intensity as well as in volume of outlay, gambling is concentrated to a disproportionate extent within certain ecological zones and among specific social strata. A strong degree of association between a number of indices relating to social deprivation and gambling was shown to exist. Where income is relatively low, occupational training and skills slight, material possessions few, physical environment drab, dreary and monotonous, social amenities meagre and access to cultural goals scarce, there gambling appears to flourish and to prevail. Does such association indicate not merely that those who have least gamble the most, but furthermore that indulgence in gambling is coextensive with low level of educational attainment, deficient social perception and inadequate personality structure and organization? Is gambling socially dysfunctional where it is most deeply ingrained, does it further impair and handicap those sections of the community among whom a complex and cumulative series of social disadvantages and deprivations are already pervasive and diffused? I would submit that the material adduced overwhelmingly suggests otherwise.

The plain fact is that, within the situational reality of the majority of working men, gambling makes sense. Their avowed reason is almost exclusively pecuniary, the primary articulated motivation is overwhelmingly the quest for money. Ask the working man why he gambles and he will justify his action in economic terms. Is not, after all, the daily loss of his small sums an insignificant price to pay for the hope of a big strike, 'the big tickle', the windfall? A fistful of notes in his pocket, allowing him to do a few of those things daily existence denies. Whether his own personal predilection for transient grandeur runs in the direction of magnanimously outfitting his family or his home (what intense joy it must be, for once, not to have to undergo the complex humiliations of the hire-purchase application forms); whether it will furnish him with resources adequate to command superior attention for his views when able to back his opinions with regular, all-inclusive orders of drinks; whether it will allow him for a short while to discard his usual confinement to 'petty gambling', so deeply despised and yet a realistic necessity, in favour of the majesty of the really big and noble stake, is of little account.

What does matter is that, to him, thrift, application and self-denial have a different set of realities. What point is there in saving, when unpredictability and mysterious remote controls govern your life? Even if in pursuit of the 'big strike' you will allow yourself to lose money you do not possess, if ends cannot be made to meet, you can always catch up by working a little extra overtime. Meanwhile your mates, your family and if it comes to it, the 'Welfare' will help you out. To scrimp and save to lay by a few pounds to see these eroded by inflation, wiped out and exposed in their foolish inadequacy in a sudden family emergency or, worst of all, to leave your few accumulated possessions to be fought over when you die—no other single cause, by all accounts, exerts comparable power as a detonator of family unity—is poor sense. To use this money in the hope of a big strike—who knows, you might even win enough to put down a deposit on a house—is surely superior rationality.

Distant goals and deferred gratification where sudden illness, economic slump or even the boss's displeasure might wreck your neatly laid plans are non-starters.* It is not his present-time orientation, his inability to think of the future, but rather his awareness of how chancy and beyond his own power of control the future is, which makes the concept of forgoing till tomorrow what you might get fun out of today hollow, meaningless, and irrational.

But there is, in this situational context, more to the activity of gambling than the hope of material reward and gratification. Enveloped by the sameness and drabness in his everyday life, subject not merely to occupational monotony—this after all was eternally the lot of the working man, whose forefathers were not the skilled craftsman of romantic history, but the agricultural serf and labourer whose daily grind allowed meagre scope for variety —but, more sadly, to the corrosive visual monotony of the proletarian urban landscape. Deprived by the lack of education and developmental elbow room of the vision towards self-improvement and spiritual self-realization, what else other than gambling can provide the thrill, the feeling of being part of the throbbing vital congregation, the illusion of belonging, of being part of the living scene, of participation in events beyond your own paltry boundaries, reified by the actuality of money staked?†

* As one of the characters in Liebow's *Tallys Corner* (p. 67) exclaims: 'I want mine right now.'

† As one bookmaker suggested to me: 'They stake their couple of bob and you'd think they own the horse '

Nor does belief in 'luck', in content though different from the emotions described by those who liken it to supernatural divination, play an insignificant role. Where chance and hazard seem to predominate in daily life, where effort and reward rarely travel hand-in-hand, confidence in a systematic regulated pattern of life is unlikely to prevail. Existence is likely to be viewed in terms of 'ups and downs', of unforseeable capricious swings of the unfathomable pendulum of fortune. What better index of whether your luck is in or out, whether now is the right or the wrong moment to take a crucial decision, than the way the horses are running for or against you, the fluctuations of your fortune in the betting shop.*

Not unlikely, involvement in betting on horseracing and greyhounds, with its intricate study of a multitude of complex variables, will replace for the working man the features of decision-taking and judgement which his life ordinarily lacks. Study of form, demanding intense concentration, application and rapid resolution might well provide an artificial substitute universe of 'work', stimulating and mind-exerting as it ought to be in reality. In all probability, the regular habit of handling a diverse network of variables, of trying to derive a system from an initially chaotic mass, will help to establish a mental set, at the very least, not totally devoid of familiarity with logical structure and sequential order. It will create a habit of mental processes available for importation into other spheres, while the store of specific shared knowledge of experience and expertise will infuse a much needed dose of confidence, of competence or possibly even excellence in a limited, however communally prestigeful, field of action.

Involvement in shared culture and communications—and it must not be forgotten that, with the exception of the rapidly disappearing local pub, the betting shop, the dogtrack and the bingo hall provide the only institutional facilities of spontaneous social group interaction in this particular environment—not only reinforces communality and corporate values, but serves as a platform for display of the full range of social talents and skills; not, in this environment, the externally status-awarding accomplishments of self-advancement and achievement, but rather the

* After all, even the conventionally respectable middle-class proverb enjoins one to 'Strike while the iron is hot'.

community-enhancing skills of fortitude, of nonchalance in the face of misfortune, of indifference to meanness, of humour, tolerance and mutuality. Nor must the part played in the service of socialization of both the newcomer, as well as the subcultural norm deviant, be underrated. In these terms, gambling may well be regarded as a structurally positively-functional component of the social system.

Notes

1. See Rowntree, B. S. and Lavers, G. R. (1951), and Zweig,F. (1) (1949).
2. I feel obliged to repeat that I did, in the course of my empirical research, not collect systematic statistical data and that therefore the proportions and percentages quoted in the present section, though based on detailed and extensive records, are by no means claimed to be precise.
3. The period of my empirical research coincided with such major national events as the crucial pre-devaluation crisis, the Arab-Israeli six-day war and a very violent phase of American race-riots.
4. The structure, organization and managements of Trade Unions were universally regarded with intense cynicism and scorn.
5. See Chinoy, E. (1955) and Goldthorpe, J. H. (1966).

Tables

Table I. Number of Betting Office Licences in Force

	ENGLAND		WALES AND MONMOUTHSHIRE		SCOTLAND		TOTAL GREAT BRITAIN	
	Number	Number per 10,000 of Population	Number	Number per 10,000 of Population	Number	Number per 10,000 of Population	Number	Number per 10,000 of Population
1961	6,647	1.54	649	2.47	1,505	2.91	8,802	1.73
1962	10,318	2.37	1,240	4.71	1,782	3.44	13,340	2.60
1963	11,453	2.60	1,268	4.78	1,667	3.21	14,388	2.77
1964	12,167	2.74	1,279	4.80	1,579	3.03	15,025	2.88
1965	12,310	2.86	1,316	4.92	1,512	2.90	15,638	2.97
1966	12,307	2.84	1,316	4.89	1,618	3.11	15,741	2.97
1967	12,704	2.81	1,272	4.72	1,559	3.00	15,535	2.91
1968	12,878	2.81	1,283	4.73	1,621	3.12	15,782	2.94

Source: Betting, Gaming and Lotteries Act 1963: Permits and Licences, presented by the order of the House of Commons pursuant to Act Eliz. II 1963.S.O c2, Sch. 1, H.M. (London 1961–8).

Table II. Estimated Number of Employees in Employment in Great Britain

	Employees in Betting	Annual Rate of Increase %	Employees in all Industries and Services	Annual Rate of Increase %
1959	36,400		21,565,000	
1960	37,400	2.7	22,036,000	2.2
1961	40,000	6.9	22,373,000	1.5
1962	43,000	7.5	22,572,000	0.8
1963	42,700	−0.7	22,603,000	0.1
1964	47,300	10.8	22,892,000	1.3
1965	53,000	12.1	23,147,000	1.1
1966	56,300	6.2	23,301,000	0.7
1967	57,300	1.8	22,828,000	−2.0
1968	57,300	Nil	22,645,300	−0.8
Increase		1959–68 %		1959–68 %
1959–68	20,900	57.4	80,300	0.37

Source: Department of Employment and Productivity, Statistics Division (Ref. Stats C1/ASB), 1969.

Table III: Estimated Annual Gambling Turnover by Mode of Outlay (in £ millions)

	1967	1968	Rate of Change 1967–8 %
(1) Bookmakers on-course			
(a) Dogs	76	55	−27.6
(b) Horses	60	51	−15.0
	136	106	−22.0
(2) Bookmakers off-course all betting (Cash and Credit)	969	938	−3.2
	1,105	1,044	
Less laying-off 9%	99	94	
Total all Bookmakers	1,006	950	−5.5
(3) Horserace Tote	34	31	−8.7
(4) Dograce Tote	70	70	Nil
(5) Football Pools	128	126	−1.6
(6) Fixed Odds	7	5	−28.6
(7) Premium Bonds	26	27	+3.6
(8) Bingo	65	78	+20.0
(9) Casinos	57	49	−14.0
(10) Gaming Machines	94	90	−4.2
(11) Others	10	10	Nil
	£1,497	£1,436	−4.2

Sources:
Items 1–7 inclusive allow themselves to be calculated with a fair degree of accuracy and postulated with considerable confidence.

Items 1 and 2—bets laid with bookmakers on- and off-course—have since 1 October 1966 been subject to General Betting Duty, originally at 2.5 per cent of turnover and since 1 October 1968 at 5 per cent. Off-course bets embrace those laid in betting shops as well as on credit accounts. As a result, taxation returns—supervised by Customs and Excise inspectors and statutorily certified by qualified accountants—reflect the gross income fully and turnover totals allow themselves to be derived.

Items 3 and 4—Horserace and Dograce Tote—have for many years now been mechanically operated and controlled and monthly takings have, since 1938, been recorded by the Horserace Betting Levy Board (or its predecessor) and the Greyhound Racing Association respectively.

Item 5—Football Pools—have since 1948 been subject to Turnover Duty varying from 10 per cent of turnover at inception, to 25 per cent from October 1966 and finally at 33⅓ per cent since October 1968.

Item 6—Fixed Odds—have been subject to duty at a rate identical to that ruling for football pools since August 1964.

Item 7—Premium Bonds—have since their introduction in 1957 been Government sponsored and Treasury controlled.

The remaining items, nos. 8–11 are less firmly founded on reliable data and are, though based on careful sifting of all the available information, tentative and subject to a greater possible degree of error.

Item 8—Bingo—Duty, at rates varying according to rateable value of premises, has been collected from all promoters since 1 October 1966. In his Budget Speech in April 1969 the Chancellor of the Exchequer, in imposing an increased rate of duty of 2.5 per cent on all stakes, expressed the view that a total amount of between £1.5 and £2 million tax would accrue in a full Tax Year.* As the amount of Licence Duty collected in 1968 totalled £0.97 million—approximately one-half the anticipated duty at new revised rates—it is safe to assume that in 1968 duty collected represented 1.25 per cent of Turnover and that, in consequence, Turnover would have been £77,832, 000. In 1967, the total duty collected amounted to £0.57 million. The rate of duty imposed on licensed premises was increased by 50 per cent in the 1968 Budget and it therefore follows that the rate of duty in 1967 stood at 0.835 per cent of Turnover, producing an estimated Turnover of £64,602,100.

Item 9—Casinos—Casinos have been subject to Licence Duty at rates varying according to rateable value of premises since October 1966. According to official views presented to the Standing Committee on the Gaming Bill, it was considered desirable to impose a duty of approximately 5 per cent on all casino turnover. It must be assumed, therefore, that the new rates of Duty imposed in the 1969 Budget, representing an increase of one-third over the previous rates, are designed to implement this intention. On this basis Turnover figures for the years 1968 and 1967 can be estimated as follows:

1968: Licence Duty rates ruling from 1 July were 75 per cent of rate imposed in the 1969 Budget and were, consequently, 3.75 per cent of Turnover. Licence Duty rates for the first half of the year, equal to the rate originally imposed in October 1966, were two-thirds of the rate ruling in the second half of the year, therefore 2.5 per cent of Turnover. (Licence Duty rates were increased by 50 per cent from the second half of the year.)

Duty collected 1 January–30 June:	£112,300	
being 2.5 per cent of Turnover		£4,492,000
Duty collected 1 July–31 December	£1,673,400	
being 3.75 per cent of Turnover		44,512,440
Estimated Turnover 1968		£49,004,440

* *The Times*, 16 April 1969 and H.M. Customs and Excise, Press Notice no. 37, 15 April 1969.

1967: Licence Duty rate was the same as that ruling for the first half of 1968, namely 2.5 per cent of Turnover. Duty collected was £1,417,900 and if this is assumed to be 2.5 per cent of Turnover, estimated Turnover for 1967 is *£56,716,000*.

Item 10—Gaming Machines—According to the 'Report on Enquiry into Gaming' 1963 (Cmd. 2275) there were, in 1963, a total of 24,699 gaming machines operating in 15,124 Clubs, providing annual 'Net Takings', i.e. input of all monies less prizes delivered by the machine plus any rental charges paid, of £10.3 million. It is widely held that gaming machines do, on average, pay out 80 per cent of their takings; therefore the following computation would be valid for 1963:

24,699 machines providing

> £10.3 million net takings (gross profit); 20 per cent of total
> £41.2 million pay-back, 80 per cent of total
> £51.5 *million*, Turnover for 1963.

Average net taking (gross profit) per machine: £417 per annum.

On this basis the Turnover for the years 1967 and 1968 can be computed as follows:

1967: Total number of gaming machines = 36,112;*
36,112 machines @ £417 net taking per machine
= £15.05 million gross profit,
+ rise in National Income 1963–1967 = 25.3 per cent†

> £ 38.1 million
> £18.86 million net taking; 20 per cent of total
> £74.44 million pay back; 80 per cent of total
> £93.30 *million* estimated Turnover for 1967.

Licence Duty collected: £2,890.100 = 3.08 per cent of Turnover
1968: Licence Duty collected: £2,783.000. If this represents 3.8 per cent of Turnover (identical to 1967), then:
Estimated Turnover 1968 = *£89.70 million*.

Item 11—Others—This represents a host of miscellaneous minor gambling activities, such as amusement arcades offering prizes, Irish sweepstake investments and commercially organised raffles. An annual sum of £10 million, though unsupportable by any statistical information, is generally agreed to be a reasonable and fair estimate.

---

* Press and Information Office, H.M. Customs and Excise Press Announcement: Betting and Gaming Duties—Revenue Statistics, 18 December 1967, Table 56.

	1963 £m	1967 £m	*Increase*%
National Income	24,845	31,148	25.3
Gross National Product	27,163	34,292	26.2
Consumers' Expenditure	20,195	25,323	25.3

Central Statistical Office, National Income and Expenditure, 1968 (London, H.M.S.O.); Table 1, p. 3.

Item—Laying-off—Machinery set up by the Department of Customs and Excise does now, for the first time, permit inclusion of the item of laying-off, the well-established practice of bookmakers of passing on bets which are in excess of their own capacities of being carried independently, or which would—as is more common—seriously unbalance their books on a particular event in the direction of excessive commitments in the event of one particular outcome—or a series of outcomes in the case of multiple bets—to other bookmakers. As, contrary to popular assumption, bookmakers who succeed in their profession are themselves immune to the lures of gambling and carry on their trade by the traditional observance of the economic rules of constantly balancing their books in favour of profits against losses, they counteract above contingencies by passing on (laying-off) bets they do not wish or cannot afford to retain to the few very large bookmaking establishments who, due to the large scale of their operations, are ensured of a complete spread of risks and whose final distribution of bets taken overall does anyhow determine the starting prices. In consequence, some of the units of money invested by the bettor with one bookmaker will appear in returns of turnover in the books of two or even more.

The full extent of the practice of laying-off is, under present regulations, unascertainable, but it is considered by the Customs and Excise officers concerned to be between 8 per cent and 10 per cent, and as there is no convincing reason for accepting or rejecting either the higher or the lower of these two levels, a compromise figure of 9 per cent of Turnover has been adopted.

Table IV. Estimated Annual Gambling Turnover by Gambling Activity

Rank Order	Activity	1967		1968	
		£m	% total	£m	% total
1	Horseracing	876	58.6	842	58.7
2	Dogracing	234	15.7	209	14.5
3	Football Pools	128	8.6	126	8.8
4	Gaming Machines	94	6.4	90	6.3
5	Bingo	65	4.4	78	5.4
6	Casinos	57	3.2	49	3.3
7	Premium Bonds	26	1.8	27	1.9
8	Others	10	0.7	10	0.7
9	Fixed Odds	7	0.6	5	0.4
		1,497	100	1,436	100

Source: see Table III.

Table V. Total Amounts Staked in Betting Shops

	1967 £m	1968 £m
Bookmakers off-course	969	938
Less laying-off	87	84
Total	882	854
Betting Shops 90% of Total*	(882) 794	(854) 769
Plus 50% of outlay on horse and dog Tote combined†	52	51
Total amounts staked in betting shops	£846	£820
Percentage of annual turnover spent in betting shops	56.5	57.1

* The returns of H.M. Customs and Excise on whose records and reports these computations are based allow no distinction to be derived between bets placed at betting shops and bets placed by way of credit accounts with off-course bookmakers whose premises are not open to the public. Since the creation of betting shops it has become general assumption that around 90 per cent of the total cash value of all bets placed off-course are made at betting shops. This distribution, for example proposed by Paling and Glendinning in their 1964 report 'Pattern for New York' is very substantially borne out by the statistical survey data cited in Chapter III.

† A substantial, though indeterminate, proportion of bets placed off-course are, at bettors' behest, placed at Tote odds rather than at book-makers' odds. Such bets are by the recipient bookmaker transmitted to the Tote and are contained in the turnover figures of Tote promoters. It is estimated that this practice applies to approximately 50 per cent of all the money wagered on the Tote.

Thus for 1967: Horserace Tote: £34 million; Dograce Tote: £70 million; Total: £104 million; 50 per cent of total = £52 million.

Source: H.M. Customs and Excise, Betting and Gaming Duties, Monthly Revenue Statistics, and Reports on Betting and Gaming Duties, 1967 and 1968.

Table VI. Estimated Gambling Turnover 1947 (£ millions)

Horseracing	400
Dogracing	300
Football Pools	70
Other Forms	25
Total	£795

Source: As submitted to the Royal Commission on Betting, Lotteries and Gaming 1949/51 by the Churches' Council on Gambling.

Table VII. Estimated Gambling Turnover 1962 ($£$ Millions)

As submitted to the New York State Legislature		Item no.	Summarized		
1 Betting Offices	900		(a) Horseracing*		
2 On-track Tote	15	2 & 5	Tote	31	
		3	On-course bookmakers	45	
3 On-track bookmakers	45				
4 Credit bookmakers	100	1 & 4	Off-course bookmakers	900	
				——	976
5 Tote investors	16		(b) Dogracing		
6 Football Pools	74	7	Tote	56	
7 Dog Tote	56	8	On-course bookmakers	44	
8 Dogtrack bookmakers	44	1 & 4	Off-course bookmakers†	100	
				——	200
9 Bingo	40	6	Football Pools		74
	——	9	Bingo		40
Total	£1,290		Total		1,290

* As suggested at the foot of Table III, 90 per cent of all money staked with bookmakers relates to bets on horseracing and the remaining 10 per cent is placed on dogracing.

† The estimate, as submitted to the New York State Legislature, does not allow deduction in respect of the bookmakers' practice of laying-off bets, but does not, on the other hand, incorporate any amounts in respect of Gaming Machines, Casino Gaming and Miscellaneous Gambling. It is considered that the amount of the former—laying-off—at 9 per cent of the total of all money wagered with bookmakers ($£976$ million + $£200$ million = $£1,176$ million), amounting to $£88$ million, does almost exactly counterbalance the combined amounts in respect of the latter—Casinos $£29$ million, Gaming Machines $£47$ million (one half the 1967 total) and Other $£10$ million—totalling $£85$ million. The final sum is therefore, subject to the above reservations, held to be $£1,290$ million.

Source: S. Roman and H. D. Paley, 'Report to the New York State Legislature, New York', December 1962.

Table VIII. National Income and Selected Items of Expenditure

	1947 £ m	1962 £ m	1967 £ m	Percentage Increase (a) 1947– 67	(b) 1962– 67
National Income	7,893	23,353	31,148	290.2	33.3
Total Personal Income	9,476	25,624	33,435	252.7	30.5
Expenditure on					
1 Housing*	683	1,946	2,976	335.7	52.9
2 Clothing	905	1,751	2,139	136.3	22.1
3 Durable Goods	N.A.	1,476	2,021	—	36.8
4 Books†	126	271	382	203.2	40.9
5 Alcoholic Drinks	682	1,115	1,585	132.4	42.1
6 Tobacco	680	1,242	1,512	122.3	21.8
Estimated Turnover on Gambling‡	795	1,290	1,497	88.5	16.0

* Includes: Rents, Rates, Water Charges, Maintenance, Repairs and Improvements by occupiers and also an adjustment for subsidies.

† Includes: Books, Newspapers and Magazines in the approximate ratio of: Books, 20 per cent, Newspapers, 40 per cent, Magazines, 20 per cent, Miscellaneous, 20 per cent.

‡ See Tables III, VI and VII.

Sources: The data for 1947 are extracted from The White Paper on National Income and Expenditure for the United Kingdom, 1946–9 (Cmnd. 7933), Table 21.

The data for 1962 and 1967 are extracted from Central Statistical Office; National Income and Expenditure, August 1968.

Table IX. Estimated Gambling Turnover and Expenditure (£ million)

| | 1967 | | | 1968 | | |
	Turnover (Table III)	Promoters' Gross Profit	Tax	Turnover (Table III)	Promoters' Gross Profit	Tax
1 Bookmakers on- and off-course	1,006	120.7	27.6	950	104.0	47.2
2 Horserace Tote	34	3.8	0.8	31	3.4	1.4
3 Dograce Tote	70	7.9	1.7	70	7.9	3.0
4 Football Pools and Fixed Odds	135	27.0	33.6	131	26.2	39.1
5 Premium Bonds	26	2.6		27	2.7	
6 Bingo	65	6.5	0.6	78	7.8	1.0
7 Casinos	57	11.4	1.4	49	9.8	1.8
8 Gaming Machines	94	18.8	2.9	90	18.0	2.9
9 Others	10	1.0		10	1.0	
Total	1,497	199.7	68.6	1,436	180.8	96.4

Sources: Betting and Gaming Duties, Revenue Statistics, H.M. Customs and Excise, April 1968 and April 1969.

Table IXA. Estimated Net Expenditure on Gambling (£ million)

	1967	1968
Promoters' Gross Profit	199.7	180.8
Tax	68.6	96.4
Total Net Expenditure	£268.3	£277.2

Explanandum (Refers to Tables IX and IXA)

Item 1—Bookmakers on- and off-course—According to information privately supplied by an executive officer of the Horserace Betting Levy Board, the total levy upon bookmakers is aimed to represent 6.5 per cent of the bookmakers' Net Profit and Net Profit, in turn, forms 12 per cent of the total Net Turnover. As Gross Profit represents all deductions, other than tax, made by promoters it is equivalent to Net Expenditure.

Item 2—Horserace Tote—The annual reports of the Horserace Totalisator Board for the 3 years preceeding 1967 establish that an average percentage of 11.28 per cent was retained by the Board from the money taken in bets each year.

Item 3—Dograce Tote—This is operated under conditions very similar to those prevailing in respect of the Horserace Tote and therefore an identical procedure for elucidating Net Expenditure has been adopted.

Item 4—Football Pools and Fixed Odds—From amounts staked on Football Pools and Fixed Odds varying percentages, ranging from 18 per cent to 30 per cent are deducted by different promoters for commission and expenses. A deduction of 20 per cent is considered a reasonable average. 'Again I have assumed', writes Hubert Phillips, 'that, of the gross revenue (a) 30 per cent is paid in tax (b) 20 per cent is retained for promoters' commission and expenses (c) 50 per cent is returned to investors as dividends.'*

Item 5—Premium Bonds—It is estimated that 10 per cent of all money invested in Premium Bonds is consumed by administrative costs and expenses. Premium Bonds are free from taxation.

Item 6—Bingo—A large part of this activity occurs in an environment in which the social or charitable elements dominate over the purely economic. Although the larger part of the industry is no doubt efficiently directed towards profit maximization, even within this group a great deal of activity takes place in premises—cinemas, dance halls, bowling alleys— in which multiple usage permits cost reductions per unit. It will therefore not be unreasonable to propose a gross profit level of 10 per cent.

Item 7—Casinos—In this activity one cannot assume other than profit maximization together with relatively high operating costs and comparative

* H. Phillips, *Pools and the Punter* (London 1955), ch. II, 'The Anatomy of the Pools', p. 5.

freedom from severe competition. A gross profit of 20 per cent seems a likely estimate.

Item 8—Gaming Machines—It is widely held that gaming machines do, on an average, pay out 80 per cent of their takings and that gross profit, therefore, is 20 per cent (see notes at foot of Table III).

Item 9—Others—A deduction rate of 10 per cent seems reasonable in respect of this miscellaneous group.

Table X. Total Consumer Expenditure. Selected Items and Estimated Expenditure on Gambling, 1967

	Total 1967 £ m	GAMBLING as Percentage of Item %	Amount spent on GAMBLING per each £1 spent on Item £ p		Per each £1 spent on GAMBLING spent on Item £ p		Percentage of Total Consumer Expenditure absorbed by Item %
Total Consumer Expenditure Expenditure on	25,323	1.1	—	1	90	45	—
1 Housing	2,976	9.0	—	9	11	10	11.7
2 Food	5,522	4.9	—	5	20	40	21.8
3 Clothing	2,139	12.5	—	12½	8	00	8.4
4 Durable Goods*	2,021	13.3	—	13½	7	50	7.9
5 Books	382	70.2	—	70	1	40	1.5
6 Entertainment†	420	63.9	—	64	1	60	1.6
7 Alcoholic Drink	1,585	16.9	—	16½	5	90	6.2
8 Tobacco	1,512	17.7	—	17½	5	60	5.9
9 GAMBLING (see Table IXA)	268.3	—	—		—		1.1

* Includes: Motor Vehicles, Furniture and Floor coverings, Radio, Electrical and other Durable goods.
† Entertainment and other recreational services.
Source: Central Statistical Office, National Income and Expenditure (London 1968), Table 27: Consumer's expenditure at current prices, pp. 36–7.

Table XI. Divergencies in Gambling Patterns

	Number of Men per 10 Women who	Number of Working-class Men per 10 Middle-class Men who	Number of Married Men aged 18–34 per 10 Single Men 18–34 who	Percentage of Adult Population taking Part in
1 Ever gamble	15	11	17	55
2 Bet on horses	13	18	15	28
3 Bet on dogs	55	22	9	7
4 Do the football pools	18	14	18	53
5 Go to bingo	3	40	27	11
6 Go to casinos/ gaming clubs	16	4	6	8
7 Place bets twice per week or more	22	25	N.A.	2
8 Place bets three times per week or more	18	12	N.A.	7
9 Place bets no more than 2–3 times per year	6	5	N.A.	10
10 Spend less than 25p per week on gambling	7	9	7	39
11 Spend 25p to 50p per week on gambling	6	9	8	10
12 Spend 50p to £1 per week on gambling	39	15	16	5
13 Spend over £1 per week on gambling	42	18	18	3
14 Play or watch sport	15	10	9	86
15 Go to the cinema	10	7	8	50
16 Go to dances	12	5	7	40
17 Go to a public house	15	11	9	74

Source: Betting Habits and Attitudes, vol. I (Commentary), vol. II (Tables), Research Services Ltd (London August 1968), Ref. J. 5752/PRH.

Table XII. Difference between Regular Bettors and Occasional Bettors (Criterion of regular bettor-betting on horses)

	MEN			WOMEN		
	% who bet on horses	(a) % who do not bet on horses	Number of Regular Bettors per 10 Occasional Bettors who	% who bet on horses	(b) % who do not bet on horses	Number of Regular Bettors per 10 Occasional Bettors who
Percentage of Total	37	63		26	74	
1 Bet on dogs	28	2	140	6	Nil	—
2 Do the football pools	71	44	16	42	18	23
3 Go to casinos/gaming clubs	14	6	23	11	3	26
4 Go to bingo	20	8	25	33	17	19
5 Attend race meetings	29	1	290	—	—	—
6 Play or watch sport	92	83	11	76	51	15
7 Go to the cinema	47	52	9	51	47	11
8 Go to dances	35	41	9	38	32	12
9 Go to a public house	79	71	11	68	45	15
10 Stake 12½p or less on football pools per week	13	24	5	—	—	—
11 Stake 50p or more on football pools per week	15	4	37	—	—	—
12 Do the football pools all year	26	16	16	—	—	—

Sources: National Opinion Polls Ltd, *Political Bulletin*, January 1963, Special Supplement 1 'Gambling'; The Gallup Poll, Surveys Conducted July 1964, January and February 1966; Research Services Ltd, *Betting Habits and Attitudes*, A Survey conducted August 1968 (2 vols. plus supplement).

Table XIII. Serious Social Problems

Percentage answering 'Yes' to question: 'Do you consider any of these as raising a very serious social problem in Britain today?'

	March 1965		May 1967		December 1968		Rate of Growth 1965–8	FRANCE Dec. 1968	
	%	Rank Order	%	Rank Order	%	Rank Order	%	%	Rank Order
Drug-taking	56	4	85	1	83	1	48	53	5
Crimes of violence	70	1	69	2	78	2	10	N.A.	
Bad housing	66	2	61	3	72	3	9	N.A.	
Immigrants; Coloureds	55	5	55	5	69	4	25	N.A.	
Juvenile delinquency	58	3	54	6	63	5	9	79	2
Organized large-scale crimes	52	6	59	4	63	6	21	82	1
Gang warfare	N.A.		N.A.		53	7	—	35	8
GAMBLING	31	7	36	7	47	8	51	39	7
Rape	N.A.		N.A.		37	9	—	56	4
Drunkenness	28	9	31	8	35	10	25	77	3
Heavy Smoking	27	10	26	11	30	11	11	N.A.	
Homosexuality	26	11	31	9	29	12	12	32	9
Prostitution	29	8	30	10	28	13	-0.3	43	6
Number of Items	11		11		13			9	
Total mentions for 11 original items	498		537		595				

Sources: The Gallup Poll, Surveys conducted March 1965, May 1967 and December 1968.

Table XIV. Betting Shop Density and Socio-Economic Characteristics: Greater London

	Betting Shops		3 Population	4 Persons per Acre	5 Over 1 Person per Room	% of Households	
	1 Number	2 Per 10,000 Population				6 Lacking Hot Water Tap	7 With Hot Water Bath, WC
Greater London	2,249	2.83	7,671,220	19.4	7.1	20.5	65.6
1 Kingston-upon-Thames	40	0.77	142,010	15.3	3.6	9.9	81.9
2 Sutton	43	1.03	165,190	15.4	3.1	8.1	85.5
3 Havering	95	1.50	246,930	8.5	4.4	5.6	91.0
4 Harrow	39	1.57	204,040	16.3	3.1	6.0	90.3
5 Redbridge	56	1.73	245,810	17.6	3.6	9.3	79.1
6 Bromley	52	1.75	295,760	7.5	3.4	8.7	85.7
7 Richmond-upon-Thames	83	1.77	174,040	12.8	3.7	12.9	75.0
8 Hillingdon	65	1.80	227,820	8.4	4.1	4.2	91.3
9 Bexley	78	1.82	213,810	14.3	2.8	7.5	85.7
10 Brent	55	1.99	282,490	25.9	9.4	23.8	63.3
11 Croydon	53	2.02	322,570	13.5	4.4	13.1	77.0
12 Enfield	116	2.08	264,760	13.2	3.2	12.6	75.0
13 Lewisham*	69	2.17	278,450	32.5	7.4	23.0	61.7
14 Kensington & Chelsea*	69	2.22	203,140	68.8	12.1	20.7	55.4
15 Greenwich*	29	2.33	226,980	19.4	5.4	16.3	69.8
16 Wandsworth*	37	2.39	218,970	37.0	7.8	28.1	53.2
17 Merton	41	2.60	180,630	19.3	3.5	11.6	79.0

* denotes Inner London Borough.

Table XIV *contd.*

| | Betting Shops | | 3 Population | 4 Persons per Acre | 5 Over 1 Person per Room | % of Households | |
	1 Number	2 Per 10,000 Population				6 Lacking Hot Water Tap	7 With Hot Water Bath, WC
18 Ealing	59	2.66	292,750	21.4	6.6	15.8	72.0
19 Harringey	138	2.80	246,570	32.9	8.5	31.6	47.1
20 Waltham Forest	45	2.86	234,530	23.9	3.4	20.9	58.7
21 Barnet	11	2.91	308,950	14.0	4.1	9.2	81.4
22 Barking	102	2.94	167,010	19.8	6.1	13.3	80.5
23 Hounslow	61	2.94	200,530	13.9	4.5	14.0	75.6
24 Lambeth*	47	3.18	320,780	47.6	10.5	29.8	54.3
25 Hammersmith*	118	3.46	203,240	50.9	12.1	37.4	42.1
26 Southwark*	43	4.16	295,900	41.6	10.8	34.0	48.9
27 Camden*	31	4.21	217,090	40.5	10.6	30.5	50.2
28 Newham	123	4.65	255,030	28.4	7.0	30.9	41.0
29 Hackney*	17	4.75	244,210	50.7	12.9	35.6	45.1
30 Islington*	121	5.86	235,340	64.0	16.4	46.4	32.9
31 Tower Hamlets*	67	6.17	196,830	40.4	13.1	36.4	51.1
A City of London*	40	8.26	4,850	7.2	—	0.9	90.2
B City of Westminster*	150	5.91	254,210	47.7	9.8	26.7	55.5

* denotes Inner London Borough.

Sources: General Register Office, Sample Census for England and Wales, 1966 (Greater London: County Report, 1967 and County Leaflet, 1968); Town Clerks and Clerks to the Justices, Boroughs of London, 1968.

TABLES 251

Table XV. Betting Shop Density and Socio-Economic Characteristics. Greater London

	1 Betting Shops per 10,000 Population	2 % Dwellings Owner-Occupied	3 Cars per 100 Households	4 % Cars Housed in Internal Garage	5 % Residents born in Commonwealth, Colonies, Protectorates	6 % Residents in Social Class I & II	7 % Residents in Social Class IV & V
Greater London	2.83	44.8	48	37.4	5.2	17.0	22.4
1 Kingston-upon-Thames	0.77	64.8	66	52.5	2.5	25.6	14.3
2 Sutton	1.03	65.5	67	58.6	1.8	25.5	14.8
3 Havering	1.50	65.9	67	56.2	0.9	17.7	20.4
4 Harrow	1.57	71.1	69	59.3	2.5	27.4	13.9
5 Redbridge	1.73	68.1	62	43.2	2.1	22.2	15.7
6 Bromley	1.75	63.2	71	59.8	2.0	28.6	14.8
7 Richmond-upon-Thames	1.77	55.6	59	39.2	3.2	25.5	15.3
8 Hillingdon	1.80	60.5	71	56.9	2.2	19.9	18.7
9 Bexley	1.82	70.1	64	61.3	1.7	18.3	18.7
10 Brent	1.99	60.5	71	59.8	9.3	16.7	22.6
11 Croydon	2.02	59.6	61	46.7	4.1	22.7	15.8
12 Enfield	2.08	64.3	59	46.7	2.3	19.7	17.5
13 Lewisham*	2.17	37.2	42	24.9	5.4	12.1	25.3
14 Kensington & Chelsea*	2.22	19.9	39	10.2	11.6	29.8	18.1
15 Greenwich*	2.33	38.3	47	33.7	9.8	13.1	26.2
16 Wandsworth*	2.39	28.7	49	14.5	6.9	13.1	23.2
17 Merton	2.60	57.3	53	42.2	3.1	18.8	17.4

* denotes Inner London Borough.

Table XV contd.

	1 Betting Shops per 10,000 Population	2 % Dwellings Owner-Occupied	3 Cars per 100 Households	4 Cars per 100 Housed in Internal Garage	5 % Residents born in Commonwealth, Colonies, Protectorates	6 % Residents in Social Class I & II	7 % Residents in Social Class IV & V
18 Ealing	2.66	55.9	53	39.1	6.2	16.3	21.4
19 Harringey	2.80	43.9	38	16.5	10.4	13.4	22.8
20 Waltham Forest	2.86	49.1	45	27.1	2.9	12.8	22.7
21 Barnet	2.91	59.6	66	50.2	3.6	29.0	14.2
22 Barking	2.94	24.7	45	25.3	1.1	7.4	33.0
23 Hounslow	2.94	54.0	57	42.9	3.9	15.1	21.0
24 Lambeth*	3.18	24.9	34	17.2	8.8	11.6	26.3
25 Hammersmith*	3.46	22.5	31	7.2	8.1	10.4	26.1
26 Southwark*	4.16	14.4	33	15.3	5.1	8.4	32.6
27 Camden*	4.21	17.9	32	14.9	8.6	19.8	23.1
28 Newham	4.65	36.2	36	10.2	4.3	6.9	25.1
29 Hackney	4.75	15.5	28	10.8	9.8	8.0	29.0
30 Islington	5.86	20.6	26	7.1	12.4	8.4	32.1
31 Tower Hamlets*	6.17	3.7	25	11.6	5.7	5.6	37.3
A City of London*	8.26	24.7	44	28.6	3.3	30.4	22.0
B City of Westminster*	5.91	10.2	32	14.9	8.6	27.1	21.9

* denotes Inner London Borough.

Sources: General Register Office Sample Census for England and Wales, 1966 (Greater London: County Report, ??? and County Leaflet 1968); Town Clerks and Clerks to the Justices. Boroughs of London, 1968

Bibliography

Titles on the Nature of Gambling

Adam, Ruth and Morgan, John (1964) 'Britain: A Nation of Gamblers', *New Statesman*, 3 April 1964.

Allen, David D. (1962) *The Nature of Gambling*, Coward McCann Int., New York.

American Academy of Political and Social Science
(1) (1950) *The Annals*, vol. 269, Special Issue: 'Gambling'.
(2) (1963) *The Annals*, vol. 347; Sellin, Thorsten, 'Organised Crime: A Business Enterprise'; Woetzel; Robert K., 'The Overview of Organised Crime: More v. Morality'.

Ashton, John
(1) (1893) *A History of English Lotteries*, Leadenhall Press, London.
(2) (1898) *The History of Gambling in England*, Duckworth, London.

Banton, Michael (1965) *Roles. An Introduction to the Study of Human Relations*, Tavistock Publications, London.

Becker, Howard S. (1963) *Outsiders: Studies in the Sociology of Deviance*, The Free Press, New York.

Bell, Daniel (1960) *The End of Ideology*, The Free Press, Glencoe, Ill.

Benson, Perkins E.
(1) (1925) *Betting Facts*, Student Christian Movements, London.
(2) (1962) *Gambling in English Life*, The Epworth Press, London.

Bergler, Edmund
(1) (1958) *The Psychology of Gambling*, Bernard Harrison, London.
(2) (1943) 'The Gambler: A Misunderstood Neurotic', *Journal of Criminal Psychopathology*, **4**, pp. 379–93.

Berne, Eric (1964) *Games People Play*, Grove Press, New York.

Blanche, Ernest E. (1949) *You Can't Win*, Washington D.C. Public Affairs.

Bloch, Herbert A.
(1) (1951) 'The Sociology of Gambling', *American Journal of Sociology*, LVII, no. 3, pp. 215–21.
(2) (1962) 'The Gambling Business: An American Paradox', *Crime and Delinquency*, vol. 8, no. 4, pp. 355–64.
(3) (1962) *Disorganisation: Personal and Social*, Alfred A. Knopf, New York.

Booth, C. (1902) *Life and Labour of the People in London,* London.

Bott, Elizabeth (1959) *Family and Social Network,* Tavistock Publications, London.

Burns, Tom (1967) *Leisure, Work and Social Structure,* Paper presented to the British Sociological Conference, London, April 1967.

Caillois, Roger (1962) *Man, Play and Games,* Thames and Hudson, London.

Casino Association of Great Britain
    (1) (1967) 'Views of the Casino Association of Great Britain on an Effective Control of Gaming', privately circulated report, April 1967.
    (2) (1967) 'What can Happen if Gambling is Driven Underground', privately circulated report.

Casson, F. R. C. (1965) 'Compulsive Gambling since the 1961 Act', *Medical News,* 2 January.

Chaftes, Henry (1960) *Play the Devil: A History of Gambling in The United States from 1492–1955,* Clarkson N. Potter, New York.

Charles, R. H. (1924) *Gambling and Betting,* T. & T. Clark, Edinburgh.

Chenery, J. T. (1963) *The Law and Practices of Bookmaking, Betting, Gaming and Lotteries,* Sweet and Maxwell, London (2nd edn.).

Chinoy, E.
    (1) (1955) *Automobile Workers and the American Dream,* Doubleday, New York.
    (2) (1967) *Society: An Introduction to Sociology,* Random House,

Christian Economic and Social Research Foundation (1968) *Families with Social Problems,* London.

Church of England National Assembly (1950) *Gambling: An Ethical Discussion,* Social and Industrial Commission.

Churches' Council on Gambling, London
    (1) *Gambling Since 1960,* Annual Report and Financial Statement to 31 December 1962.
    (2) *Gambling—Why?* Annual Report and Financial Statement to 31 December 1963.
    (3) *Gambling and You,* Annual Report and Financial Statement to 31 December 1964.
    (4) *Gambling: A Nation's Responsibility,* Annual Report and Financial Statement to 31 December 1965.
    (5) *Gambling: Time to Think Again,* Annual Report and Financial Statement to 31 December 1966.
    (6) *Gambling: An Attempt to Estimate,* Annual Report and Financial Statement to 31 December 1967.
    (7) *Gambling . . . a Bad Risk for Britain,* Annual Review for the Year ended 31 December 1968.

Churchill, Seton (1894) *Betting and Gambling,* James Nisbett, London.

Clinard, Marshall B. (1963) *Sociology of Deviant Behaviour,* Holt, Reinhart and Wilson, New York.

Cohen, Albert K. (1964) *Deviance and Control,* Prentice-Hall, New York.

Cohen, John
  (1) (1954) 'Ideas of Work and Play', *British Journal of Sociology*, no. 4.
  (2) (1956) *Risk and Gambling: The Study of Subjective Probability*, Philosophical Library, New York.
  (3) (1958) 'The Nature of Decision in Gambling', *Acta Psychologica*, **13**.
  (4) (1958) 'Subjective Probability, Gambling and Intelligence', *Nature*, no. 181.
  (5) (1959) 'Preference for Different Combinations of Chance and Skill in Gambling', *Nature*, no. 183.
  (6) (1960) *Chance, Skill and Luck: The Psychology of Guessing and Gambling*, Penguin Books, London
  (7) (1964) *Behaviour in Uncertainty*, Allen and Unwin, London.
Cohen, John and Cooper, Peter (1960) 'A Study of a National Lottery: Premium Savings Bonds', *Occupational Psychology*, **34**.
Coser, Lewis A. (1962) 'Some Functions of Deviant Behaviour and Normative Flexibility', *American Journal of Sociology*, LXVIII, no. 2, pp. 172–81.
Cotton, Charles (1674) *The Compleat Gamester*, Henry Broome, London.
David, F. N. (1962) *Games, God and Gambling*, Griffin, London.
Davies, Arthur C. et al. (1966) *Focus on Drink and Gambling*, Temperance Council of the Christian Churches, London.
Davis, Claude B. (1956) *Something for Nothing*, Lippincot, New York.
Devereux, Edward C. Jr. (1949) *Gambling and the Social Structure: A Sociological Study of Lotteries and Horse Racing in Contemporary America*, unpublished Ph.D. Thesis (Harvard University, 1949).
Donnison, D. V. (1967) *The Government of Housing*, Penguin Books, London.
Dos Passos, John R. (1904) 'Gambling and Cognate Vices', *Yale Law Journal*, **14**, November 1904, pp. 9–18.
Downes, David (1966) *The Delinquent Solution: A Study in Subcultural Theory*, Routledge and Kegan Paul, London.
Dowst, Robert S. (1959) *The Odds, the Players, the Horses*, Dodd Mead, New York.
Dowst, Robert S. and Craig, C. (1960) *Playing the Races*, Dodd Mead, New York.
Drake, St. Clair and Clayton, Horace C. (1945) *Black Metropolis*, Harcourt Brace, New York.
Dumazadier, Joffre (1967) *Toward a Society of Leisure*, translated from the French by Stewart E. McClue, The Free Press, New York.
Encyclopedia of the Social Sciences, Gambling, vol. IV (1930)
  (1) Stockig, Collins, 'General and Historical', pp. 555–8.
  (2) Seagle, Williams, 'Legal Aspects', pp. 558–61, Seligman, Johnson, New York.
Fabricand, Burton P. (1965) *Horse Sense*, David McKay Co., Inc., New York.
Festinger, L. and Katz, D. (1953) *Research Methods in the Behavioural*

Sciences (part 1, ch. 2, 'Field Studies') Holt, Rinehart & Winston, New York.

Foote Whyte, William (1955) *Street Corner Society*, The University of Chicago Press.

Fowler, Norman
 (1) (1963) 'Next Move for a Gambling Nation', *Crossbow*, April 1963.
 (2) (1967) 'A Policy for Gambling', *Bow Group Memorandum*, London, December 1967.

France, C. J. (1902) 'The Gambling Impulse', *American Journal of Psychology*, VII, no. 13, pp. 364–407.

Freeman, T. B. (1959) *The Conurbations of Great Britain*, Manchester University Press.

Freud, Sigmund (1952) *Dostoewski and Parricide: Collected Papers*, v, The Hogarth Press, London.

'Gambling' in
 (1) (1914) *Encyclopedia of Religion and Ethics*, James Hastings (ed.), Charles Scribner & Sons, vol. 6, pp. 163–7.
 (2) (1954) *Lutheran Encyclopedia*, Erwin L. Lucker (ed.), Concordia Publishing House, Saint Louis, Mo., pp. 401–2.
 (3) (1909) *Catholic Encyclopedia*, The Encyclopedia Press, New York, vol. 6, pp. 375–6.
 (4) (1903) *The Jewish Encyclopedia*, Funk and Wagnalls, New York, vol. 5, p. 563.
 (5) (1941) *The Universal Jewish Encyclopedia*, The Universal Jewish Encyclopedia Inc., vol. 4, p. 508.

Gataker, Thomas (1619) *On the Nature and Use of Different Kinds of Lots*, E. Griffin for W. Bladen, London.

Gemelli, A. and Alberoni, F. (1961) 'Experimental Study in the Concepts of Chance', *Journal of General Psychology*, no. 65, pp. 3–24.

Glass, Ruth and Westergaard, John (1965) 'London's Housing Needs', *Centre for Urban Studies*, Report no. 5, University College, London.

Goffman, Erving
 (1) (1963) *Behaviour in Public Places: Notes on the Social Organisation of Gatherings*, The Free Press, New York
 (2) (1969) *Where the Action is*, Allen Lane The Penguin Press, London.

Goldthorpe, John H. (1966) 'Attitudes and Behaviour of Car Assembly Workers', *British Journal of Sociology*, September 1966.

Goldthorpe, John H. and Lockwood, D. (1963) 'Affluence and the British Class Structure', *The Sociological Review*, vol. 4, July 1963, pp. 133–163.

Goode, W. J. and Hatt, P. K. (1952) *Methods in Social Research*, McGraw-Hill, New York.

Gorer, Geoffrey (1966) *The Danger of Equality and Other Essays*, The Crescent Press, London.

Green, Peter (1924) *Betting and Gaming*, Student Christian Movement, London.

Greenson, Ralph (1947) *On Gambling*, American Imago, vol. IV, pp. 61–77.

Hardy, Charles O. (ed.) (1924) *Readings in Risk and Risk Bearing*, Chicago University Press.

Harris, C. (1927) *The Use of Leisure in Bethnal Green*, Lindsay Press, London.

Herman, Robert D. (ed.) (1967) *Gambling*, Harper & Row, New York.

Hobson, J. A. (1905) *The Ethics of Gambling*, Macmillan, London.

Horton, P. and Leslie, G. R. (1965) *The Sociology of Social Problems*, Appleton, New York.

Huizinga, Johan (1949) *Homo Ludens*, Routledge and Kegan Paul, London.

Hyman, Herbert H. (1955) *Survey Design and Analysis*, part III, The Free Press, Glencoe, Ill.

Jackson, Brian (1968) *Working Class Community*, Routledge and Kegan Paul, London.

Kaplan, Max (1960) *Leisure in America: A Social Enquiry*, John Wiley, New York.

Katz, Leonard (1962) 'Monetary Incentive and Range of Pay-offs as Determinants of Risk Taking', *Journal of Experimental Psychology*, no. 64.

Klein, Josephine (1957) *Samples from English Culture*, 2 vols., Routledge and Kegan Paul, London.

Koenig, Rene (1964) Opp Karl-Dieter and Sack Fritz, *Das Spielen an Geldautomaten*, Report of the Forschungsinstitut für Soziologie, Universität of Cologne (translated under 'Gambling on Gaming Machines', with Appendix and questionnaires by Otto Newman, London 1967, unpublished).

Landis, P. (1964) *Sociology*, Ginn & Co., New York.

Larabee, Eric and Meyersohn, Rolf (1958) *Mass Leisure*, The Free Press, Glencoe, Ill.

Laskin, Richard (1964) *Social Problems*, McGraw-Hill Co. of Canada.

L'Estrange, C. Ewen (1932) *Lotteries and Sweepstakes*, Heath Cranton, London.

Levison, Horace C. (1963) *Chance, Luck and Statistics*, Dover Publ., New York.

Liebow, Eliot (1967) *Tally's Corner: Washington D.C.: A Study of Negro Streetcorner Men*, Routledge and Kegan Paul, London.

Lockwood, D. (1960) 'The New Working Class', *European Journal of Sociology*, 1, 2.

London, Jack (1903) *The People of the Abyss*, London.

Longrigg, Roger (1964) *The Artless Gambler*, London.

Luce, R. D. and Raiffa, H. (1957) *Games and Decision*, Chapman Hall, London.

Ludovici, L. J. (1962) *The Itch for Play*, Jarrold, London.

Macoby, E. E. and M. (1954) 'The Interview' in G. Lindsey (ed.), *Handbook of Social Psychology*, Addison Wesley, Mass.

Malinowski, B. (1926) *Crime and Custom in a Savage Society*, Routledge, London.

Marx, Herbert L. (ed.) (1952) *Gambling in America*, The H. W. Wilson Co., New York.

Mayhew, Henry (1851) *London Labour and London Poor*, Spring Books, London.

Mays, J. B. (1961) *Growing up in the City; a study of juvenile delinquency in an urban neighbourhood*, Liverpool University Press (Social Research Series).

Merton, Robert K. (1967) *Social Theory and Social Structure*, The Free Press, New York.

Merton, Robert K. and Nisbet, R. A. (ed.) (1961) *Contemporary Social Problems*, Harcourt, New York.

Merton, Robert K. and Kendall, P. L. (1946) 'The Focused Interview', *American Journal of Sociology*, LI, no. 6, pp. 541–57.

Meston, Rt. Hon. Lord (1963) *Shaw's Guide to the Betting, Gaming and Lotteries Act*, Shaw and Sons, London.

Miller, S. M. and Riesman, F. (1961) 'The Working Class Sub-culture: A New View', *Social Problems*, vol. 9, no. 1, pp. 86–97.

Miller, Walter B. (1962) 'Lower Class Culture as Generating Milieu of Gang Delinquency', in M. E. Wolfgang, L. Savitz, N. Johnston, *The Sociology of Crime and Delinquency*, John Wiley and Sons, New York, section v, pp. 277–89.

Moody, Gordon E.
  (1) (1965) Hidden Dangers.
  (2) Notes on the Use of Gambling for Fund Raising.
  (3) (1950) Gambling—an Ethical Discussion.
  (4) (Undated) Gambling and Financial Stability.
  (5) (Undated) Wanted a Debunking Campaign.
  (6) (Undated) Our Topsy-Turvy World.
  (7) (Undated) Gambling and Citizenship.
  (8) (Undated) Gambling and the Magistrate's Court.
  (9) (Undated) Gambling in Disguise.
  (10) (Undated) Gam-Anon: The Gam-Anon Way of Life.
  (11) (Undated) Gambling and Education in Christian Citizenship.

Morris, Robert P. (1957) 'An Explanatory Study of Some Personality Structures of Gamblers', *Journal of Clinical Psychology*, no. 13, pp. 191–3.

Mortimer, R. C. (1947) *The Elements of Moral Theology*, A. & C. Black, London.

McGall, G. J. (1963) 'Symbiosis: The Case of the Hoodoo and the Numbers Racket', *Social Problems*, no. 10, 4, pp. 361–70.

McGothbin, W. H. (1956) 'Stability of Choice among Uncertain Alternatives', *American Journal of Psychology*, no. 69.

McKinsey, J. C. C. (1952) *Introduction to the Theory of Games*, McGraw-Hill, New York.

McKnight, Gerald (1964) *The Complete Gambler*, Souvenir Press, London.

Nadel, S. F. (1951) *The Foundations of Social Anthropology*, Cohen & West, London.

Nation, The (1960) 'Gambling Inc.: The Treasure of the Underworld', special issue, vol. 190, 22 October.

Neumann, J. von and Morgenstern, O. (1957) *The Theory of Games and Economic Behaviour*, University Press, Princeton.

Neville, Ralph (1909) *Light Come, Light Go*, Macmillan, London.

New Society (1965) 'Betting Shop Dream World', 5 May.

Ogburn, W. F. and Nimkoff, M. K. (1964) *A Handbook of Sociology*, Routledge and Kegan Paul, London (5th edn.).

O'Hare, Richard J. (1945) 'The Socio-Economic Aspects of Horse Racing', unpublished Ph.D. dissertation, Catholic University of America: *Studies in Sociology*, vol. 12.

Perruci, Robert D. (1967) 'The Neighbourhood Bookmaker: Entrepreneur and Mobility Model', Working Paper no. 10, *Institute for the Study of Social Change*, Department of Sociology, Purdue University, Lafayette, Ind.

Peterson, A. W. (1952) 'The Statistics of Gambling', *The Journal of the Royal Statistical Society*, LXV, part II, pp. 199–218.

Peterson, Virgil W. (1951) *Gambling: Should it be Legalised?*, Charles C. Thomas, Springfield, Ill.

Phillips, Hubert (1955) *Pools and the Punter*, Watts & Co., London.

Pickering, W. S. F. (ed.) (1961) *Anglican-Methodist Relations*, Paton, Longman & Todd, London.

Pringle, Henry (1935) *Gambling in the United States: Its Forms, Extent and Injury*, Washington Board of Temperance.

Raab, E. and Selznick, G. (1959) *Major Social Problems*, Row, Peterson & Co., Evanston, Ill.

Ranulf, Svend (1938) *Moral Indignation and Middle Class Psychology*, Levin & Munksgaard, Copenhagen.

Reid, E. and Demaris, O. (1965) *The Green Felt Jungle*, Heinemann, London.

Reik, Theodor (1942) *From Thirty Years with Freud*, Hogarth Press, London.

Robb, J. H. (1954) *Working Class Anti-Semite*, Tavistock Publications, London.

Rodman, Hyman (1963) 'The Lower Class Value Switch', *Social Forces*, XLII, no. 2., pp. 205–15.

Roman, Samuel and Paley, Henry D.
    (1) (1962) *Report to the New York State Legislature*, New York.
    (2) (1966) *Off Track Betting*, Report, New York.

Roston, R. A. (1965) *Some Personality Characteristics of Male Compulsive Gamblers*, University of California, Los Angeles, Report presented at the 73rd Annual Convention of the American Psychological Association.

Rowntree, B. S. (1905) *Betting and Gaming*, Macmillan, London.

Rowntree, B. S. and Lavers, G. R. (1951) *English Life and Leisure: A Social Study*, Longmans, London.

Rubner, Alex (1966) *The Economics of Gambling*, Macmillan, London.

Ryden, Halsey L. (1959) 'A model for the experimental utility of gambling', *Behavioural Sciences*, vol. 4, pp. 11–18.

Scarne, John (1961) *Scarne's Complete Guide to Gambling*, Simon & Schuster, New York.

Scodel, A. *et al.* (1959) 'Some Personality Corelates of Decision-Making under Conditions of Risk', *Behavioural Sciences*, no. 4, pp. 19–28.

Simmel, Ernst (1920) Zur Psycholanalyse des Spielers, *Internationale Zeitschrift für Psychoanalysis*.

Skinner, Frank W. (1968) *People Without Roots*, a Study Undertaken in the London Borough of Tower Hamlets 1966–67; London.

Skousen, W. C. (1963) 'Challenging the Gambling Syndicate', *Law and Order*, no. 11, pp. 10–15.

Smith, Leslie (1963) 'The Gambling Boom', *New Society*, London.

Smith, Liewellyn H.
    (1) (1931) *The New Survey of London Life and Labour*, King, London.
    (2) (1939) *A History of East London*, Methuen, London.

Sombart, Werner
    (1) (1913) *The Jews and Modern Capitalism*, T. Fisher Unwin, London.
    (2) (1930) 'Capitalism', in *Encyclopedia of the Social Sciences*, vol. 3, pp. 195–208, Macmillan, New York.

Spinley, B. M. (1953): *The Deprived and the Privileged*, Routledge and Kegan Paul, London.

Tec, Nechama (1964) *Gambling in Sweden*, The Bedeminster Press, New Jersey.

Thomas, W. I. (1901) 'The Gambling Instinct', *American Journal of Sociology*, VI, no. 2, pp. 750–63.

Thorner, Isidor (1956) 'Ascetic Protestantism, Gambling and the Price System', *American Journal of Economics and Sociology*, vol. 15, no. 2, pp. 161–72, New York.

Toennies, F. (1887) *Community and Association* (English translation; The Michigan State University Press, Michigan, 1957).

Weinberg, Kirson S. (1960) *Social Problems of Our Times*, Prentice Hall, New York.

White, R. Clyde (1955) 'Social Class Differences in the Use of Leisure', *American Journal of Sociology*, LXI, no. 2, pp. 145–50.

Willmott, P. (1963) *The Evolution of a Community*, Routledge and Kegan Paul, London.

Wykes, Alan (1964) *Gambling*, Alders Books, London.

Young, M. and Willmott P. (1957) *Family and Kinship in East London*, Routledge and Kegan Paul, London.

Zola, Irving K. (1963) 'Observations of Gambling in a Lower Class Setting', *Social Problems*, vol. 10, no. 4, pp. 353–61.

Zweig, Ferdynand
    (1) (1949) *Labour, Life and Poverty*, Gollancz, London.
    (2) (1952) *The British Worker*, Macmillan, London.
    (3) (1961) *The Worker in an Affluent Society*, Heinemann, London.
    (4) (1965) *The Quest for Fellowship*, Heinemann, London.

Commissions and Official Reports

Betting Act: 1853.

1923 House of Commons Select Committee on Betting Duty.

The Royal Commission on Lotteries and Betting 1933: Report Cmnd. 4341.

Betting and Lotteries Act: 1934.

Mass Observation and National League against Gambling: 'Investigation': 1947 (unpublished report).

The Royal Commission on Betting Lotteries and Gaming: 1949–51.

Government Social Survey 1949–50: 'Betting in Britain' (N.S. 710/714).

U.S. Congress: 82nd Congress: 2nd and 3rd Interim Reports (G. Reports 307: Kefauver Committee); Gov. Printing Office, Washington, D.C. 1951.

Massachusetts Crime Commission: Report 1957.

Betting and Gaming Act: 1960.

Report of the Departmental Commission on a Levy on Betting on Horse Races: H.M.S.O.: Cmnd. 1003, April 1960.

United Kingdom: White Paper on National Income and Expenditure: 1960–8.

Family Expenditure Surveys: Ministry of Labour: 1961–8.

Betting and Gaming Act: Permits and Licences: H.M.S.O. 1961–8.

Horserace Betting Levy Board: Annual Reviews: 1961–8.

U.S. Congress: Committee on Government Operations: 'Gambling and Organised Crime': Washington, D.C. 1962.

New York State: Annual Reports by the State Bingo Commission: 1962–6.

Betting, Gaming and Lotteries Act: 1963.

Report on Enquiry into Gaming under Section 2 of Finance Act 1963: H.M.S.O.: Cmnd. 2275: 1964.

London: Report of the Committee on Housing in Greater London (Milner Holland Committee); Cmnd. 2605, London 1965.

Customs & Excise: Notice No. 452: General Betting Duty: 1966.

—: Notice No. 451: General Betting Duty—Bookmakers: 1966.

—: Notice No. 453: Gaming Licence Duty: 1966.

—: Notice No. 454: Gaming Machine Licence Duty: 1966.

Economic Report on 1966: H.M. Treasury: 1967, 1968.

General Register Office: Sample Census 1966; England and Wales; County Report: Greater London; H.M.S.O. 1967.

Gaming Act: 1968 Eliz. 2 c 65.

General Register Office: Sample Census; England and Wales; County Leaflet: Greater London; H.M.S.O. 1968.

General Register Office: Sample Census; Economic Activity Leaflet: Greater London, H.M.S.O. 1968.

The Royal Commission on Betting, Lotteries and Gaming: Minutes of Evidence: Cmnd. 8190.

Metropolitan Borough of Bethnal Green: Annual Reports of the Medical Officer of Health.

Index